Just the Funny Parts

Just the Funny Parts

. . . And a Few Hard Truths About Sneaking into the Hollywood Boys' Club

NELL SCOVELL

DEY ST.
An Imprint of WILLIAM MORROW

DEY ST.

FIRST EDITION

Library of Congress Cataloging-in-Publication Data has been applied for.

ISBN 978-0-06-247348-6

18 19 20 21 22   DIX/LSC   10 9 8 7 6 5 4 3 2 1

Every good story needs . . .

A BEGINNING

Frances and Rubin Cohn
Rhoda and Louis Scovell

Cynthia and Mel Scovell

A MIDDLE

Colin Summers

AND AN END

Rudy Summers
Dexter Summers

Contents

STAGE 3:
GET ME A YOUNGER, CHEAPER NELL SCOVELL!

STAGE 4:
WHO IS NELL SCOVELL?

Foreword

by Sheryl Sandberg

For decades, archaeologists assumed that prehistoric cave paintings were the work of male hunters who wanted to capture their dramatic feats. But a recent study revealed a hidden truth. One researcher looked at the artists' "signatures"—handprints stenciled on the walls—and compared the relative lengths of fingers to those of modern humans. The data showed that 75 percent of the early cave painters were women.

This revelation is important for our understanding of prehistoric human culture. It also means that the last time women held most of the jobs in the entertainment field was about twenty thousand years ago.

The entertainment industry is notoriously tough on women. Then again, so is *every* industry. The challenges Nell has faced during her TV career will seem familiar to many women and be eye-opening for many men. Nell overcame those obstacles in the ways most women do: by working hard, taking risks, making her career a jungle gym instead of a ladder, and having a partner who was a true partner. Nell didn't just help me write *Lean In*, she lived it.

Whoever said feminists weren't funny never met Nell. Her sly sense of humor is one of the main reasons why I've asked her to collaborate again and again. Comedy makes the good times— and the bad times—better. While working on *Lean In*, Nell and I found ways to laugh in the face of gender bias. And while working on *Option B*, as hard as it was, we found ways to laugh in the face of death. One of the most irreverent stories in *Option B* involves Nell at her beloved mother's funeral. Nell has four siblings and she opened her eulogy by holding up an envelope and declaring, "I have in this envelope the name of Mom's favorite child."

Humor is a release. It breaks the tension in stressful situations. And as *Just the Funny Parts* shows, Nell has been in *a lot* of stressful situations. She knows the pressure of being the lowliest writer on a TV staff as well as the pressure of being a showrunner. I love that she is passing along the inside knowledge she gained during three decades in the trenches. Nell's voice is filled with honesty and wisdom—even when it occasionally shakes with rage.

Humor can also give us hope when there is no hope, which is why women have *always* been funny. They just haven't always received credit for it. As Nell maintains, if Larry David were living in eighteenth-century France and heard the peasants had no bread, his response—"Let them eat cake"—would have made people laugh. But when Marie Antoinette said it, they chopped off her head.

Like the cave painters working in the shadows, women have long toiled behind the scenes in Hollywood. That's why it's important that writer/directors like Nell speak up. Her story is inspiring, not because she was unstoppable, but because when she *did* get stopped, she found ways to keep writing, continue being creative, and always but always, maintain her sense of humor.

I've seen firsthand Nell's commitment to support and advocate for other women. She once told me about a talented young TV writer who reached out to vent after a soul-crushing meeting. The woman said she couldn't take the rudeness and rejection any longer. She was tired of competing for the "one female slot" on comedy shows. Nell gave her a pep talk, sharing tips on how to deal with the frustration. A week later, the young writer emailed her, excited.

"You have been such an inspiration for me to follow my writing dreams," she wrote, "that I wanted you to be one of the first to know that I just got my very first staff writing job."

The young woman mentioned the name of the project, which Nell recognized because she'd been up for the "one female slot" herself. Nell laughed as she relayed the story. She was truly happy for her colleague.

Both Nell and I look forward to the day when there are no "female writers"—just writers. We share an unshakeable belief that having an equal number of men and women sitting at the table where decisions are made will make this world fairer and better. It will also make the world funnier. ◆

Just the Funny Parts

Introduction

That which doesn't kill me . . .

. . . allows me to regroup and retaliate.

—My personal motto

IN 1991, A FRIEND TOLD ME A JOKE THAT MADE ME BOTH laugh and shudder. We were strolling through the Universal Studios lot where I worked on the sitcom *Coach* and felt awed by my surroundings. Our writers' offices were located in Lucille Ball's old dressing room. On the way to the commissary, I passed Alfred Hitchcock's bungalow. After lunch, I might sneak onto Soundstage 12 and visit the Visitor's Center of the original *Jurassic Park*. That day, my friend and I were heading to the backlot to check out the clock tower from *Back to the Future*.

I was feeling excited about my own future. Although my first five TV jobs had ended abruptly, my career had finally taken off. I even had an upcoming meeting with a feature film producer who wanted to hear my "fresh" ideas. My friend, who had more experience in the industry, listened to me gush and then jumped in.

"You do know the joke about the four stages of every writer's career, right?"

I shook my head. He launched into an old show business joke, using my name to illustrate.

What are the four stages of every Hollywood writer's career?

Stage 1: Who is Nell Scovell?
Stage 2: Get me Nell Scovell!
Stage 3: Get me a younger, cheaper Nell Scovell!
Stage 4: Who is Nell Scovell?

The joke was like a DeLorean time machine and I instantly glimpsed the unfolding of my entire career. Just three years earlier, I'd been an unknown. Now I was hovering between Stage 1 and Stage 2. My rise probably meant an experienced writer was getting pushed out, and someday that experienced writer getting pushed out would be me. My fresh take would become stale and I'd return to obscurity.

The "four stages" joke has made me laugh for decades. It's funny in the same way that getting attacked by a bear while standing in front of a "Caution: Bears" sign is funny. It's a warning that prepares you for tragedy while doing nothing to prevent it.

Stage 1—"Who is Nell Scovell?"—is a question I've pondered more than anyone on the planet. For those who have never given it a moment's thought, let me fill in the broad strokes. Nell Scovell is a TV writer, producer, and director who has worked on popular series like *The Simpsons, NCIS*, and *Late Night with David Letterman*, as well as cult favorites like *Charmed, The Critic*, and *MST3K*. We all know "Sabrina" is the first name of the teenage witch who fronted the hit ABC series in the nineties. But you might not know that Sabrina's last name was "Spellman" because Irving Spellman was one of my dad's closest friends and I chose that witchy surname when I created the series.

Looking back on my career, I feel lucky and grateful, and all the other things women are supposed to feel so that people will like us. But I genuinely *do* feel lucky and grateful because the average TV writer's career lasts about eleven years and I managed to beat the odds.

My first TV job could easily have been my last. I was 26 when I flew from NY to LA to meet with an executive producer about writing on a late-night comedy show for the brand-new FOX network. During my flight, I came up with pages of ideas and jokes for the meeting. I shouldn't have bothered. The executive producer talked nonstop, laying out his plans to combine comedy and journalism that would shake up the late-night format. After half an hour, he wrapped up his monologue and asked me a question.

"So are you okay with moving to Los Angeles?"

"Yes," I said. And since I finally had an opening, I continued. "I jotted down some ideas if you want—"

He didn't want.

"Great," he said, jumping up from his chair.

He told me his next call would be to my agent and that he was looking forward to working together. I practically skipped across the parking lot to my rental car. I had gotten the job *and* learned my first lesson about Hollywood meetings: the more you let people talk about themselves, the more they will like you.

The show hired ten writers, nine men and me. The team in the office next to mine was hilarious and I couldn't wait to get to work every day and spend time with them. The three of us ate meals together, wrote sketches together and, after work, we'd play Pictionary and miniature Ping-Pong. It was only their second TV job and we all cared deeply about making the show a success. We figured if it flopped, our careers would be over. You've probably never heard of *The Wilton North Report* but those writers—Conan O'Brien and Greg Daniels—did just fine. Greg went on to co-create *King of the Hill*, NBC's *The Office*, and *Parks and Recre-*

ation. Conan went on to become Conan. Actually Conan was always Conan, it's just that his audience expanded beyond our office hallway.

With Conan O'Brien, 1986

Historically, talk shows are developed around a charismatic host. Not *The Wilton North Report*. Two weeks before we launched, the executive producer still hadn't filled the position. Ellen DeGeneres auditioned and came across as both friendly and edgy, the ideal talk show host. The Executive Producer passed on her.

In a panic, he dispatched Conan, Greg, and me to scout talent at a comedy club. The three of us struck up a conversation with Jay Leno who happened to be hanging out in the lobby. Jay was already a household name as guest host of *The Tonight Show*. It would be another two years before NBC handed him the reins . . . and another seventeen years before Jay handed them to Conan . . . and then another nine months before Jay snatched them back. But that night, Jay was the coolest person in the world for chatting with three nerdy twentysomethings. At one point, I made a smartass comment and Jay pointed at me.

"You're funny," Jay declared. "You should do standup."

"What, me? No!" I said.

"Why not?"

"Because I'm a writer, not a performer."

"Aw, c'mon," Jay coaxed, gesturing toward the showroom. "Don't you look at the people up there and think, Hey, I could do better than that?"

"No. I look at those people, even the bad ones, and think, 'Wow. They're really brave.'"

Jay stared at me and then with perfect timing said, "You shouldn't do standup."

The last thing I wanted was to attract attention. Gloria Steinem once said, "For me, writing was a way of staying invisible because I felt invisible, only a little seen through words." I agree with one adjustment: I didn't feel invisible, but I did feel like I was getting away with something and if I just kept my head down, they'd let me keep doing it. Keeping a low profile also suited my New England upbringing where you're only supposed to be in the papers three times: when you're born, when you marry, and when you murder your husband. Or something like that.

My plan was sly: stay out of the spotlight but near the action. It worked. I've stood on the red carpet at the Academy Awards as Daniel Craig passed by inches from me. I may have even touched the back of his tuxedo jacket—unless you think that's creepy, in which case, I definitely did not. I've sat in a hotel suite late at night with Mark Zuckerberg and Andy Samberg working on a funny opening for a Facebook conference. And I've played Fuck-Marry-Kill with Key and Peele during an interview for *Vanity Fair* before the 2015 Emmys.

My career has let me put words in the mouths of iconic performers like Bette Midler, Bob Newhart, Craig T. Nelson, and Miss Piggy. Those performers make everything funnier. It's like having Serena Williams as your doubles partner. If you can just get your serve in, she'll do all the work for the win.

And just because you're invisible, doesn't mean you're powerless. For five years, I contributed jokes to the White House Correspondents Dinner, including one in 2012 where the punchline was the stage direction "WINK."

That night, I was responsible for making the leader of the free world shut his right eye. For a nanosecond, I was the most powerful person on the planet. Clearly, that power went to my head because now I'm tossing off my cloak of invisibility. After a career capturing other voices, it's time to dig deeper into the question, "Who is Nell Scovell?" I can already hear the conversation with a network executive:

Does it have to be "Nell"? What if you turned "Nell" into "Neal"?

A placard that greeted me on a first day of a new job.

ME: *Why would I do that?*
EXEC: *You want men to read your book, right?*
ME: *Right.*
EXEC: *Then you gotta have a male main character. Helps them relate. Oh, and maybe Neal should be into Thai boxing. That's big these days. Think about it.*

Okay, I did. And although Neal sounds awesome, his story just isn't that unusual. There are probably a dozen Thai-boxing Neals who have written for TV, but when I started, it was hard to find any woman doing what I wanted to do. That's why in 1988, I was so excited when a manager connected me with Marilyn Suzanne Miller, one of the three original female writers on *Saturday Night Live*. Marilyn agreed to meet me for coffee near Gramercy Park and I was eager to soak up her wisdom.

She kept her sunglasses on throughout our coffee date and while I don't recall the exact words, her advice basically boiled down to this: *TV is a horrible business. You'll be lucky if it doesn't destroy you. Run. Run for your life.*

I left the coffeeshop, rattled. I remember thinking that if I were ever in the position to speak with younger writers, I would not be so discouraging. Besides, my experience would be different from hers. Marilyn had to break the glass ceiling. Now, in part thanks to her, we were a decade closer to equality. If there were obstacles in my way, I would clear them. If there were people in my way, I would prove them wrong. I would rise up fighting.

Thirty years later, I want to thank Marilyn for trying to warn me. She was right. I quickly discovered that in Hollywood, the glass ceiling is not actually made of glass. Instead, it's made of that Terminator metal that shatters then reconstitutes and reforms. I even thought about calling this book, *Just the Angry and Bitter Parts*, but I want to keep my promise not to be discouraging. Also, that would be an eight-volume set.

Television can be a horrible business, but my advice is not to run.

There have been times that I wanted to bolt, like during the final week of directing my second film. We were on location at a Women's Club in Vancouver, shooting a low-budget cable movie that I'd co-written with my sister Claire. After a strong morning, we came back from lunch and the set fell apart. Three hours later, we were two-and-a-half hours behind. During a scheduled break, I found a coat closet to hide in and sobbed. I called my friend Jesse Dylan and through gulps explained that it felt like the director of photography was sabotaging me and I didn't know what to do.

Jesse is an experienced director so I expected him to give me some practical advice: *Line the actors up in a row. Go tight on their faces.* Instead, he uttered three words that changed everything.

"Go down fighting."

It was exactly what I needed to hear. I picked myself off the floor and headed back to the set to do the best I could with the situation I had.

I think about Jesse's advice often. In Hollywood, you rise up fighting or you go down fighting. Either way, you're fighting.

Now back to the funny parts.

Stage One

WHO IS NELL SCOVELL?

CHAPTER 1

Every Character
Needs a Backstory

Q: What was the smartest dinosaur?
A: Roget Thesaurus

The first joke I recall writing, circa fifth grade.

I WAS BORN AT BOSTON LYING-IN HOSPITAL ON TUES-
day, November 8, 1960. On Wednesday, the entire state of
Massachusetts celebrated. Those two events were not connected. On my birthday, Boston-bred John F. Kennedy defeated
sweaty Richard M. Nixon at the voting booths. Kennedy became
the youngest president ever elected and that day marked a cultural shift that led to the youth movement, the civil rights movement, the feminist revolution, the sexual revolution, and the rise
of pop culture. But I'm sure you have a cool birthday too.

Three out of my four grandparents immigrated to the United
States in the early 1900s. My paternal grandfather Louis Scovell
fled Smorgon, Belarus, as a teenager, and came in through Ellis

Island. Louis used to tell stories about his teenage years in "the old country" and having to bring the cows back to the barn while German bullets whizzed by his head. I will tell my own grandchildren about being forced to play dodge ball in middle school while wearing a horizontal-striped spandex uniform. I've suffered, too.

Middle school PE uniform
aka The Comedy Writer Maker

Louis had minimal education but plenty of smarts. He married Rhoda Orentlicher, of the Tarnopol Orentlichers, who came to America at the age of four. Over the centuries, Tarnopol flipped between Poland and Austria and since Rhoda was drawn to books and music, she preferred to self-identify as Austrian. My father, Mel, used to joke that each year his mother's birthplace moved closer to Vienna until eventually it was within the city limits. Rhoda kept a kosher home but Louis loved bacon so much, he convinced a doctor to write a note saying bacon was necessary for his health. Told you he had smarts.

My maternal grandfather Rubin Cohn was born in London, which sounds posh until you learn that his Polish mother gave birth while waiting to board a ship to New York. Buddy (as we called him) grew up in Greenwich Village and took any available job: rolling cigars, selling shoes. Eventually, he became a hat manufacturer. Buddy's wife, Frances Cohen, was born in Brooklyn although she never knew the exact date, so we celebrated her birthday on Thanksgiving. Her parents put her to work as a child, sewing appliques on dresses, which makes her one of Brooklyn's original "artisanal lifestyle enhancers." Frances loved science and dreamed of studying medicine. The closest she could get was to become a podiatrist who filed callouses and treated ingrown toenails on Park Avenue.

Louis went into the retail shoe business and he and Rhoda settled in the working-class town of Brockton, Massachusetts, where my father was born and raised. Brockton produced two world-class boxers, Rocky Marciano and Marvelous Marvin Hagler, proving that people would rather get punched in the face than stay in Brockton. My mother, Cynthia, nicknamed Sooky, was born in the equally badass factory town of Fall River, Massachusetts. Like many first-generation Americans, my parents discovered that the key to upward mobility was (1) not living in Europe during Hitler's reign; and (2) focusing on education. By 1951, Mel had graduated from Yale and was stationed at Fort Eustis near the College of William & Mary where Sooky was majoring in math. Mel says they were introduced because they "were the only two Jews in Virginia."

Sooky fell in love with Mel because he made her laugh. Sooky made Mel feel loved. Less than a year later, they married and moved to the Boston area. In eight years, they made five kids: Julie, Alice, me, Ted, and Claire. You may have noticed that I'm right in the middle. Yeah, I noticed that, too.

The five of us were tight-knit, bookish, and only slightly less neurotic than J.D. Salinger's Glass family. We loved one another and the way we expressed this was by constant and merciless teasing. We made fun of one sister for having a small head (she doesn't) and another for having allergies (I do—leave me alone). We made up songs like the "I'm always right" song which was sung to the tune of Chopin's "Grande valse brillante" and featured lyrics that looped, "I'm always right. You're always wrong." While building snow forts in the backyard, my brother Ted enjoyed blocking the path of his sisters who desperately needed to go inside and pee. Then he'd make us laugh until it was too late. We were relentlessly cruel and yet completely devoted to one another. This was the best possible training for a career in a TV writers room.

My parents provided us with a comfortable and stable childhood. We moved once—a full *five* miles from Belmont to Newton. Sometimes I feel like my uneventful upbringing puts me at a disadvantage in my chosen profession. I'm a little jealous of writers who come from Southern Gothic families filled with alcoholics and vampires. The first time I met comedy legend Merrill Markoe, she asked me to contribute to a side project where she compiled stories from women with narcissistic mothers.

"Why do you think I have something to offer?" I asked.

"Well, you're funny," Merrill said. "And a lot of my funny female friends had mothers who just focused on themselves."

"I'm sorry to disappoint you," I said. "But I had the warmest, nicest mom."

Sooky was cheerful and helpful and my staunchest defender. At my third-grade parent-teacher conference, the teacher complained that I made too many jokes during class. She asked my mother to talk to me about toning it down. My mother said she'd pass the message along. And she did. . . .

On my fortieth birthday.

My mother waited *thirty-two years* until I was an established comedy writer to tell me that my third-grade teacher had notes on my personality. Sooky found a way to protect without smothering. Her unconditional love is one of the reasons that I could withstand so much criticism and rejection over the years. It's my Harry Potter scar.

Sooky died in 2004 at seventy-two from pancreatic cancer. At her funeral, I spoke about how I never saw my mother embarrassed. That's because to feel embarrassed you have to want to be seen in a particular light . . . and then fail. My mom never pretended to be something she wasn't. There was nothing phony about her. Basically, she was the antithesis of Hollywood.

While my mom offered support, my dad offered challenge. Mel liked it when his kids got good grades. And when we didn't? We were all too scared to find out. His philosophy on life was clear: be logical, be ethical, be honest. No lies were tolerated in my family, not even white lies. Here's an actual conversation I had with my dad after emailing him a caricature of me that appeared in *Vanity Fair.*

ME: Hey, did you get the caricature I sent you?

DAD: Yes, I saw it. *(long pause)* It's not flattering but it looks like you.

Complete honesty is a truly admirable way to raise your children until one decides to go work in the TV and movie business. Then she will feel blindsided. The constant barrage of lies in the

Eight Lies Writers Hear All the Time

1. I'll read your script this weekend.

2. This is brilliant! We just have a couple of notes.

3. If we hire anyone, it'll be you.

4. Hey, your show . . . your vision.

5. We can't pay you, but it's good exposure.

6. Nothing is happening in town right now.

7. We're looking for someone who can think outside the box.

8. We want the lead to be a strong woman.

entertainment industry confused and dismayed me, especially in the beginning. Eventually, I cracked the code: if something seems like good news, it's probably a lie.

My tendency to tell the truth has definitely hurt my career. In the early nineties, I had a meeting with a producer who had the rights to make a movie version of an old TV series. The producer mentioned that he wanted Jim Belushi for the lead. My lousy poker face gave me away.

"What, don't you like him?" the producer asked.

"Not really," I said, bluntly. "I just never thought he had half the talent of his brother."

The producer opened his arms in disbelief.

"Look who's shitting on Jim Belushi?!"

I didn't get that job, but my dad would've been proud of me.

As a kid, I often sat on the arm of Mel's reclining chair and helped him solve British crossword puzzles, deciphering anagrams and puns. My dad loved wordplay. Driving along the highway in the early seventies, Mel suddenly called to the backseat:

"Kids, who does Sonny love and how much?" We had no idea what he was talking about. Then he pointed at a hotel sign in the distance: Sheraton. ("Cher, a ton.")

My dad also passed along his love of science fiction to me. During the summers, my sisters devoured Charlotte Brontë and Jane Austen while I sat in a turquoise butterfly chair reading Ray Bradbury and Philip K. Dick. In college, I took an independent study in fantasy novels with Thomas Shippey, a visiting professor from the UK who was dubbed, "Tolkien's last protégé." Professor Shippey was actually friends with Harry Harrison, who wrote "Make Room, Make Room," the novella that became the movie *Soylent Green*. I thought that was the coolest thing. What was less cool was when Prof. Shippey mentioned that he wrote fiction under a pseudonym.

"What name?" I said. "I want to read it."

"I can't tell you," he said.

"Why not?"

"Because the books are rather misogynistic," he answered.

My love for science fiction extended to TV shows, including the original *Star Trek* and *The Twilight Zone,* which both ran in syndication during my high school years. I also memorized *The Prisoner*'s defiant Number Six declaration, "I will not be pushed, filed, stamped, indexed, briefed, debriefed, or numbered. My life is my own." That made my little teenage heart beat faster. Actually, it makes my fiftysomething heart beat faster, too.

On the weekends, my siblings and I watched black-and-white screwball comedies from the 1930s and 1940s. *The Thin Man* series and the Marx Brothers delighted us. Groucho, Harpo, and Chico were agents of chaos, apt to break into song, and siblings who got on each other's nerves. No wonder we loved them. We were also lucky to come of age when Woody Allen was dating Diane Keaton and not a family member. Mel took us to the theater to see *Sleeper* and my favorite, *Love and Death.*

Still for sheer giddiness, you couldn't beat *Young Frankenstein*. Gene Wilder's gentle oddness complemented Mel Brooks's irreverent broadness. *Young Frankenstein* also featured Teri Garr and Madeline Kahn who were adorable and hysterical. Years later, I got to hang out with Teri and watched as some friends offered her a joint.

"No, thanks," she said. "I get high on life."

Most Hollywood memoirs dish about celebs doing drugs. I'm going in a different direction.

In my early teens, two new sketch comedy shows started airing on TV and I knew they were special because my parents thought they were weird. *Monty Python's Flying Circus* smashed highbrow into lowbrow and I memorized sketches about drunken philosophers, ex-parrots, and arguments about arguments. Only a handful of friends got the humor and it bonded us. At school, we'd greet each other:

"'Ello, Mrs. Premise."

"'Ello, Mrs. Conclusion."

Saturday Night Live was far more popular, premiering in October of my high school freshman year. In the days before YouTube, if you wanted to understand why kids were talking about "land sharks" on Monday, you had to keep your sleepy ass up late on Saturday. The sensibility of Monty Python appealed to me more, but *SNL* had something the British troupe didn't have: funny women. The first *SNL* cast featured three women and four men—groundbreaking for its time. I admired Gilda Radner, the original manic pixie dream girl, but I *adored* the tougher, more strait-laced Jane Curtin. She held her own against Dan Aykroyd and, even as a conehead, Curtin came across as strangely real.

Closer to home, my aunts Jane and Pinky—Mel's sisters— would regularly crack up any room they were in. Aunt Jane liked opera, ballet, and fart jokes. And she wasn't afraid to "work blue" as the Borscht Belt comics would say. At a family gathering, she once sidled over to me.

"Hey, I've got one for you," she said. "Mabel and Molly are rocking on the porch of a retirement home." Jane switched to a wistful old lady voice: "Mabel, do you remember the minuet?" Then in a coarser voice, "Molly, I don't even remember the men I fucked."

It took me fifteen years to get that joke.

Aunt Pinky's humor was darker. Once, my sister Alice was sprawled on the couch reading *Little Women* when Pinky walked by, tapped her on the shoulder, and said, "Don't get too attached to Beth."

Jane and Pinky were early role models and a reason why I've always known that women are as funny as men. Throughout my childhood, I never saw any evidence to the contrary. Who's funnier than Jean Hagan in *Singin' in the Rain*? Or droller than Myrna Loy lining up martinis in *The Thin Man*? I cheered when Johnny Carson went on vacation and Joan Rivers guest hosted *The Tonight Show*. And sure, Bob Newhart was the star of *The Bob Newhart Show,* but costars Suzanne Pleshette and Marcia Wallace topped him all the time.

The ability to make people laugh is not tied to any physical characteristic including skin color, hair color, nose size, penis size or lack thereof. People of every religion can be funny especially when they're making fun of their own religion. Gay people *do* seem to be a little funnier than straight people, but maybe straight people go into closets and tell jokes. For me, Kurt Vonnegut settled the matter in seven words: "Some people are funny. Some are not."

I was fortunate to be surrounded by funny people from birth. Still, wisecracking was viewed as a hobby, not a profession. My dad is hilarious . . . and ran not-for-profit healthcare centers in low-income communities. Aunt Pinky was the most sarcastic person I knew . . . and conducted research at Columbia University. My own career path pointed in two directions: doctor or lawyer. Since my grandmother wanted to study medicine but couldn't pursue that dream, I went to college planning to achieve it for her. A Teaching Assistant in my Intro Biology class said, "No, you won't." A C+ in the easiest science class freshman year destroyed any hope of becoming a surgeon. Now I always advise high school students, "Don't follow your dreams; follow your talents." Writing came far more easily to me than science. I turned to that instead, although I still play surgeon once a year. Every Thanksgiving, I insist on carving the turkey. Haven't saved a patient yet.

CHAPTER 2

Sports and SPY

Writing is the hardest thing to do and the easiest thing to piss on.

—Irving Brecher, Oscar-nominated screenwriter

A T EVERY PANEL ABOUT TV WRITING THAT I'VE SAT on, an audience member will invariably ask, "How did you break in?"

Invariably, I will answer, "That's a terrible question."

This usually gets an uncomfortable laugh because no one's expecting the nice panel lady to be so rude. I answer bluntly to make an impression, then I explain that if you ask a thousand different writers "How did you break in?" you'll get a thousand different answers. But if you ask a thousand different writers "*Why* did you break in?" you'll get the same answer: we wrote.

A writer's career begins long before securing that first job or agent. Arranging words in entertaining ways can take many forms: essays, plays, standup, sketches, poetry, magazine articles, songs, and tweets. There's an old saying that "a writer writes" but that's just the start. A writer writes . . . *a lot* . . . and then shares that work with others.

My friend Amy Hohn described the process perfectly. One day, during a long walk through Central Park, she said, "The only way to move forward creatively is to allow yourself to be judged." I stopped in my tracks and dug out a pen so I could jot down her observation. I've even thought about having it tattooed on my body, maybe in Chinese characters if that's shorter.

Writing is not what you start. It's not even what you finish. It's what you start, finish, and put out there for the world to see. Sometimes we're afraid to share our work because we know those twin jerks—criticism and rejection—are out there waiting to beat us up. Once the assault begins, there are three possible responses: (1) run away from the jerks; (2) defend yourself against the jerks; (3) assume the position and say, "Thank you, sir, may I have another." The third choice hurts like hell, but the jerks often have useful feedback.

Some writers fear the blank page. To me, that's like fearing an empty dog dish—the page is just something you fill every day. Other writers insist, "I hate writing . . . but I love *having written*." I'm the freak who enjoys the process of writing, especially those moments when I fall into a flow and become totally absorbed by a project. As a middle child, it was hard getting my voice heard so being able to express myself without interruption feels like a luxury.

Age 11, working at the kitchen table on a paper about marsupials. Did you know an opossum's penis is bifurcated like a barbecue fork?

John Irving observed, "Before you can write anything, you have to notice something." This may explain why I initially gravitated to journalism. Reporting is all about noticing. In high school, I became News Editor of *Denebola*, the oddly named Newton South High School newspaper. When I got to college, I was eager to continue down the path of serious news journalism.

The second week of my freshman year, I entered the stone and brick building of *The Harvard Crimson* where a group had gathered to "comp" (i.e., compete) to join the paper's staff. Editors addressed the group, making pitches for their various departments: news, opinion, the arts magazine. A senior wearing a rumpled overcoat and holding a cigar took the floor. He looked like he was auditioning for the part of Oscar Madison in a Sarasota dinner theater production of *The Odd Couple*. It was a short audition. He uttered just two sentences: "Anyone who's cool, stick around. We're gonna talk about writing sports."

An airhorn went off in my head.

I'd never been cool in my life and someone had just offered me an opportunity to change that. Sportswriting wouldn't be a stretch for me either. I'd been manager of the boys' track team in high school and my brother was a ranked New England tennis player. Being a Boston sports fan was easy in the late sixties and seventies. The Bruins were world champions. The Celtics were world champions. The Red Sox were (almost) world champions. The Boston Patriots were not the champions that the New England Patriots are today, but I liked the young quarterback Jim Plunkett. I took dinner theater Oscar Madison up on his offer. I stuck around and became a sportswriter. I'm still waiting to be cool.

The decision was made impulsively and remains one of the best of my life. Covering straight news didn't quite suit me. I always felt like I was playing at being serious. My brainy *Crimson* colleagues like Nicholas Kristof, Susan Chira, and David Sanger were reporting on apartheid protests while I spent fall weekends on the banks of the Charles River, covering crew sculls gliding through perfectly arched bridges as the sun burnished the red and gold leaves. Who's the brainy one now?

Sports Editor John Donley taught me that a game's final score was the news hook, but the real story concerned the characters on the field and the history between the teams. Competition is deeply emotional. It's not just who wins and loses; it's the *thrill* of victory and the *agony* of defeat. For one of my first college assignments, I interviewed actor Tommy Lee Jones, who played offensive guard on the legendary Harvard 1968 football team, which staged a sixteen-point comeback in the final forty-three seconds against Yale. The *Crimson* headline the next day blared *Harvard Beats Yale 29-29*. On the tenth anniversary of "The Game," I spoke to Jones about its significance.

"Ending my career with that particular game against Yale was like dying and going to heaven," he told me.

That's *Fugitive*-level drama.

Fledgling sportswriters were taught to sweat over the first paragraph—the lede—where the goal is to inform *and* amuse. Once, when covering a regional track and field event, the men's team tied for second place after a day of competition and the perfect lede popped into my head. Back in the Crimson building, I smiled as I banged out my killer opening, which played off an old saying. I wrote:

```
If a tie for first is like kissing your sister
then a tie for second is like French kissing her.
```

I finished my story and handed it to the copyeditor. He read the lede, then looked up at me.

"Is this a joke?"

I nodded. "Funny, right?"

"No, it's in really bad taste."

I watched him slash a line through my lede.

"What are you doing?" I cried.

"We can't print this," he said.

The editor and I argued over what was appropriate. I lost. The fact that I couldn't see his point about the line's tastelessness was an early sign that I might be more suited to comedy than journalism. I truly believe that if you're a comedy writer and have never been told "You've gone too far," then you haven't gone far enough. I also believe that if you're constantly told "You've gone too far," then maybe you're an asshole.

My colleagues in the sports "cube"—as our tiny office was called—were fun and supportive. I moved up the ladder and sophomore year became one of three Associate Sports Editors who reported to newly crowned Sports Editor Jeffrey Toobin. Jeff is now a CNN legal analyst, best-selling author, and one of the most entertaining people on the planet. He still loves sports. In 2008, Jeff was providing commentary during a vice presidential debate and got busted when eagle-eyed viewers spotted him watching a National League playoff game on his laptop. Come on. It was a *vice* presidential debate.

Junior year, I toyed with the idea of comedy writing and attended an introductory meeting at *The Harvard Lampoon*. The humor magazine's premises were dark and a little smelly even to a college student. The *Lampoon* editor running the "comp" meeting was intimidatingly tall and had an enormous head. His instructions seemed designed to scare us off. "Compers" would be required to turn in three pieces which would be thrown on the floor. *Lampoon* editors would then read and write comments on the back where the criticisms could be viewed by everyone. The potential for public humiliation seemed high, but did I let this guy stop me from pursuing my dreams?

Yes. Yes, I did. I never went back to the *Lampoon*. Over a decade later, I was chatting with then-*Simpsons* writer Jeff Martin and we discovered that we'd been in the same college class and hadn't known each other.

"You should've comped for the *Lampoon*," he said, enthusiastically. "We would have loved you."

I was touched, then noticed he was intimidatingly tall and had an enormous head. He'd been the comp director who had scared me off. Now he wasn't scary at all. I'd been foolish back in college not to even try. I refused to allow myself to be judged and I didn't move forward creatively.

Heading into senior year, my plan was to throw myself into writing a thesis on "The Influence of Ecclesiastes on Early Twentieth Century American Literature." Fortunately, an August phone call changed that plan.

Out of the blue, a *Boston Globe* sports editor tracked me down while I was still at home in Newton. He'd read some of my *Crimson* articles and was wondering if I'd be interested in joining a team of four college students covering high school sports for the city newspaper. It was like getting called up to the big leagues. I ditched Ecclesiastes and went pro.

The other three "schoolboy correspondents" were enrolled at Northeastern University. I later learned a fourth NU student had been selected—a female—but she fell out at the last minute. When that first choice fell through, it would have been easy for the editors to say, "Well, we tried for diversity," and then hire another male. They didn't. And whenever I hear a TV producer say, "We'd love to have more female writers, but we just can't find any," my response is, "You're not looking hard enough." Vince Doria, who led the *Globe*'s award-winning sports coverage in the eighties, did more than just make an effort, he made a difference.

On a typical week at the *Globe*, I might write a field hockey roundup and profile a cross-country runner. Each Saturday, I'd cover a high school football game in some remote Massachusetts

town. I'd spend the week taking a crash course in the town's football history, then freeze my ass off watching the game while my
roommates were back in our dorm room sleeping off their Friday night fun. The deadlines were brutal. On the drive back to
the newsroom, I'd start composing the copy in my head. I once
screeched into the *Globe* parking lot, threw my blue Ford into
park, jumped out, and slammed the locked door just as I noticed
my keys dangling from the ignition. I stared in horror for a beat,
then realized I had no time to consider what an idiot I was. I
sprinted toward the building to file my story.

Working at the *Globe* taught me how to swear, guzzle lousy
coffee, and find towns in Massachusetts that are still not on
Google Maps. It was a treat to sit desks away from world-class
sportswriters Will McDonough, Lesley Visser, and Leigh Mont-
ville. Most of the full-time *Globe* reporters ignored the college
correspondents, but veteran Mike Madden used to stop by my
desk to offer encouragement. One day, he threw me a great piece
of advice about journalism.

"Specialize," he told me. "There will always be better writers
out there, but if you're the expert on a subject and that subject
comes up, they'll call you."

About a week later, he stopped by my desk again.

"I was just thinking, I've never seen a woman in the press
box at boxing matches." He handed me a flyer for a local boxing
event. "That would be a good specialty. You should go," he said.

I sensed that he was right, but I wasn't cut out for boxing.
In all my favorite sports, an athlete got a penalty for throwing a
punch. I tossed the flyer away and then watched as boxing exploded in the second half of the eighties. If I'd taken Mike's advice and started doing my homework in 1981, I would have been
positioned perfectly.

There was another hitch. Sportswriting in general had begun
to lose its appeal to me. My direct editor at the *Globe* was a "just

the facts, ma'am" kind of guy who wasn't looking for a clever lede. After I graduated from college, I hoped to find an editor that appreciated humor.

I moved to New York and took a day job as an executive assistant, answering phones for a CEO on the Forbes 500. I took any writing job that came my way, including my first paid magazine assignment from *Cosmopolitan*. Helen Gurley Brown was still at the helm and the editor commissioned me to write an essay: "My Three Ghastly Weeks with a Grade C Lover." I saved almost all my early writing, but somehow this piece has been lost to time. Not an accident.

My writing career was slow to take off because I acquired an unfortunate habit in my early twenties. Some spend their post-college years in a haze of pot smoke; I liked to get married. I did it twice. And got divorced twice. All before the age of twenty-six. I guess you could call me a romantic. Seriously, only a true romantic would throw herself into a second marriage just six months after the first one failed.

My first husband was my college sweetheart and a second-year student at NYU law school. He was brilliant and kind and knew *exactly* what he wanted to do with his life. I was twenty-two and floundering. When he was selected for a prestigious clerkship, I left my job as an executive assistant and moved to the District of Columbia several months ahead of him. I'd taken a low-paying job answering constituent mail for a Massachusetts congressman. The work was serious and I was unhappy. Our marriage collapsed. By the time he got to D.C., I was on my way back to New York.

Feeling wobbly about my life, I started dating the son of the CEO I'd been working for. We'd hung out a lot at the office and got along great. He was seven years older and really wanted to get married. In my eagerness to cover up my first marital misstep, I made an even bigger one.

The second marriage was troubled from the start. We exchanged vows at my family home in Newton and then flew to Nantucket for a short weekend honeymoon, with a longer trip to China planned for the fall. I woke up the next morning in a quaint B&B to the sound of my brand-new husband pacing. Okay, it was more like stomping.

"Is something wrong?" I asked.

"I've got to get off this island," he said, agitated. "I'm suffocating!"

Metaphor much?

We left Nantucket and drove around New England for two days with no destination. It was madness. *The Adventures of Buckaroo Banzai Across the 8th Dimension* had come out a couple of years earlier and my brain played a loop of Buckaroo's pronouncement, "No matter where you go, there you are."

Our lives should have been happy, living in a lovely apartment overlooking the Central Park reservoir. Yet we argued over everything, even over where to eat dinner.

"If I want Italian and you want Japanese, why can't you compromise and have Italian?" my husband once said to me, redefining the word "compromise." We never made it to China. I hung in for over a year and then pulled the plug. He did not object.

After two divorces, I felt utterly humiliated. Fortunately, I had a supportive family. My father tried to make me feel better. "Look, you didn't have kids," he told me. "So the way I see it is you had two *very* serious boyfriends."

I would never recommend anyone follow my lead, but the failed marriages did help me in a few ways. Like many young women, I entered the workforce assuming someday I'd get married, have kids, and then leave my job to raise them. After two divorces, I scratched "getting married" as a life goal. Been there, been there, done that, done that. I became determined to never again let a relationship derail my work. Writing became my salvation—a professional way to prove my value after those personal failures. My divorces also taught me not to get trapped in a bad decision. I keep two pillows in my office emblazoned with my favorite sports quotes. One pillow says, "Never change a winning game." The other says "Always change a losing game." I know it's not always possible to walk away from a "losing game." Some tough situations must be endured. But if change becomes an option, I'll grab it.

In the summer of 1986, I was still looking for a nonhumiliating way out of my second marriage (plane crash?), when a new magazine called *SPY* approached my then-husband looking for investors. He wasn't interested, but tossed me the prospectus and said, "This sounds like something you'd like." Let the record show, my ex was right about *one* thing.

SPY billed itself as a "satirical monthly" with the tagline: "Smart. Funny. Fearless." The magazine's mission was to eschew fawning profiles and call out the hypocrisy of the rich and powerful. This irreverent attitude is common now—it's called the Internet—but you can arguably trace the origin of the "snark ages" back to *SPY*.

I contacted magazine cofounders Kurt Andersen and Graydon Carter and they invited me down to their unfurnished, raw office space

Kurt Andersen   E. Graydon Carter
EDITORS

Thomas L. Phillips Jr.
PUBLISHER

George Kalogerakis   Susan Morrison
DEPUTY EDITORS

Drenttel Doyle Partners
DESIGN DIRECTORS

Mark Michaelson
ART DIRECTOR

Santiago Cohen
ASSISTANT ART DIRECTOR

Karin Silverstein
PICTURE EDITOR

Joanne Gruber
COPY EDITOR

Nell Scovell
REPORTER

Joseph Mastrianni
EDITORIAL ASSISTANT

Eric Kaplan
CUB REPORTER

Kathleen Adams   Caroline Howard (photo)
Lisa Lampugnale   Anne Mortimer-Maddox
RESEARCH

First *SPY* masthead. Researcher Lisa Lampaugnale later changed the spelling of her last name to Lampanelli and became the "Queen of Mean." She was always nice to me.

in the Puck Building. Seated on folding chairs, I pitched ten story ideas. They hired me as *SPY*'s first reporter.

Sheryl Sandberg likes to quote the advice, "If you're offered a seat on a rocket ship, don't ask what seat. Just get on." *SPY* was a rocket ship and changed the trajectory of my life. Going to the office was a welcome distraction. People were funny but gruff. There was a lot of teasing and shouting over partitions. In short, it felt like home.

Given my recent experience, it's not a coincidence that my beat for the magazine became spotlighting the foibles of New York's wealthy. I started with crea-

tures so entitled that they had an extra set of legs. The article "How Rich Is That Doggie in the Limo?" gently mocked A-list dog owners and included ingenious photos of pampered pets shot in soft-core porn lighting.

My reporting started at the townhouse of Pat Buckley, wife of William F., who bragged about how

From "How Rich Is That Doggie in the Limo?"

her King Charles Spaniels were related to President Ronald Reagan's dogs (i.e., the First Pets). Another pet owner said she kept her miniature poodle on a strict diet because Air France had an eleven-pound limit for pets traveling in Le Club class. A Park Avenue veterinarian told me that he was performing a lot more cosmetic surgery, including wart removal and eye lifts for Shar-Peis.

"How Rich Is That Doggie in the Limo?" was supposed to skewer these over-the-top pet owners. Instead, the piece was received warmly. It was the mid-eighties and excess was in. Regis Philbin even booked me on his cable access talk show. My next feature needed to take sharper aim.

The Duchess of Windsor had a pillow embroidered with the

motto: "You can never be too rich or too thin." I wanted to debunk this claim by profiling wealthy women who were both. Kurt liked the concept but was skeptical that women would discuss their weight with a reporter. I thought these women would leap at the chance to brag about their will power. My hunch proved correct.

"The last time I weighed myself, I was under one-fifteen, but I was wearing a big fur coat and shoes at the time," Nan Kempner, a well-connected socialite, told me over the phone. Once she spoke on the record, others followed. The story's lede featured wordplay out of my sportswriting past.

In New York, there is an inverse relationship between a woman's dress size and the size of her apartment. A size 2 gets a 14-room apartment. A size 14 gets a two-room apartment.

Susan Morrison, long-time editor of *The New Yorker*, edited the article and made it edgier. Art Director Alexander Isley designed an eye-catching layout with insets of these women's bony necks and twig arms.

Opening spread

The New York Post's Page Six picked up the March 1986 piece with a banner headline: "Flat Facts about the Slim and Solvent." Syndicated columnist Ellen Goodman riffed on my observation. Years later in his book *Snark*, critic David Denby praised "Too Rich and Too Thin" as "a lovely piece of Juvenal." At least, I think it was praise. I'd never heard the word "Juvenal" but "lovely" sounded positive.

SPY quickly grew into a cultural phenomenon thanks to the genius of Kurt and Graydon. Kurt kicked off each issue with a beautifully crafted essay that wove together politics and pop culture to reveal the *zeitgeist*. Kurt was also the first person I ever heard use the word *zeitgeist*. I so admired Kurt's distinctive voice that for years I tried to copy it, totally missing the point. Graydon was an equally gifted writer whose outward charm masked his scathing prose, especially when the magazine was mocking a certain "short-fingered vulgarian."

Kurt and Graydon deployed me as an all-purpose reporter. I contributed to every section of the magazine: short pieces for the front, centerfold maps, and charts and sidebars for cover stories like "Colleges of the Dumb Rich," "Wall Street Crooks," and "Little Men." I believe part of my success as a reporter was that I sounded young. I'm still convinced that the elusive Edwin Schlossberg (husband of Caroline Kennedy) took my call and gave me a quote because his assistant thought I was working for a high school newspaper and he wanted to be nice.

As *SPY* became more popular, it also became harder to get interviews on the record. In the early days, people would pick up their phones and speak freely. After a year, potential targets had become more guarded. I was growing frustrated when my home phone rang in March 1987.

"Please hold for Tina Brown," a voice said.

The British editor-in-chief of *Vanity Fair* jumped on the line. She said hello, then got straight to the point.

"I've seen your work in *SPY*. Come work for me."

Tina made a great pitch, dangling an enticing offer of forty grand a year, which was more money than I ever thought I'd make. *SPY* had started me on a salary of a hundred dollars a week and to make extra cash, I babysat for Graydon's kids. (Actually, the babysitting was cool. I had no social life at the time and his kids were terrific.)

For many reasons, the decision to leap to *Vanity Fair* was easy although telling Graydon that I was leaving *SPY* was hard. At least, he was gracious.

"You're making the biggest mistake of your life," he warned me.

About five years later, Graydon became *Vanity Fair*'s editor-in-chief. We had a good laugh about that in his swanky new office.

My early contributions for Tina were short, quirky pieces that she dubbed, "Nell things." Slowly, I was starting to develop my own style, mostly high-concept with a visual component. The *Vanity Fair* issue featuring a nude, pregnant Demi Moore on the cover included a "Nell thing," entitled "Tropical Art." That piece asked noted art collectors, "If you were stuck on a desert island, what three paintings would you bring along?" Madonna, Jackie Mason, Brooke Astor, David Salle, Mort Janklow, and Robertson Davies all played along, which is the eighties in a nutshell.

At twenty-seven, I no longer felt like an aimless failure. I had built a nice career. I had built a bit of confidence. I had built a happy life. Then one Sunday while running errands, I bumped into *SPY* copyeditor Joanne Gruber. It was great to see her and catch up. Then at the end of our conversation, she paused to weigh her words.

"Nell," she said, hesitantly. "I don't mean this an insult, but I think you could write for TV."

An airhorn went off in my head.

CHAPTER 3

The Setup

<pre>
                    RUTH
     I thought you might need an extra pair of
     hands.

                    GARRY
     (to camera) That would double my sex life.
</pre>

Dialogue from my spec script for
It's Garry Shandling's Show

T RYING SOMETHING NEW SHOULD BE THE EASIEST thing in the world. If you succeed, great. And if you fail, you have the perfect excuse: "Hey, I've never done this before." I decided to take Joanne's advice and give TV writing a shot.

All my knowledge of TV writers came from watching *The Dick Van Dyke Show*. Rob Petrie, Buddy Sorrell, and Sally Rogers had a lot of fun writing for character Alan Brady (played by Carl Reiner). Still, their workplace seemed about as realistic as the astronaut program on *I Dream of Jeannie*. Nothing in my upbringing pointed toward a career in TV. Geographically, Boston and Hollywood are about as far apart as you can get in the continental United States. Philosophically, they're even further. Several local boys managed to make the leap. Ben Affleck, Matt Damon, and Mark Wahlberg have become three of our biggest movie stars and two of our finest actors. But growing up in Newton, it was hard to find even a tenuous connection to show business. Leonard Nimoy's parents lived in the same elderly Jewish housing complex as my maternal grandparents. Granny (Frances) said the *Star Trek* star visited one day and I almost lost my mind. The next time I was in the building's lobby, I inhaled deeply, thrilled to be breathing the same air as Mr. Spock.

Forty years later, I met Leonard at a book party for Lynn Povich's memoir *The Good Girls Revolt*. We bonded over our ancestors shared address and then chatted about art. When I mentioned I was Co-Executive Producer of *Warehouse 13* on the Syfy Channel, Leonard cocked an eyebrow.

"Really? And how did you become interested in science fiction?"

"I was drawn to it at an early age," I said. "You don't choose it; it chooses you."

"That's a good point," he said. "It certainly chose me."

Then Leonard roared with laughter.

While I voraciously consumed movies, TV, and plays growing up, I had a limited view of the entertainment industry. Performing seemed like the only way in and by the age of twelve, I'd peaked. During the summers in the late sixties, I was cast in three musicals at The Barn Playhouse in New London, New Hampshire. My roles included Tevye's youngest daughter, Bielke, Snow child #3 in *Carousel*, and Princess Ying Yaowalak in *The King and I*. (Yeah, I was a white kid playing an Asian girl long before Emma Stone was even born.) The actress playing Anna in *The King and I* was married to the Barn's musical director, Stephen

Schwartz. He went on to become the award-winning composer/ lyricist of *Godspell, Pippin,* and *Wicked.* I went on to sit in the audience of *Godspell, Pippin,* and *Wicked.*

Me, lower right. My sister Claire sits behind me. My brother Ted sits in the lower left. My sister Alice is in the top left.

Writing as a way into TV had never occurred to me. When my *SPY* editor raised the possibility, she pointed out a door that I'd been walking by every day but had never thought to try the handle.

If real estate's mantra is "location, location, location," show biz's mantra is "talent, talent, talent." No, wait. That's what it *should* be. Instead, it's "connections, connections, connections." While I'd been too scared to comp for *The Lampoon* in college, I knew a former editor who had moved to LA to work on HBO's *Not Necessarily the News.* The Old Boy Network came through for me. Rob LaZebnik offered to send some of my *SPY* pieces to his very young, very aggressive agent, Gavin Polone. Rob's kindness paid off when I introduced him to my younger, novel-writing sister Claire. At first, she made fun of Rob's funny last name, and then two years later took it as her own in front of friends, family, and a judge. Rob found me my first agent and I found him his first wife. I've since switched agents many, many times. Rob and Claire are still going strong.

Gavin signed me based on my magazine work. He explained that the standard way to break in to television was to write a "spec"—short for speculative—script for an existing series. He would pass along my writing sample to studio executives and showrunners to try to get me placed on a staff. Around this same time, I ran into *SNL* writers Tom Gammill and Max Pross who had been friendly with my sister, Alice, in college. Tom offered me a tip: "Hey, you should go see Albert Brooks's movie *Real Life*. It's playing in the Village this weekend. I think you'd really like it."

Real Life changed my life. This 1979 fake documentary follows a family on camera in a parody of the first reality show, "An American Family." Albert Brooks plays "Albert Brooks," the filmmaker, who keeps inserting himself into the story. He breaks into song. He frets about gaining weight. He manages to be simultaneously insecure and smug.

While Groucho, Woody Allen, and Mel Brooks winked at the camera, Albert played his part straight. He said hilarious things but never acknowledged them. I became a complete convert after this two-line exchange in *Real Life* where Mrs. Yeager, the mom, becomes rattled after the cameras follow her into the gynecologist's office.

"I want to be alone," Mrs. Yeager says.

"Okay," responds Albert. "Can we come with you?"

I walked out of the film tingling. Albert's tone was both absurd and grounded. His sense of humor inspired me. I wanted to write that way, too.

For my spec script, I should have turned to one of the popular shows of the time: *The Cosby Show, Family Ties, The Golden Girls, Cheers*. Instead, I decided to write an episode of the sitcom that made me laugh the hardest: *It's Garry Shandling's Show*. Like *Real Life*, its premise was absurdly self-referential. Garry played "Garry" who lived in a condo with three walls, facing an audience whom he addressed directly (which is why it's called "breaking the fourth wall"). This cult classic is not as well known or well-regarded as Garry's second series, *The Larry Sanders Show*, but I'm one of the weirdos who enjoyed it more.

My agent Gavin represented a writing team at *Shandling*—Al Jean and Mike Reiss—and they forwarded some produced scripts for me to analyze. Once I understood the structure, I worked out a story, bouncing ideas off Alex Isley who I knew from *SPY*. Alex pitched jokes back and showed me early on that a friend who provides vocal encouragement is great, but a friend who provides actual help is even better.

When you're writing a spec, the rules are unclear: Do you have to think of every plot point yourself? Write every line? Is it fair for friends to give you feedback? Add jokes? With rare exceptions, comedy writers get help. In Steve Martin's memoir *Born Standing Up*, he tells a story about his first joke that ever aired on TV: "It has been proven that more Americans watch television than any other appliance." Hilarious, right? And *sooo* Steve Martin. Except Martin admits that he didn't write it. The joke sprang from the mind of his then-roommate, comedian Gary Mule Deer. With Mule Deer's permission, Martin pitched the line at *The Smothers Brothers Comedy Hour* and people loved it. Martin further admits that two colleagues pointedly asked him if he'd written the joke and Martin said he took full credit, adding that if he'd been hooked up to a lie-detecting machine, "It would have spewed smoke."

It's wonderful that Martin included this confession because no one would ever question his comedy chops, but even he got help from a friend. Obviously, the majority of a spec script had better come from your brain because if hired, you'll have to deliver. Still, TV is a collaborative medium and learning how to receive input from others and separate good ideas from bad is a big part of the job.

In a couple of weeks, I'd pounded out a complete spec script. *It's Garry Shandling's Show* often featured cameos of stars and I copied that format. I wrote a scene set in the kitchen, where Garry and his pudgy friend Leonard are exchanging diet tips.

>   **LEONARD**
> I have a photo of Dom DeLuise on my
> refrigerator door. It discourages me from
> digging into the chocolate, chocolate chip
> too often.

>   **GARRY SHANDLING**
> That old trick. I've got something even
> better.

(*GARRY OPENS THE REFRIGERATOR DOOR TO REVEAL DOM DELUISE SITTING IN THE REFRIGERATOR, READING A BOOK AND EATING A PIECE OF PIZZA. DOM EXTENDS THE SLICE TOWARD GARRY.*)

>   **DOM DELUISE**
> You hungry?

>   **GARRY SHANDLING**
> No. I just lost my appetite.

I even added a callback. During a party scene, Garry returns to the kitchen and opens the refrigerator. The rotund actor is still there as Garry grabs a bottle of champagne.

>   **DOM DELUISE**
> What's that?

>   **GARRY**
> It's Perignon, Dom.

My agent sent my spec to his clients Al and Mike and asked for feedback. A couple of days later Gavin called and I heard my first "happy agent" hello. Al and Mike had liked the script enough that they gave it to *Shandling* showrunner and cocreator Alan Zweibel. Alan had called Gavin to say that the show wanted to buy my script. They'd even fly me to LA so that Alan and Garry could give me notes for a rewrite.

I started jumping up and down like a rookie who'd hit a home run in his first at-bat. Literally and figuratively, I was on my way to Hollywood. A week later, I nervously walked into the *Shandling* offices at Sunset Gower Studios. I stopped by Al and Mike's office to thank them for their help. We talked about the business and they offered me three invaluable pieces of advice.

1. Never be afraid to write on spec.
2. Don't ask friends for work.
3. Take any job that comes your way. You never know where it might lead.

The first piece of advice is pure gold. There are so many reasons to write on spec. Sometimes you get an idea that's weird and you know it won't sell on a pitch so you have no choice but to write it on spec. Sometimes you get an idea that you love but don't want to endure the painfully slow pitch process so you write it on spec. And sometimes you want to try a new genre and the best way to experiment is to write on spec. I become a better writer every time I finish a script so it never feels like a waste of time. Over the years, I've completed seven full-length movies on spec, sold two, one was produced, and I'm still holding out hope for the rest.

Al and Mike put me at ease before Alan's assistant summoned me to his office. We made small talk while we waited for Garry. I'd seen all of Garry's standup specials, which gave me a sense of what to expect: a brilliant, perceptive, and neurotic star. Ten minutes later, Garry hustled by the room, wearing sunglasses. He doubled back and regarded me quizzically. Alan introduced us and reminded him that I'd written the script they bought. Garry nodded approvingly.

"You write like a guy," he said.

I beamed. One of my favorite comics had just paid me a compliment. It was only in the rental car later that his warm words give me a slight chill. I knew Garry meant the comment as praise, but by bringing up my gender, it also carried a hint of negation. Had I sold out other women by smiling when he said that I "wrote like a guy"? I tried to think of what would have been a better response. I replayed the moment in my head and came up with these *mots d'escalier*:

"You write like a guy," Garry says in the do-over.

"Oh," I say with a dismissive wave. "That's just something I did in the snow once."

Etching your name into a snowbank with pee seemed like the only writing where men truly do have a clear advantage over women. I wasn't fast enough to think of this retort at the time. And I still cherished Garry's praise. For many years after, if I was struggling at a job, I'd remind myself, "Garry Shandling thinks I'm funny" and it boosted my spirits.

Garry joined us in Alan's office and sat on the couch just long enough to declare that he wasn't in the mood to give notes. He apologized and asked if it would be okay if we discussed the script some other time. I was returning to NY the next day so I glanced at Alan who came to the rescue. He said they could give me notes over the phone. Garry approved the plan, then said he was heading to the set.

"You want a tour?" he asked.

It was my first time ever on a sitcom set. My brain tried to make sense of what I'd seen on TV and now stood inside. Everything looked smaller thanks to the sky-high stage ceilings. I was mesmerized by "Garry's" living room, his couch, his Mercedes golf cart! I noticed a Ping-Pong table off to the side. Garry explained that they were shooting an episode that parodied the Robert Redford movie, *The Natural*, substituting baseball with Ping-Pong. I laughed. As we passed the table, I lingered.

"Do you play?" Garry asked.

"We had a table in our garage growing up and my brother and I used to play after dinner most nights," I answered.

"Want to hit?"

"Sure," I said, picking up a paddle.

"You know I'm good," Garry said as he moved to the other side of the table. It was a statement of fact, not a brag. He was simply letting me know what to expect.

We started to volley. I kept up. When I slammed a forehand past Garry, he cocked his head.

"Let's play a game."

We did, and I surprised him. Oh, I didn't win. But I did make it into double digits. We placed our paddles down. Garry shook my hand and thanked me for coming in.

I returned to New York. When I walked into my studio apartment, there was already a message from Alan on my answering machine. He and Garry had talked some more and decided not to move forward with my spec script. Instead, they had a new story idea for me to write. If I called him tomorrow, he'd fill me in.

This was disappointing. What I thought was a home run had turned out to be a long foul fly. But I was still at the plate. The next day, I called Alan who pitched me my new assignment in two words: "Haunted Condo."

I laughed out loud. The premise was bare bones: an old tenant in the complex named Lydia Cavanaugh dies and her ghost won't vacate her apartment, which upsets the condo association.

I expanded the story and wrote a new script in a week. It went faster than the first and at least one joke has withstood the test of time:

>   GRANT
> There are some who say Lydia Cavanaugh was a witch.
>
>   GARRY
> There are some who say Geraldo is a journalist.

To get a script from NY to LA in the eighties required military precision. Gavin would arrange for someone in the agency's NYC mailroom to pick up a manila envelope left outside my apartment door. The envelope would be "pouched" across the country overnight, and then someone in the agency's LA mailroom would drive it to the studio the next day. Hitting Send is *so* much easier.

A couple of days after I turned in the new draft, Gavin called and I heard my first "sad agent" hello. It's the oldest story in the book: girl gets script, girl loses script, girl gets another script, girl loses that one, too. Alan told Gavin that although they weren't going to shoot the Haunted Condo episode, they would pay me a full script fee of $11,000. That took some of the sting away. In two weeks, I'd made the same as three months of journalism.

I hung up the phone and tried to sort out my feelings. I'd been so excited, then so disappointed and now those feelings were cancelling each other out. This left me feeling numb. Over the past thirty years, I've felt numb a lot. I learned not to get too happy about good news or too distraught about bad. It's not just me. I once called my friend Chris Keyser after his pilot script got picked up to production.

"Congratulations!" I said.

"Thanks!" he replied, cheerfully. "Just another step on the path to inevitable disappointment."

Being realistic about the odds doesn't mean you don't care about a project; it means you acknowledge that others control what happens to that project. One friend who has a shelf of Emmys summed it up: "Be as happy as you can be for as long as it lasts, but sustained joy is not part of the deal."

In this sense, my *Shandling* experience was the perfect way to lose my TV virginity. The highs and lows set realistic expectations and the "inevitable disappointment" was offset by so many rewards. I made money. I got to play Ping-Pong with one of my comedy idols. And to prove Al and Mike correct that "you never know where a job might lead," I ended up working with them again on several projects including *The Simpsons* and their own outstanding, animated show, *The Critic*.

Writing that first spec proved the *SPY* editor had been right: I *could* write for TV. More importantly, I'd enjoyed the scriptwriting process. It's always better to like doing something than to be instantly good at it. If you're successful but hate the process, you'll stop doing it. If you suck, but the work intrigues you, you'll keep at it and get better.

Five months after my *Shandling* adventure, I got hired on a new FOX late-night show. It was the fall of 1986 and I moved to LA and rented an apartment with my sister Claire in the Fairfax section of West Hollywood.

The Wilton North Report (named after cross streets) combined comedy with journalism and opened each night with a Weekend Update–style look at the news. A crew of correspondents taped reports and conducted in-studio interviews. This format had a lot of overlap with *The Daily Show,* which premiered ten years later and had the advantage of digital technology, only a half hour to fill, and a charismatic host.

After passing on Ellen DeGeneres, the Executive Producer settled on two bland male hosts who came from morning radio. In the week leading up to the *Wilton North* premiere, we held mock run-throughs. I wrote a *SPY*-ish piece where I made snarky comments about magazine ads. For example, I held up model/actress Kelly LeBrock's famous "Don't hate me because I'm beautiful" ad and said, "No, Kelly, we don't hate you because you're beautiful. We hate you because you can't act." The crew laughed and later that day, the Executive Producer called me into his office and asked if I'd do the same bit on the premiere in two days. I was stunned. The last time I'd performed was as Amaryllis in a high school production of *The Music Man*. (Were you there? I killed.) If I agreed, I'd have to perform live on national TV on a night that would be reviewed by every newspaper in the country. It was an insane request and I gave an insane answer.

"Yes."

I would never have volunteered for the mission, but when called, I served. There was a lot of chaos and little rehearsal time. As a lifelong nail-biter, I was hugely concerned about holding up the ads and the camera picking up on my nervous habit. I shouldn't have worried. My hands were shaking so much that you barely noticed the chewed-up nails.

Live from LA: A deer in headlights.

Close-up of my chewed nails.

I got through the piece quickly—maybe a little *too* quickly. Most of the reviews ignored my short segment and focused on the hosts. The *San Francisco Chronicle* was an exception. They included this as one of the show's "highlights."

□ A cute commentary on sex in advertising by "Wilton North" writer Nell Scovell, whose funny smile and clear wit were enhanced by her undisguisable nervousness.

Not to nitpick but you really don't need the word "undisguisable" in that sentence.

I did one more on-camera segment for *Wilton North* where I interviewed a Pee-wee Herman doll. My hands shook less, but I still wasn't bitten by the camera bug. I saw the way Conan O'Brien, who was also writing on the show, relished his time on-camera and how much he added to the material. For me, it made more sense to write for Conan—like a New Year's Eve 1988 bit where I had Conan pucker up close to the camera so that anyone home alone could get a smooch.

In early January, there were rumblings that *Wilton North* would be cancelled. Conan, Greg Daniels, and I spend hours in our offices trying to divine whether we'd have jobs in a month. At one point, Conan grabbed a marker and said, "Here's how the executives will decide our futures."

Drawing by Conan O'Brien, 1988

We lost that coin toss. *The Wilton North Report* was gone two weeks later.

Both my first and second TV jobs ended in utter failure. But as every sportswriter knows, third time's the charm.

CHAPTER 4

The Big Twist

*A man steps into an elevator and sees a beautiful woman
inside. As the doors close, he turns to her and says, "Excuse me,
can I smell your pussy?"*

She recoils in disgust. "You most certainly cannot!"

"Oh," he says, "then it must be your feet."

—Joke told to me by Eddie Gorodetsky

I LOVE THIS JOKE. IT STARTS WITH A SENSE OF MENACE then pivots to stinky feet—even babies laugh at stinky feet. When I'm directing, this is one of my go-to jokes to tell the crew to break the ice. It's short, a little shocking, and ultimately harmless. It lets crew members, who are still mostly male, know they can swear around me. Also, for the rest of the shoot, prop guys and gaffers are pulling me aside to tell me their favorite dirty joke.

Comedy surprises you. Often the surprise comes from a shift of perception and reveals a surprising motivation. It's the twist you never saw coming, but once it arrives, it makes total sense. Like most great jokes, this chapter has a big twist at the end. You'll never guess what happens. Even with me telling you that you'll never guess, you'll still never guess. But when we get there, it will make total sense.

Fresh off *Wilton North*'s cancellation, I returned to the east coast in early 1988, eager to find another TV job. My top choice was *Late Night with David Letterman* and I asked my agent about the hiring process. He said I would need to write a submission that included ideas for desk pieces (pieces Dave would do at the desk) and remotes (pieces shot outside the studio). In a couple of weeks, I pulled together enough material for what is today referred to as a "packet." The trick was to match *Late Night*'s mischievous tone. I included one gag where Dave gets a song stuck in his head and throughout the hour the song intrudes on the show at random times through the set's speakers, distracting Dave, the audience, and the guests.

Gavin passed the packet along to the show's head writer. A few weeks later, he called with a "happy agent" hello. My *Letterman* material had gotten me a meeting . . . just not with *Letterman*. The *Smothers Brothers Comedy Hour*, a relaunch of the once-popular prime-time sixties variety series, was looking for writers. Gavin had given my material to producer (and former *Dick Van Dyke Show* writer) Ernie Chambers. Ernie was in New York City for one day and wanted to meet me. Could I have breakfast with him the next morning? Yes! And did I know the Smothers Brothers? Are you kidding?

Actually, I barely knew them at all. The Smothers Brothers' original show aired from 1967 to 1969 and I wasn't that into political humor at age seven. I knew the brothers were named Tom and Dick, and that one played the bass and the other the guitar, but I couldn't have told you which played which. Today, Google would have gotten me up to speed, but Sergey Brin and Larry

Page were still in high school. I ran to the only place where you could watch old television episodes: a museum.

Sitting in a cubicle at the midtown Museum of Broadcasting and Radio, I watched three episodes of *The Smothers Brothers Comedy Hour*, laughing loudly enough to disturb others. Dick played the bass and the straight man. Tom played the guitar and the fool. The template for these sketches was ingenious: the brothers would start singing a song until Tom interrupted. Dick would react annoyed as Tom launched into a bit about something topical. That bit would build to a punchline and then the brothers would return to the song. So often comedy sketches don't know how to end so going back to a catchy song created a natural and satisfying finish.

Tom and Dick started their careers as clean cut, All-American folksingers and their variety series was promoted as a hip alternative to *The Ed Sullivan Show*. The show's tone changed as the country grew divided in the late sixties. Tom started to give airtime to "radical" voices who opposed the Vietnam War and promoted civil rights.

Despite network warnings, the Smothers Brothers remained political, openly promoting peace. In the second season, the brothers committed an even worse sin: they grew facial hair. By the third season, sponsors complained and in April 1969, CBS abruptly pulled the plug. Months later, the writing staff—which included Steve Martin, Lorenzo "Carlton the doorman" Music, Mason "Classical Gas" Williams, and Carl "Jaws" Gottlieb— won an Emmy for Outstanding Writing Achievement in Comedy, Variety or Music.

Slowly, the country evolved toward Tom's way of thinking. Watergate took down Nixon and everyone now agrees that the Vietnam War was a colossal clusterfuck. Two decades after the original series was cancelled, CBS invited the Smothers Brothers back for an hourlong special. The old writing staff returned and ratings soared. Variety shows had been declared dead, but CBS sensed a faint pulse. The network ordered five additional episodes. The only problem was that the program couldn't secure the all-star writing staff beyond the reunion. That's where I came in.

I headed to my breakfast meeting with Ernie and immediately a slight misunderstanding arose. Based on my material, Ernie thought I was currently on staff at *Letterman*. I had to explain that he had read my submission, but I had never worked there. It was awkward, but it secretly pleased me that someone thought my pitches sounded like they *could* have aired on *Letterman*. Ernie kept an open mind and hired me. Two weeks later, I was flying to LA for a few months of work. I had no plan on where to sleep or how to get around. I was twenty-seven and didn't care about logistics. Besides, a rental car could solve both problems.

My first night in LA, I joined my new boss for dinner. Tom Smothers plays an idiot on TV, but in real life he's brilliant, thoughtful, and unpretentious. We talked about comedy partnerships and his admiration for Laurel and Hardy. At the end of the dinner, Tom asked where I was staying.

"At a hotel for the moment," I said. "I'm still trying to figure it out."

"If you want, you could stay with me," he said. "CBS rented me a huge place. There's a maid's room you could sleep in."

Tom described the West Hollywood apartment: a stately brick building just down the road from the Chateau Marmont, huge living room, big fireplace. Movie stars Clark Gable and Myrna Loy once resided there. Bette Davis and Christopher Guest still did.

"And we could drive to work together," Tom added.

I was taken aback. How do you respond to an offer like that?

Apparently, you say, "Yes."

It was probably inappropriate for me to move in with my boss. Still, it made some sense. I was the help so why not live in the maid's room? I didn't worry about Tom crossing any lines.

He was famous. He had hung out with the coolest people on the planet and smoked pot with Harry Nilsson and John Lennon. He had hot-tubbed with Tuesday Weld. He was twenty years older than me.

Okay, I was new to Hollywood.

My first night in the maid's room, I was in bed wearing just a t-shirt and reading a book when I heard a knock on my door.

"Nell, you still up?"

My heart started beating faster. Maybe I'd been wrong and the situation was about to get uncomfortable. I pulled on pants and opened the door. Tom was holding a book.

"I wanted you to have this," he said.

He handed me a copy of *Shadow Dancing in the USA*, a book of essays by journalist Michael Ventura. Tom said good night and walked away. A twist! I slipped back into bed and flipped open the cover. Tom had inscribed the first page with a simple message: "I hope you enjoy the book."

Tom turned out to be a superb roommate. Each morning, we'd drive to the office in his white Mercedes and talk about books and politics. The commute became my favorite part of the day—the only time that's ever been true for me in LA. Maybe the only time that's ever been true for *anyone* in LA.

The first day of work, I met the rest of the writing staff who all had twenty years on me. Head writer Mason Williams was soft-spoken and cerebral, apt to quote George Bernard Shaw. He was openly disdainful of Hollywood and yet he had three Grammys and an Emmy. Mason didn't like showbiz, but showbiz sure liked Mason. The room also included Jim Stafford, a novelty singer who'd scored a hit in the mid-seventies with a song cowritten with David Bellamy. "Spiders & Snakes" made it to number three on the charts when I was fourteen. The premise was a boy and girl go for a walk and he keeps harassing her by shaking frogs in her face and looking for critters to drop down her shirt. She, however, is interested in a more mature relationship and informs him, "I don't like spiders and snakes."

Stafford parlayed his folksy appeal and boyish good looks into a summer variety replacement series in 1976. It didn't last long. Nor did his 1978 marriage to country music legend Bobbie Gentry, who wrote and sang the mega-hit "Ode to Billie Joe." Gentry's song relates the Gothic tale of a Mississippi teenage couple spotted throwing something mysterious off a bridge. The lyrics never make clear what the couple tossed or why Billie Joe McAllister went back later and jumped into the murky waters himself. The reason for his suicide was a pop culture riddle and when someone asked Stafford about living with his famous ex-wife, he archly replied, "Let's just say, I know why Billie Joe McAllister jumped off the Tallahatchie Bridge."

It was a great joke. Unfortunately, Stafford's dim view of women extended beyond ex-wives. He preferred hanging with the guys, smoking cigarettes, and playing guitar. As far as he was concerned, I didn't belong. To a certain extent, he was right. If you were singing "one of these things is not like the others," I was the obvious answer. I was also the only one who was young enough to have grown up on *Sesame Street* and get that reference.

From left to right: Jim Stafford, me, John Hadley, Mason Williams, Bob Arnott. Just because the guys were older, didn't mean they were mature. Note Bob Arnott still at the making "bunny ears" stage.

At *SPY* and *Wilton North*, our humor was snarky and nothing was sacred. One day at *Smothers*, we were headed to the stage when someone brought up the late Mamas and Papas lead singer Mama Cass Elliot. The rumor at the time—now debunked—was that Mama Cass had choked to death on a ham sandwich. I was walking behind Tom and made some wisecrack like, "She should've had the soup." Tom wheeled around with a stern look.

"Cass was amazing," he scolded me. "And I loved her."

Tom's reprimand has stayed with me ever since. I felt so mean and small. He was right to scold and remind me that an important rule of comedy is: know your audience. I should have known they were friends. Truly one of the sweetest clips on the Internet is Mama Cass singing "Dream a Little Dream of Me" to a sleepy Tom in 1968. I apologized at the time, but the moment still eats at me, much like—(*Nell, don't!*).

Each week, the five writers had to generate a cold open, two musical bits for the brothers, and intros for their guests. I got assigned a lot of intros, which often meant meeting the artists. Once, Tom sent me to interview singer-songwriter John Hartford who wrote "Gentle on My Mind," the only song I ever learned to play on the guitar. John turned down a dressing room, preferring to relax in his tour bus that was parked in the studio lot. When I boarded, half a dozen card-playing band members whipped their heads in my direction.

"Hi," I said. "Tom wanted me to talk to John."

Without a word, the band members threw down their cards and hustled off the bus. It struck me as odd until someone later explained that one of the "rules of the road" is when a lady gets on the bus looking for the boss, the crew disappears. Fast.

Intros tended to be more clever than funny and I was desperate to come up with a solid bit for Tom and Dick. I sat in my tiny office and churned out sketches. In one, I had Tom tell Dick that he had an idea for a movie. Dick asks what kind.

TOM: It's a love triangle.

DICK: A love triangle sounds good. Who'd be it?

TOM: You and me.

DICK: You and me and . . . ?

TOM: . . . a triangle.

In a sketch designed to lead in to "I Can't Help Falling in Love with You," I had Tom confess to Dick that he's dating a much younger woman.

DICK: (to audience) Now I know what you're thinking and I disagree. I think it's fine that my brother's going out with someone his junior.

TOM: She's a senior. (beat) Marshall High School.

Tom kind of liked that last one and personally edited it, penciling notes in his neat cursive. Tom's comments include a lot of "Not right yet" and "This gives the wrong impression." It was hard to capture the brothers' complicated onstage relationship and make Tom just the right shade of stupid. It was also important that the bits be socially relevant. Sketch after sketch of mine fell short.

For the second episode, the brothers were looking for a bit to pair with the song, "Give Me That Old Time Religion." I started working on an idea about Cain and Abel.

"They were brothers just like us," Dick would say, "only they got along better."

I filled out the sketch. Tom liked the broad strokes as well as the final punchline. He and Mason did a pass and "Cain and Abel" went into the script. Even more amazing, it stayed in.

Standing in the wings during the taping, I felt like Steve Martin in *The Jerk* when he sees his name in the phonebook. Tom and Dick launched into the song, then Tom interrupted to talk about his favorite Bible stories like "Joseph and his coat of many collars." The jokes were landing. The audience was laughing. As the bit neared the end, Tom went off-script. He often ad-libbed to make his performance edgier, which was fine so long as he landed on, "And that's why Abel was killed." He needed to use that *exact* wording to properly set up Dick's final zinger. But Tom wasn't going near the line. Dick tried to prompt him. Tom kept spinning. The energy in the room dipped and my grin dropped. Tom had forgotten what he needed to say. I started to panic. Then, suddenly, he pivoted.

"And that's why Abel was killed," Tom said.

"No," Dick responded. "Abel was killed for interrupting his brother."

The audience roared as the brothers launched back into singing, "Give me that old time religion." People applauded at the end. My heart swelled. When Tom came offstage, he spotted me in the wings and approached. He leaned in close with a twinkle in his eye.

"I had to make Dickie sweat up there," he confided.

A twist! Tom hadn't forgotten the line. He knew *exactly* what he was doing. And in that moment, I realized that it wasn't just Dick; we all play straight man to Tom Smothers.

Around the third and fourth episode, the mood shifted at work. We'd burned through the material we stockpiled during preproduction and no longer had time to hone new sketches. Tom and my carpooling days were over. Before production started, I'd moved out of his maid's room and onto the couch of Marcy Carriker, the show's Associate Producer. Marcy and I were both short, brunette, and in our twenties and she became the life preserver that kept me from drowning in a sea of middle-aged men. A bond often naturally develops between the female employees on predominantly male shows. Even if the two women are as different as humans can be, there'll be times when they huddle and whisper, "Did that just happen?" At one job, I regularly stopped by another woman's office to ask, "Am I corporeal? You can see and hear me, right?"

Marcy was an exceptional roommate: kind, generous, and a remarkable storyteller. Back then she was obsessed with true crime and would recount the horrific details of her favorite homicides. Sometimes a grisly murder-suicide was just the thing to take my mind off the increasingly tense writers' room.

Heading into the fourth out of six episodes, the network was still weighing a pickup. Tom was on edge. One way to increase the possibility of more episodes is to make changes in your creative team, which signals to the network that the production is still trying to find the right formula. In a sad twist, Mason was demoted abruptly and Jim Stafford was elevated to head writer. This made me nervous. Stafford favored sketches that ended with Tom calling his brother a "butt brain." He also didn't seem to value, or even want, my input. The first Friday after the personnel shakeup, Tom sent all the writers off to come up with ideas for a cold open over the weekend. I arrived on Monday morning with a page of pitches. I stopped by Stafford's office to hand them in.

"Thanks, Nell," he said. "But you know some of the boys and I got together by the pool yesterday and we worked it all out."

My fears were coming true. You can't succeed when you're not even allowed to participate.

As Stafford got more powerful, he got bolder. Guitar great Chet Atkins was booked on the show and I walked from the offices to the stage to sit in the empty audience and watch him rehearse. Stafford was waiting to rehearse, too—he was now appearing on every episode—and sat next to me. We listened as Atkins sang a gorgeous tribute to his deceased father.

When the song ended, I gushed about Atkins which gave Stafford an idea. "If you like him, Nell, here's what you should do," he said. Then he suggested that I go offer Atkins "a blow-job." This comment came out of nowhere. One second my mind was on Atkins singing about his father and death and the next Stafford was suggesting something you don't associate with either of those. A twist!

I decided it was best to treat this as a joke and laughed. Every woman knows that forced "huh-huh-huh." Still, something about Stafford's comment threw me. It wasn't the crudeness. Maybe it was the setting. Stafford and I were isolated and that made the moment creepy. Coincidentally, a photographer was on the set that same day and asked to snap our photo. The result captured our dynamic for all of time. Stafford tossed his arm around my shoulders and leaned his head against mine, invading my space. I react politely to his overfamiliarity, as women in the workplace are expected to do, but my smile is not my usual toothy grin. It's tight-lipped and restrained. My body is curled up in a ball and my right hand is visibly clenched.

With Jim Stafford

Detail of my clenched hand

The sense of desperation was mounting as we started our final week of production. Would this episode be the last? Finally, word came in: CBS wanted six more episodes. We all cheered, although my status was unclear. My contract was only for the initial order and now Stafford was in charge. I asked my agent to see where I stood. Stafford told Gavin that no decisions had been made on the writers. He'd be figuring it out over the break.

I would have been more freaked out by the uncertainty except something distracted me. The day before we taped our last episode, another writer pitched a last-minute cold open that parodied a recent spate of tell-all memoirs. The bit involved three Smothers' employees stepping forward to hawk their books. The parts were cast at the last minute. Tom cast Ken Kragen, his actual manager, to play his fake manager. He hired Steve Martin's old roommate Gary Mule Deer to play a gossipy beekeeper. The third employee was described in the script like this:

(NELL, DRESSED AS A FRENCH MAID, ENTERS AND STANDS BESIDE KEN. SHE ALSO CARRIES A BOOK.)

It was part of the show's DNA to have writers double as performers so when Tom asked me to pitch in, I was pleased. Still, the costume gave me pause. After months of wearing baggy jeans and Agnes b. striped shirts, I now had to dress like a fifties sexual fantasy. Also, I'd been sitting on my butt for two months eating junk food and was worried my thighs weren't exactly "camera ready." The costumer fitted me that morning and, hours later, I wriggled into fishnet stockings, patent leather pumps, an off-the-shoulder black bodice, and a short black skirt with stiff crinoline. A stylist piled my hair in an up-do and stuck on a stupid doily hat. Fake eyelashes. Lipstick. Eh, voilà.

My writers' room colleagues approved of the look. "Now that's more like it!" one said.

I didn't get terribly nervous because my one line was spoken in unison with Gary and Ken so there was little to screw up. The bit was over in a flash. The director shot us from the waist up so the fishnets and skirt were completely unnecessary. I was back in my civvies before Harry Belafonte sang the season's last number.

The wrap party was held onstage. I didn't know whether I was saying goodbye to people for a month or forever. As it turned out, I had one more chance to see some of the writers when Stafford decided to throw a small pool party that weekend. Part of me wanted to skip seeing the pool where he and "the boys" worked, but I worried that if I didn't stop by, it would look like I didn't want to be a member of the team. I came up with the perfect solution: I'd arrive late and take off early.

It was getting toward evening when I stopped by. The crowd was thin—no Marcy, no Tom, no Mason. Stafford greeted me enthusiastically. I tried to be as cheerful as possible. (Last impressions and all that.) I made small talk with some guests and then, per my plan: "Would you look at the time!"

I found my host to say thanks.

"I'll walk you out," Stafford said.

We were passing through his house to the front door when he offered to show me around. The last stop was his bedroom. He ushered me in, shut the door, and immediately started kissing me up against the wall. It was *so* weird. Why was he kissing me and, even weirder, why wasn't I pulling back? My brain was churning, but my body seemed frozen in shock. For weeks, I'd been so desperate to get Stafford's approval. Ha, I was getting it now! But what did it mean? Had I been wrong? Did he actually like me?

You don't kiss someone unless you like them, right? Maybe that's why I wasn't pulling back. If making out meant he liked me, I didn't want to do anything to make him *not* like me. He held my future in his hands. And then, ohmigod.

He started maneuvering us to the bed. We fell on top of his covers, fully clothed, and continued making out. At one point, I ran my fingers through his hair.

"Careful!" he snapped. "I have a piece."

I peered closer and saw a thin molded piece of plastic glued to the front of his scalp with fake hair coming out. I'd never noticed it before.

"Wow," I thought. "That's a good piece." But before I could contemplate his hair further, Stafford made his next move. He unzipped his pants and used his hand to guide my head down. This is so, so hard to admit but . . .

Reader, I blew him.

A twist! You didn't see that coming, did you? I sure as hell didn't.

And then it was over—one and done. The entire incident took less than ten minutes. There was no reciprocity. My clothes never came off. He had a party to get back to and I had to be, you know, *anywhere else on the planet.*

Racing to my car, I thought, "What an interesting turn of events just happened to someone who looks a lot like me."

Reality rushed back in before I made it home. I knew what had happened and my heart sank. During the act, I had felt a false sense of pride that so many women feel, that smug feeling that Stafford wanted something from me which meant I was the one in control. The truth was not so flattering. I had been manipulated.

Oscar Wilde is credited with the quote: "Everything in the world is about sex except sex. Sex is about power." Stafford had just reminded me of a woman's true purpose and it wasn't writing jokes. He had gotten what he wanted or maybe even what he thought he deserved—the same tribute he suggested I offer Atkins.

When Stafford started kissing me, I worried that if I rejected him, he'd retaliate by not hiring me. Later, it struck me that the reverse outcome was just as undesirable. If Stafford hadn't taken me seriously as a writer before, this would not make things better. And if I did return to the room, would I feel like I'd gotten the job for abilities other than my writing? Would more be expected?

I never had the chance to find out. I was back in NYC when Gavin called with a "sad agent" hello. Stafford wasn't bringing me back on staff. I imagine he never intended to.

After I hung up the phone, I replayed the beats in my head: I feared that Stafford would penalize me . . . so I submitted to him . . . and he still penalized me. In a way it was funny. This "joke" provided a classic shift in perception which reveals a surprising motivation: I saw myself as a determined, hardworking writer and Stafford saw me as a way to get off.

And that's when it hit me: I *really* don't like spiders and snakes.

Stafford and I never spoke or crossed paths again. It's unlikely we will since I don't get to Branson, Missouri much. If we did meet, I don't know what I'd say to him. But I know what I'd tell my younger self: don't mistake sexual power for real power. If you think gratifying a colleague or boss will help your career, think again. Gloria Steinem put it perfectly: "If women could sleep their way to the top, there would be a lot more women at the top."

There's a tendency for women who wind up in these situations to beat themselves up and declare, "I was such an idiot" or "God, how could I have been so stupid?" I'm glad I never did that. I don't believe I acted stupidly. Vulnerable and in shock, I'd made a decision out of fear and confusion.

I never considered any recourse, in part because I wanted

to move on. Besides, what recourse did I have? If the show or network had a human resources department, I wasn't aware of it. There were no handbooks on company policy or sensitivity workshops to enlighten employees. It would be three more years until Anita Hill testified against Supreme Court Justice Clarence Thomas in front of the Senate Judiciary Committee. Like so many, I hung on every word of Hill's courageous testimony. I watched a hero rise in real time.

Twenty-five years later, Hollywood still has a long way to go in changing its casual acceptance of behavior that ranges from inappropriate to criminal. In fact, sexual harassment is so embedded in show business, the industry even has a cutesy name for it: the "casting couch"—which does sound a lot nicer than the "rape sofa."

Predatory behavior often becomes an open secret. Back in the nineties, female assistants at William Morris would warn one another not to get in an elevator with client Bill Cosby. In 2005, Courtney Love was asked to give advice to "any young girls" planning on moving to Hollywood. She bravely responded, "If Harvey Weinstein invites you to a private party in the Four Seasons, don't go." So many coworkers, agents, lawyers, and managers looked the other way while the assaults continued. And so many of these same people have behaved inappropriately themselves. I worry that Weinstein actually raises the bar on bad behavior. As long as a producer doesn't walk into a hotel room naked, clutching a tiny bottle of lotion, he can now consider himself a gentleman.

I understand there's no greater love in this world than that of an Executive Producer for a vulnerable intern, assistant, or actress. But if you're a powerful man, control your impulses. Ruling out sex with employees and professional contacts leaves three billion possible partners minus maybe two hundred. And, of course, you can reverse the genders and the same holds true.

Heading into the second season, Stafford also jettisoned Mason and one other writer. New writers were added to replace us—all male. The penis party was in full swing. The *Smothers Brothers Comedy Hour* lasted for ten more episodes before getting cancelled.

Since then, I've stayed in touch with Tom who ended up marrying Marcy—a twist! Marcy remains one of my closest friends. She and Tom have two great kids and our families have spent many happy days at their vineyard together. I still look back on my time at the show fondly and the good far outweighs the bad. Tom and Mason were patient mentors. I watched world-class musicians perform up close. And I got to work with a hero of mine.

Martin Mull wasn't the biggest name to appear on the show, but he was the one I was most excited about. At sixteen, I was obsessed with *Fernwood 2 Night*, a short-lived Norman Lear series that starred Martin as Barth Gimble, a smarmy, leisure-suit-wearing host of a cheesy talk show. Fred Willard played his guffawing sidekick. *Fernwood* was my introduction to anti-humor. The show fascinated me in part because I didn't always get the jokes, like when Barth deadpanned lines like: "For those of us who saw the tragedy of Vietnam firsthand on TV . . ."

All the writers gathered when Martin came in to pitch us a possible cold open. He ran through the setup and some dialogue and then hit us with the punchline:

> It's time to lay to rest this entire "brothers" business. They are not brothers. It has all been a big lie. Join me, then, won't you in accepting and enjoying, Mr. Dick Smothers and his lovely wife, Tommy.

Tom roared. He sent Martin off to an empty office to fill out the monologue. Martin was halfway out the door when Tom suddenly had a thought.

"Nell," he said. "Why don't you go help him?"

Like a puppy, I leapt from my chair and scampered after Martin. He sat at a desk and I sat across, smiling as I watched him massage the beats. Occasionally, Martin would ask me about a word choice and I'd offer an opinion. Mostly, I listened and nodded and laughed. About twenty years later, it hit me: Martin Mull didn't need my help. Tom just wanted to give me the chance to observe a genius hone a bit.

Now that's a nice twist.

Martin Mull signed my script with some good advice.

CHAPTER 5

The Payoff

INT. VERMONT-INN-DAY

                   LARRY
Then it hit him like a ton of
sticks.

                   DICK
You mean "bricks."

                   LARRY
A ton of anything is still a ton, Dick.

Newhart, "Get Dick" Writer's First Draft, 1989

A PROFESSIONAL COMEDY WRITER'S JOB IS TO MAKE others laugh. Sometimes we write jokes and think, "Yes, that will work." And sometimes we write jokes that crack ourselves up. When the sticks/bricks joke first popped into my head, it made me laugh. Re-reading it twenty-eight years later, it still does.

By June 1989, I had no idea where my TV career stood. In twelve months, I'd been hired on three different series, which seemed like a positive sign. But then none of those jobs had lasted longer than three months, which seemed like a negative sign. For all the encouragement I'd received, there'd been equal disappointment. To put it in dating terms: the guy seemed really into me, but I suspected he might be gay. Still, I wanted to make this new career work. Writing for TV made way more sense than writing for magazines. And by sense, I mean money.

After months of being twenty years younger than my *Smothers Brothers* colleagues, it was great to be back in NYC and reunite with friends my own age. Most Fridays, I attended Movie Night, which was founded by magician Penn Jillette and some friends. We'd all gather at the Howard Johnson's in Times Square for brownie sundaes before heading to a midnight movie.

Movie Night rules include sitting in the front row and applauding whenever the name of the movie is mentioned. Any establishing skyline shot triggers a chorus of "Chicago!" Even if the Eiffel Tower or the Washington Monument appear in the shot, you still shout, "Chicago!"

I first met Penn and his partner Teller on assignment for *Rolling Stone* magazine to cover the release of their movie *Penn & Teller Get Killed*. The interview took place at their office in a sketchy Times Square apartment building. After I asked all my questions, Penn offered to walk me to the elevator and see me out safely. If the elevator had come right away, my life would've been very different. Instead, we waited and waited and ran out of small talk. I became self-conscious of the differential between Penn's physical presence and my own. At 6-6 and 220 pounds, he was a foot-and-a-half taller and double my weight.

"You know," I blurted out. "If a volcano erupted right now and covered us in lava, archaeologists would dig up our bones in a million years and assume I was your lunch."

Penn let his jaw drop theatrically. He stared at me for a beat.

"Do you want to go see RUN-DMC at the Nassau Coliseum

this weekend? A bunch of us are going and I've got an extra ticket."

And that's how I joined Penn's merry band of misfits. Penn's friends were a mix of magicians, artists, computer scientists, and comedy writers. We came from different fields, but all had certain things in common. We were all teetotalling, science-loving, sex-positive atheists. I started spending what Penn would call "stupid amounts of time" with him and his friends. Nothing made me happier than a voicemail in Penn's unmistakable low growl: "Eddie and I are getting dinner—you comin'?"

Penn was a flawlessly generous friend and included me in all the activities. When the group decided to see a live sex show, Penn invited me to join. I had no idea what to expect walking into the seedy Show World, the last of the Times Square peep shows. We passed rows of near-naked women in stalls and I noted the place reeked of bleach.

"That's not bleach," Penn informed me. "That's the base smell of cum. People think these places clean with bleach. They don't."

In the main showroom, a crowd of men stood in a circle watching two women who were *really* enjoying each other's company. The next act was a solo artist who began by slipping a condom on a dildo.

"I hope she's wearing a diaphragm in case the condom breaks," I whispered to Penn.

When the next act started, I told Penn that I was taking off. He nodded and someone else from the group, who had also seen enough, walked me out. I appreciated my glimpse into this alien subculture. And I loved that Penn let me join this stereotypically male excursion and never insinuated that my presence would ruin anyone else's fun. I didn't feel pressured to go or pressured to stay. Penn trusted people to make their own decisions.

Penn also invited me on a weekend scouting mission to the

desert when he and Teller started thinking about performing in Vegas. The duo had a successful run on Broadway and racked up dozens of memorable appearances on *SNL*. On *Late Night with David Letterman*, they famously released a top hat filled with cockroaches all over Dave's desk, sending the host flying out of his chair. It was a rare instance of Dave losing his cool on-air. Moving to Vegas was a solid business decision for magicians. They're really the only people you can say that about. In April 1987, about ten of us accompanied Penn to what he called a "city built on bad math." The group included Billy West—the future voice of Fry on *Futurama*—and Spike Feresten, who later wrote "The Soup Nazi" episode of *Seinfeld*.

Around the table left to right: John Fortenberry, me, Tim Jenison, Marc Garland, Spike Feresten in sunglasses, Eddie Gorodetsky, Billy West, Penn Jillette, Brad Carvey, April 1987

The group took in the classic Vegas revue "Jubilee" where we learned that the Titanic sank not because it struck an iceberg, but because the captain was distracted by topless dancers. This would explain why the band kept playing as the ship sank; the girls had to dance to *something*. I laughed so much during that trip, and I'll always be grateful to Penn for helping me feel safe and funny after a rocky year.

For work, I picked up magazine assignments and was accepted into the Disney New Writers Program, which paid me to write my first pilot. I mined my own experience and wrote *Funny Girls* about a female writing team on a late-night talk show. Unlike Liz Lemon, my leads were low-level writers working for a vain host and a head writer whose character description read:

"HEAD WRITER: Sexist and overbearing, he makes life hell."

Okay, so maybe I was still working out my issues with Stafford.

Funny Girls went nowhere. Next, I wrote a spec script for *The Ellen Burstyn Show,* which was the rare sitcom that shot in New York. Secretly, I was hoping for another quick sale like *Shandling.* My script found its way to the showrunner who kindly took the time to mark it up, scribbling notes in the margins. The remarks were not positive. The word "harsh" pops up next to a lot of my jokes. One line even got a "You don't know this, but you could never make a joke like this on TV." About three-quarters of the way through, the comments stopped. I flipped to the end to look for a final word of encouragement like "Good effort!" or "Keep trying!"

Nothing.

Even though the showrunner had impressive credits and I was a novice, I remember thinking, "He's wrong." Maybe my comedy wasn't too harsh; maybe *his* comedy was too soft. Subjectivity works both ways. Just because you allow yourself to be judged doesn't mean you have to accept that judgment.

In June, Gavin called to say the sitcom *Newhart* was looking for a couple of story editors (the lowest-level writers on staff). Bob Bendetson, the Supervising Producer, had enjoyed my *Shandling* script and wanted to meet. Conveniently, he and his wife,

Heidi, were on their way to Italy with a layover at JFK airport. If I got myself to the gate, he could interview me for the job while waiting for his flight.

This was exciting. I'd watched Bob Newhart's first series in the seventies where the legendary comedian played a psychologist who remains calm even when surrounded by lunatics. Newhart is the master of small moments, snatching laughs in the pauses, in the unsaid, and in the stare. As someone once put it: Newhart blinks funny. As a teenager, I was captivated by the way Bob and his TV wife, Emily, played by Suzanne Pleshette, interacted in their cool, modern marriage. She worked, he worked. She rolled her eyes when he expected dinner on the table. We even got to see them in their midcentury-decorated bedroom with the sophisticated bookshelf behind the headboard.

Then when I was in college, *The Bob Newhart Show* had a resurgence in syndication, spawning the first TV drinking game. Viewers had to down a shot every time a character said, "Hi Bob."

The second Newhart series—the one I was up for—was set in rustic Vermont where he played an innkeeper named "Dick" who remains calm even when surrounded by lunatics. Created by Barry Kemp, the show had flashes of absurdity. Each week, three flannel-shirted, woodsy Vermont brothers would stride into Dick's inn. Only one spoke and he routinely introduced his siblings, "This is my brother Darryl and this is my other brother Darryl." By the final season, the audience would erupt into applause as soon as the woodsy brothers entered.

On the ride to the airport, I brainstormed topical jokes so I'd have something to say if the interview stalled. I was two-for-two at getting hired after meetings and I remember feeling confident as Bob B. and I sat down at the gate. Bob B. remembers our meeting differently.

"You were so freaked out," Bob B. told me in 2017. "I was trying to calm you down, but you just kept pitching jokes. I kept saying, 'We like your writing. You don't have to keep pitching.' You just kept trying to impress me."

I do recall that after our meeting, I walked around the corner and kind of fell apart. But at least no one saw me.

"You know, after you left, Heidi walked by you," Bob B. said. "She came back and said: 'That girl is hyperventilating.'"

Despite my nervousness, Bob B. gave me a shot. *Newhart* had a 24-episode order and I was guaranteed to write on the first thirteen. If the producers were pleased with my work, they had an option to pick me up for the "back eleven." Once again, I crossed the country. I took over the lease on Marcy's West Hollywood apartment and bought my first car, a dark blue Honda Civic.

Newhart was shot at the MTM studios in Studio City. Each morning, I'd drive past the *Roseanne* stage and park across from the *thirtysomething* house. After lunch, the writers would sometimes stroll over to the northwestern corner, head down a sloping path, and arrive at the lagoon from *Gilligan's Island*. One of the main sets of a popular sixties sitcom, the lagoon was nothing but a dirty, busted-up oversized tub. And that's showbiz.

For the first time, I was part of a traditional sitcom writers' room. There were seven of us: two Executive Producers, Supervising Producer Bob B., a mid-level male Producer, and a team of two women who were Story Editors like me. The bosses were both named Mark and we'd sit in "Mark and Mark's" office to break (i.e., plot) stories.

Right away, I figured out that if I pitched a joke or plot point that got shot down, I shouldn't dwell on the rejection. Some writers berate themselves internally: "Why did I say that? I shouldn't have pitched it." But if everyone else in the room is working on their next pitch, then fixating on the previous one puts you a step behind. This approach also applies to an overall career where it's better to focus on the next opportunity rather than ruminate on missed chances and setbacks.

I also learned not to waste time with windups. There's a tendency, especially with women, to kick off pitches with caveats, like: "I don't quite have it, but I was thinking that it might be funny if maybe he said something like—and these may not be the *exact* words—but the gist is . . ." By then, who's listening?

I tend to blurt out my jokes as quickly as possible. If they fly, great. If they thud, I don't take it personally. Again, Bob B. remembers it differently.

"Every time Mark and Mark didn't like what you did, you'd look a little destroyed," Bob recalls. "I thought you were very insecure."

Of course, I was insecure. And don't forget the part about being petrified, too! I felt massive pressure to succeed. After so many false starts, I needed to last a full season and not get cut after thirteen episodes.

My first script assignment had a silly plot that involved Dick accidentally burning down his favorite French restaurant after sneaking a cigar in the men's room. Feeling guilty, Dick invites the chef to stay at the inn. Monsieur Hubert is grateful until he discovers that Dick caused the fire and vows revenge. The episode was filled with jokes about poisoned omelets and Dick being mowed down by wheels of brie. It needed a name and we landed on "Get Dick," so yes, my first script had a penis joke for its title.

I had a week to finish my "first writer's draft" and I spent most of that time scribbling in Du-par's coffee shop near the studio. Jack Kerouac fueled his work with Benzedrine. Truman Capote relied on gin. My drug of choice was a large fudge brownie topped with an inch of thick chocolate frosting. I estimate it takes a hundred calories for me to generate each page of a script. Give me a deadline and lots of carbs and I'll get the job done.

The character voices on *Newhart* were well-established and I quickly discovered that sitcom writing was more satisfying to me than sketch writing. I turned in my draft late one afternoon, handing it directly to one of the Marks. He held it to his nose.

"Smells funny," he said.

I smiled, but my stomach lurched. The nights after handing in a script are long and filled with anxiety. There's a common fantasy about turning in a draft so brilliant that the boss calls you at home that night to let you know. That fantasy has only come true for me once and it wasn't that night.

The next morning, I got into my office early and left my door open in case an Executive Producer wanted to stop by and flash a thumbs-up. Bob B. was the first to appear.

"Hey, Nell," he said in a singsong-y pitch. "Great job. Really funny script."

"Seriously?"

"What? You don't believe me? Have you read it?"

I smiled. Bob B. praised a few specific jokes, including Larry pointing out to Dick that "a ton of sticks" weighs the same as "a ton of bricks." He had some notes, but we'd go over those later. Bob B. headed to his office in the building next door.

A half hour later, Bob B. returned to my office, looking rattled. He fumbled, trying to find the right words, but there were no right words. Mark and Mark had not shared his enthusiasm for my draft. More precisely, they hated it.

"I have their notes," Bob B. said. "And there are a lot of them."

Bob B. pulled up a chair next to me behind my desk. We opened our scripts.

"The first big note is that they didn't think you had enough jokes."

Pathetically, I fished for a shred of positive feedback.

"Did they like the sticks and bricks joke?" I asked in a small voice.

"No," he said bluntly. "They thought it required too much setup. Here's what you need to do . . ."

Bob B. went down the first page, pointing at every line of dialogue and saying, "Joke. Joke. Joke. Joke. Joke."

We walked through each page. Bob B. was professional and precise and made it as painless as rectal surgery can be. I saved the marked-up draft. Pretty much every page looks like this:

This page amuses me because after giving specific criticism like "wordy" and "too jokey," Bob B. clearly just gave up and delivered the global note: "ALL BETTER." To this day when I'm editing my scripts, I'll write "DB" in the margin next to a joke. It's my shorthand for "Do Better."

My friend Rob Bragin has the best description for how writers should accept notes. He graduated from Berkeley and adopts the advice of protestors being dragged off by the police.

"Go limp," he advises. "Don't stiffen up and don't fight."

I took the Marks' notes with minimal defensiveness. Two things helped sustain me. First, it was kind of cool to be getting notes on a sitcom script. I hadn't gotten that far on *It's Garry Shandling's Show* so in a way this was progress. And second, I was so grateful that Bob B. had stopped by my office that morning with praise. It was a perfect reminder that one person's "great job" is another person's "page one rewrite."

The bones of the script didn't change although most of the dialogue did. My second draft was better received. The room did a pass and the episode went into production.

Newhart's shooting schedule began with a Monday morning full cast table read. ("Table read" is a highly technical term referring to the way actors sit around a *table* and *read* a script.) The read gives the writers a sense of whether the plot works, the jokes work, and the pacing works. More importantly, it gives writers free bagels.

At *Newhart*, the cast, the director, the network and studio execs, and the writer/producers sat at tables pushed together on the stage. An additional row of chairs for crew members, agents, and assistants ringed the perimeter. On the morning of the "Get Dick" table read, I walked onto the stage, grabbed a bagel and a freshly printed script, then beelined to the chairs on the periphery and sat down. My name was on the script but I wanted to be as unobtrusive as possible. I was too scared to sit at the center table. I was also too scared to introduce myself to Bob Newhart. No one else bothered to introduce us, either.

The table read went smoothly. For all the Marks' focus on "joke, joke, joke," the biggest laugh in the script came after Newhart delivered these three words:

> DICK
> I feel . . . bad.

The line doesn't look like a joke on the page, but it was tailored for Newhart's deadpan delivery and stopped the table read as we all gasped for breath. A skilled comedic actor will give the impression that he's pulling laughs out of thin air, but he's working off a deep understanding of human nature. That's the advantage of writing for a Bob Newhart—and especially *the* Bob Newhart.

After the read, the producers huddle with the network for notes. If the actors have any problems, they ideally express them at this point. The writers head back to the office to start the rewrite while the director starts blocking scenes. There are run-throughs on Tuesday and Wednesday, prompting additional adjustments. Thursday is camera blocking day and Friday is shoot night. Newhart used to warm up the crowd with one of his telephone standup routines. My favorite was the Englishman listening to Sir Walter Raleigh calling from Virginia to pitch him on the wonders of smoking tobacco. The listener responds warily, "I think we're gonna have a rather tough time selling people on sticking burning leaves in their mouths."

"Get Dick" (still a penis joke) turned out well and I was assigned another script. The other story editors were assigned a second script, too, but were handed a dog of a story. George, the handyman, meets a woman who he deems perfect except for one thing: she has a cartoonishly large ass and he just can't get past it. (Get it?) The female story editors rightfully protested the plot and pitched less offensive possibilities. Mark and Mark dug in their heels. Bob B. went to the story editors and tried to broker a deal.

"I kept saying, 'Just make the show about how shallow George is,'" he recalled. "I told them, 'I get your point, but this is the stupid business and those two guys are in charge.'"

The story editors softened the physical insults as much as they could before the episode shot. Tensions remained high as we approached the thirteen-episode mark when the producers had to let the staff know if our options were picked up. A week earlier, the male Co-Producer was informed that his job was secure. All three female Story Editors were kept waiting until the last day of contractual notification.

Bob B. was dispatched to deliver the verdicts. He stopped first at the team's office. Mark and Mark swung the axe. Then he stopped by my office. My neck was spared.

Yay! Or maybe, Yay? I felt awful about the other story editors and wasn't looking forward to sitting in the room without them. I also suspected that Mark and Mark didn't want me there, but Bob B. had argued my case. Twenty-six years later, I asked him pointblank if my suspicions were correct.

"Yeah," he responded sheepishly.

Mark and Mark hired a new team of male story editors for the remaining episodes. Once again, I was the only female writer in the room. Staying on staff meant I got to be part of the series' final episode, which *TV Guide*'s Matt Roush placed at #1 on the Top Ten Best Finales list. After a wacky episode where Dick sells the Vermont Inn to Japanese investors, he wakes up in bed and rouses the lump under the covers next to him. The lump rolls over, revealing he's not with the woman who played his wife on *Newhart*.

Instead, he's with Suzanne Pleshette who played his wife on *The Bob Newhart Show.*

"You won't believe the dream I just had," he tells her.

Scott Buck, me, Bob Bendetson, in the *Newhart* offices.

The audience went nuts at the meta version of "and then I woke up." It's not often that you have eight seasons to set up a punchline.

Mark and Mark and Bob B. cowrote the finale, which was nominated for an Emmy. I had one joke in that episode. During the opening scene at a town meeting, a local proudly states: "We made the flying squirrel the town bird."

On the evening of the finale, about an hour before the audience arrived, I slipped onto our soundstage. The crew was at dinner so I had the set to myself. I wanted to stand in the old *Bob Newhart Show* bedroom set that had been taken out of storage and reconstructed. It was the strangest feeling to be inside a room that I'd watched on TV as a kid. I ran a finger over the sophisticated bookshelf behind the headboard. I felt like Alice through the Looking Glass.

For all the ups and downs, I had survived the season and now had a "Written by" credit on five TV episodes. I was part of *Newhart* history—although I still hadn't formally met the star. Countless times, I'd stood on set watching the legend rehearse and if he happened to look in my direction, I'd avert my eyes. If I was at the craft services table and he approached to grab a handful of popcorn, I'd scoot away. He played the most mild-mannered characters on TV and yet, for some reason, I was terrified of him.

After a few minutes in the bedroom set, I decided to head to dinner. I walked across the stage, opened the door and was startled to find myself face-to-face with the show's star. There was no avoiding him, nowhere to scoot. There was only one thing for me to say.

"Hi, Bob."

Amazingly, he responded, "Hi, Nell."

He stepped inside and the heavy stage door shut behind him. I paused outside, blinking my eyes to adjust to the light. Our entire exchange had consisted of four words, but it felt deeply meaningful. In the joke about the four stages of a career, the first stage asks the question: Who is Nell Scovell?

Now I had an answer: Nell Scovell was a TV writer who just played the "Hi Bob" game—pro version.

Stage Two

GET ME
NELL SCOVELL!

CHAPTER 6

The Simpsons: *Fugu Me!*

INT. DOCTOR'S OFFICE

*THE DOCTOR ADDRESSES HOMER SIMPSON, WHO HAS JUST
LEARNED THAT HE ATE POISONED BLOWFISH.*

> DOCTOR
> You have twenty-four hours to live,
> Mr. Simpson.

> HOMER
> (UPSET) Twenty-four hours?!

> DOCTOR
> Well, twenty-two. I'm sorry I kept you
> waiting so long.

"One Fish, Two Fish, Blowfish,
Blue Fish" First Draft

WHERE WERE YOU ON THE NIGHT OF SUNDAY, January 14, 1990? I was alone in my West Hollywood apartment watching a cartoon on TV. Normally this would not be memorable, but as the credits began to roll, I did

something I'd never done before and have never done again: I
called my agent at home.

"Gavin, it's Nell. *(pause)* Your client. I want to write for *The
Simpsons*."

Now a cultural institution, *The Simpsons* was not universally
embraced when it debuted. Many dismissed the yellow family
as garish and too mean, which was exactly why I liked them. In
an early episode, "There's No Disgrace Like Home," the Simpsons try family counseling and are handed foam bats to hit each
other with and work out anger issues. After a few swings, Homer
asks, "Wouldn't these bats work better if we took the foam off?"
The counseling session ends with all five members of the family sitting in chairs that allow them to give each other electric
shocks. The shocks go on and on until in the background, the
city lights dim.

The characters, drawn by cartoonist Matt Groening, first appeared as interstitials on *The Tracey Ullman Show*. Sam Simon
and James L. (Jim) Brooks helped develop and expand the shorts.
FOX had only been in existence for a few years, so when Jim
pitched the series, he had personally launched more hit comedies
than the entire network.

Months earlier, I'd interviewed with Jim's production company for a job on *Tracey Ullman*. The meeting went great. Or
so I thought. They didn't offer me a job. But when my agent
pitched me to write a freelance episode for *The Simpsons*, they
remembered my name. Al Jean and Mike Reiss, who'd helped
me at *Shandling*, worked on the show and vouched for me. Since
not that many writers were clamoring to work on some weird-ass
cartoon, *The Simpsons* offered me a script assignment. We set a
date for me to come to the office and pitch story ideas.

"Where do you get your ideas?" is a question that baffles me.
It's like asking, "How do you grow your hair?" The answer is

basically the same: It just sort of happens. Things come out of your head.

Developing an idea into a script can seem equally mysterious, but my *Coach* boss Barry Kemp once boiled the complicated process down to twelve words. "Writing," Barry said, "is not an act of creation, it's an act of choice."

An episode, article, or book doesn't flow out of a pen or keyboard fully formed. Each work is built concept by concept, beat by beat, word by word. It's a process of discovery. You head down a path which leads to another and another and another until you hit a dead end. Then you backtrack to where you made a wrong turn and look for a better way through.

When I write, I feel like an optometrist, constantly flipping between lenses and asking, "Is this better? Is this?" Slowly, the work comes into focus. Here's how choices, big and small, add up to an episode using my *Simpsons* as a case study.

The Story Pitch

A story pitch sets up a situation—the "sit" in sitcom—and gives a sense of how the story might play out. It's "What if?" with a hint of "What comes next?" Most sitcom stories break down to three basic story beats:

1. Character has a problem. (e.g., Brad has two dates for the prom.)
2. Character tries to solve the problem but things get worse. (e.g., Brad tries to keep both dates happy by running between the two, until they bust him.)
3. The problem gets resolved in a surprising way. (e.g., The two dates fall in love. As they ditch Brad, he calls out, "Meg! Jenny! . . . At least, let me watch." Canned laughter—the "com" in sitcom.)

At a party: (left to right) Me, Sam Simon, then-wife Jennifer Tilly, Mike Reiss, Denise Reiss

The Simpsons employs about twenty-eight writers now, but when I walked into Sam Simon's office in the spring of 1990, there were fewer than ten. I recognized Al and Mike, and was introduced to Jon Vitti, Wally Wolodarsky, Jay Kogen, and George Meyer. Sam Simon sat behind a desk while the rest sunk into sofas. I sat on a chair rolled in from the outer office. The all-male room was welcoming but also intimidating.

"So," Sam asked. "What've you got?"

Many writers, especially those with backgrounds in standup, like to pitch off-the-cuff. I prefer to write my pitches down on a yellow pad and then read them as quickly as possible. It's less spontaneous but there are two upsides: (1) reading means I don't have to make eye contact with anyone; and (2) twenty-six years later, I still know *exactly* what I pitched.

I took a deep breath . . . it was the last one I took until I walked out of the room.

Pitch #1: Bart is at the free-throw line. There's one second left in the city-wide basketball game. Bart's team is behind by a single point. Bart makes a deal with God: If He helps Bart sink these two foul shots, Bart will never be mean to his sister Lisa again. Bart sinks the two. His team wins. He's the hero!

Bart arrives home exuberant and immediately asks Lisa if her face hurts. "No. Why?" she replies. Bart starts the punch line, "Because, it's k—" Then he remembers his vow ". . . it's kinda red on your cheeks, you might have a rash." Lisa rushes to the mirror to see. Bart notices a kick-me sign on her back. He lines up . . . then remembers his vow. Lisa noticing her shoelace is untied she bends over to tie it and coupled with the sign this is too much for Bart. He runs to Homer for advice: "If you make a deal with someone do you have to keep your end of the bargain?" "Yes," says Homer, "but only until the check clears." "What if the deal is with God?" Bart asks. "You got a problem there," says Homer. "Since God is all seeing, it's hard to skip town."

Bart is depressed. What good is being a basketball hero if he can't tease his little sister? Life has no meaning as he realizes that tormenting her was his greatest pleasure. The episode ends at the state championships with Bart's team down by a point and one second on the clock, Bart is back on the free-throw line. "Come on, Bart, do it again!" his teammates shout. Bart gets an idea. "God, let's say I throw an air ball and we'll call it even, okay?" Bart tosses an air ball. The team turns on him. Bart whispers to God: "One more to forget the whole incident." Bart throws another air ball. His team loses. Everyone hates Bart who goes home happy and teases Lisa.

Pitch #2: It's Lisa's birthday and she gets to choose the restaurant. She wants sushi. The family goes to Frank's Raw Fish Emporium. Bart orders a burger. Homer says, "You don't go to a Japanese restaurant and order a burger." To waitress, "I'll have the chicken platter." Marge tries to get Homer to try the sea eel, he refuses. "Well, how about a little blowfish, it's a delicacy." He tries it. Just then the sushi chef comes in yelling "Do not eat the blowfish! It is a poisonous delicacy!" They all look at Homer. What do they do now? Chef says to get to a hospital immediately. "In that case" says Marge "we better get the check." The restaurant says, "There's no charge . . . for the blowfish." BUT the family will have to pay for the rest of the meal. The family feels bad for Homer but worse for Lisa. After all, this has ruined her birthday.

Emergency room at hospital has very long line. Intern comes by to say they can't treat blowfish poisoning. Homer's down to his last 24 hours and has to figure out what to do before he dies—"Try to have fun, it's Lisa's birthday!"

Phone rings. The restaurant made a terrible mistake. The bill should have been $36 not $42. They can pick up the $6 tomorrow. This gives Homer a reason to live. He decides to fight the poison, turns colors, retches, but manages to survive.

Fans of the show know that Sam liked pitch #2. For the next hour, the room explored the comedic possibilities of Homer eating fugu and thinking he would die. Someone pitched that as soon as the waiter finds out that a customer has been poisoned, he should tell the chef, "Chef, you have disgraced us! Do the honorable thing." Then we cut to the chef taking an ornamental sword from the wall and raising it to commit hara-kiri.

Someone else chimed in. "Then the Chef suddenly drops the sword and rushes off while the waiter shouts after him, 'Hey, come back here! Do the honorable thing! Do the honorable thing!'"

My notes don't say who pitched this joke, but if I had to guess, I'd attribute it to George Meyer, who once told me that he thought the funniest thing in the world was a frustrated guy shaking his fist at the sky. I can picture the waiter doing that here.

Deconstructing who contributed what to a script can get messy. Jokes are often joint efforts and it's hard to say who deserves credit. The person who pitched the concept? Who honed the precise wording? Who added the additional kicker at the end? There's a story of a TV writer, who while on set, watched a line get a big laugh and then whispered to the person next to him, "I helped on the path to that joke."

It sounds pathetic but every TV writer has thought the same thing.

Once the room landed on the general storyline, we moved on to "what comes next?"

"What if Homer says, 'I guess I'll just lie down and die,'" someone pitched. But Marge has other plans. "Homer, you have twenty-four hours. Do all the things you wanted to do. Let's go!" Marge says.

Homer doesn't move. "I'm thinking," he says, channeling Jack Benny's famous response to "Your money or your life."

We laughed at the idea of keeping Homer on the couch for the entire episode, but that seemed one-note. We jumped ahead and discussed what perspective Homer could gain from a near-death experience.

"Maybe he learns, 'I'm a one-dimensional, shallow man,'" someone suggested.

"Or maybe he becomes determined to live life to the fullest . . . only to discover that he has no thoughts, no interests, and no desires," Sam said. "His last twenty-four hours on earth are

about desperately trying to find meaning in his life . . . right before it ends."

This suggestion led us down a path of Homer looking for
a hobby. Someone pitched Homer going over to Ned Flanders
house.

"I know Flanders is the neighbor," I interjected, "but I'm a
little unclear on his character."

It was so early in the series that Flanders had only appeared
a few times.

"Flanders is the All-American nice guy," someone explained.
"Very encouraging. So, of course, Homer is bitter toward him."

Sam threw out the idea that Homer recovers from the blowfish poisoning at the end of the first act and then joins a theater
group that's putting on Tennessee Williams's *A Streetcar Named
Desire*. We all laughed. Mike Reiss suggested that Homer shows
up to audition for the part of "Stanley" and the director exclaims,
"Normally I don't like it when someone dresses in character, but
you are a perfect slob." (I'm not certain this was Mike's pitch, but
it sure sounds like him.)

The third act would begin with Homer peering out from behind the curtain.

"Ooh, a full house," he says. "Twenty-five people!"

At the afterparty, the cast gathers to read the review. In a
twist, critics love the production, calling it "a tidy hour and a half
in the theater."

Homer tears up. "And to think I almost didn't live to see this."

Sam loved this idea but something about it didn't appeal to
me. Sam noticed my expression.

"What?" Sam said. "You don't like the idea of Homer being
in a play?"

I *really* need to work on my poker face.

"It's fun," I said. "But if it becomes an episode about community theater, then don't you miss out on the character explora-

tion raised by the question: If Homer had only twenty-four hours to live, how would he spend it?"

Sam tilted his head in a way that made me think that I shouldn't have said anything. But the most mportant choice you make for any episode is the story area. All other choices flow from that. Sam said he'd run both options by Jim Brooks and get his thoughts. Once he had a clear direction, they'd bring me back in to flesh out the story.

A couple of days later, Sam called.

"I guess you're the genius," he said. "Jim liked your way better."

Sam didn't abandon his funny Tennessee Williams notion. In the fourth season, "A Streetcar Named Marge," written by Jeff Martin, featured Marge joining a community theater's production of the musical "Oh, Streetcar!" That episode makes every "Best Simpsons" list so maybe I'm not such a genius after all.

Breaking the Story

With the broad strokes of a beginning, middle, and an end, the room can start to place the dots that later connect into a story. Writers often have different strengths: some are better at plot or jokes or visual gags or emotional moments. Using all the voices in a writers' room allows you to pool strengths. It's writing as a team sport.

We mapped out a loose structure: Act One would focus on the family going out for sushi and end with Homer being poisoned. Someone pitched a doctor saying, "There's a test, but ironically it takes twenty-four hours to get the results. I still recommend you take it to protect me." Another pitch had the doctor asking, "Homer, how's your eyesight? You should donate your organs . . . except your stomach."

Act Two would start with Homer making a list of things to do on his last day on earth. We brainstormed possibilities based on Homer's existing relationships: make peace with Dad, tell off boss, have a beer with the boys, listen to Lisa play her sax, teach Bart how to shave. Homer adds, "Be intamit with Marge."

Although it's never mentioned in dialogue, number eleven on the list is "Plant a tree." I wrote that into the script as a nod to my grandmother, Frances who liked the quote: "In their life, everyone should plant a tree, write a book and have a child." (Like Homer, I'm putting off the tree planting until the last possible second.)

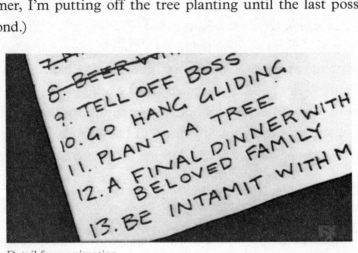

Detail from animation

The easiest way to build a story is not to use your imagination, but to simply apply logic. Maggie is a baby, so *logically* Homer would want to make a videotape for her to watch when she's older. To do that, he would *logically* need a camera. If he doesn't have one, then *logically* he needs to borrow one from his neighbor. This line of logic led to pitching a scene where Homer goes next door and finds the Flanders family pulling taffy. While saying goodbye, Flanders invites all the Simpsons to a barbecue that weekend. Homer offers to bring the thickest, juiciest T-bone steaks. As soon as the door closes, Homer chuckles, "Joke's on him. I'll be dead by then."

In addition to exploring things Homer would logically *want* to do in this situation, we discussed things he would *need* to do. Someone pitched a scene where Homer stops by to check in on his life insurance policy.

> "I'm afraid your life insurance has lapsed," the insurance agent says, peering at the policy. "Oh, sorry! It will lapse tomorrow."
> "Heh heh heh," says Homer. "How much?"
> "Fifteen thousand dollars."
> "Up it to fifteen million."
> "Isn't that a lot?" says the agent.
> "Hey, I feel lucky," says Homer.

Another scene—pitched by Jim Brooks via Sam—had Homer going to church to seek solace from Reverend Lovejoy. Instead, Rev. Lovejoy comments on how often Homer fell asleep during his sermons.

"I'm sorry, Mr. Simpson, this is probably a little small of me, but I bet right now you're wishing you'd been a better Christian."

Some of the jokes were harsh, like Grandpa Simpson telling Homer, "I know the greatest tragedy is to outlive your children . . . but it doesn't feel so bad." The meanest jokes rarely make it into the script, although they often make the room laugh the hardest.

Following a traditional story pattern, Homer's dilemma must get worse at the end of Act Two.

"What if he's speeding home and then gets stuck in traffic?" someone pitched.

I heard the word "speeding" and realized we could up the ante.

"What if he gets pulled over by a cop and thrown in jail?" I said.

That seemed overly cruel—and funny—so we decided that a cell door clanging shut would end Act Two.

Act Three tumbled out as a race against time. Homer needs to get out of jail, stop at the bar to see Moe, and get home in time to be "intamit with Marge." Someone pitched a post-coital snippet of dialogue.

"You know, Marge, I don't mind if you marry someone with money to take care of the kids," Homer says. "Like Jackie Onassis."

"Remind me which one of our friends is a Greek tycoon," says Marge. (Bonus points if you knew Marge's maiden name is Bouvier.)

For the conclusion of the story, we thought Marge could fall asleep after sex while Homer sneaks downstairs to cherish every last second. He flips through *TV Guide*. Nothing's on. The Bible on a bookshelf catches his eye. Aware of his shortcomings, he opens it up to reveal two cassette tapes.

"Ooh, the good book on tape. Phil Collins reads *Genesis*." (Bonus points if you knew Collins was the drummer in the band Genesis.)

Homer drifts off and we dissolve to the next morning. Marge finds him slumped in a chair. He snores and Marge realizes he's alive. The two celebrate.

While breaking the story in the room, I scribbled down pitches as fast as I could. I always advise writers to take their own notes. Too often, this task falls to an assistant who'll capture the gist of jokes, but miss the exact wording. Specific words in a specific order matter. Taking notes also allows a writer to annotate. I put a star next to a line that gets a big laugh, especially from the showrunner. Not only does it remind me to include that joke; it also gives me a window into the showrunner's sense of humor.

I walked out of the *Simpsons* room with over thirty handwritten pages. The next step was turning the scrawled notes into a neat outline.

The Outline

An outline lays out the acts and scenes while clarifying and tracking the attitudes of the characters. On some series, you're not given much to work with and need to fill in a lot of plot holes. *The Simpsons* room generated so much material that outlining became more an exercise in choice than creation. I had four different possible explanations for why the Simpsons decide to try sushi:

1. Marge heard about sushi at the beauty shop or pet store.
2. Lisa is bored with meatloaf and wants to try something new. Homer defends meatloaf: "Every time I find something different. A clove of garlic. A hint of cayenne."
3. Marge says her sister likes sushi "and she's got good taste." "Marge," says Homer, "That woman thinks I'm a stupid clod."
4. The family heads to Homer's favorite burger joint and discovers it's closed for health violations. The sushi place is next door.

I went with #2 since it contained the emotional component that Lisa is bored. A character with a strong attitude generates more comedy. A joke is just a joke, but an emotion can be mined. Runner-up was #4 where Homer is upset that his burger joint is shut down. ("Oh no! The rotating pie station!")

The outline pulled together quickly since Homer checking off his list of activities provided a built-in structure. In the room, pitches jump from scene to scene, but an outline requires that the writer figure out the transitions. The fugu episode took place over twenty-four hours—most sitcom stories work better in a compressed time—and we hadn't discussed a transition from the night where Homer gets poisoned to the next day. I tried this:

INT. BEDROOM - NIGHT

                HOMER
        (ADJUSTING ALARM CLOCK) Then I'll get up at
        seven to make the most of my last day.

INT. BEDROOM - 7 AM
The alarm rings. Homer rolls over and turns it off
without getting up.

INT. BEDROOM — 11:30
Homer rolls over, opens his eyes and sees the clock.

                HOMER
        11:30!

INT. LIVING ROOM - MINUTES LATER

                HOMER
        (UPSET) Marge, why did you let me sleep
        so late?

                MARGE
        You looked so peaceful lying there.

                HOMER
        There'll be plenty of time for that!

Another transition that required some thought was the moment after Marge discovers Homer isn't dead. The episode never
explains why he survives the poison. I thought Homer could return to the restaurant the next day.

                MASTER CHEF
        Ah, Mr. Simpson, so you live. Our
        blowfish is so weak it won't even kill
        a cat. I must get a new wholesaler.
        Anyway, you owe us $56.80. We have a
        policy of not charging customers who
        die from eating our sushi. But since you
        survived . . .

A typical sitcom outline has ten to twelve single-spaced pages. My *Simpsons* outline had seventeen, and that was after cutting funny lines like, "Tomorrow is the last day of the rest of my life." Finally, I needed to give the episode a title. As a Dr. Seuss fan, I went with "One Fish, Two Fish, Blowfish, Blue Fish." It stuck.

Outline Notes

A few days after I turned in my outline, I was back in the *Simpsons* office to get notes. Matt Groening and some additional writers (all male) joined the group, and we moved to a conference room next to Sam's office. The chairs were arranged in a circle. I sat to the left of Sam, and Matt sat directly across. Jim Brooks wasn't there, but he'd read the outline and given his notes to Sam.

The session did not start well. Sam thought it took too long to get the family to the sushi restaurant. I drew a big line through my first two pages. One of the best rules of screenwriting is "Start late, end early." In real life, we ring doorbells and ask, "How are you?" In TV and movies, you can just jump to the scene of the crime.

Thankfully, the notes slowed down on page three. Details were added. In the outline, the Master Chef is unavailable to slice the fugu because he's making out with a woman in the backseat of a car. Someone suggested it should be Bart's teacher Mrs. Krabappel. They had to spell her name out slowly for me. This exchange didn't make it into the script, but it still cracks me up.

> **MASTER CHEF**
> Oh, Miss Krabappel, your hair smells so clean.
>
> **MISS KRABAPPEL**
> Oh, Mr. Hirohito, can you really get me a futomaki roll?

The notes session dragged on. At one point, I looked over and saw that Matt had decided to rest his eyes for a bit, arms crossed in front of his torso at the wrists. I glanced over at Sam. I didn't know it at the time, but there was tension between the two Executive Producers. Our eyes met and Sam's took on a conspiratorial gleam.

"Don't wake him," Sam mouthed.

Tragically, Sam died in 2014. He was only fifty-nine. When he learned that his cancer was untreatable, he devoted himself to charitable work to save and protect animals. It's hard not to think about his choice in light of the theme of this episode. Sam did so much good in the time he had.

In the last two pages of the outline, Homer gets out of jail and races home to make love to Marge. I thought it would be funny to have Homer grab Marge, lead her toward the bedroom and then cut to the two lying in bed, staring at the ceiling.

"It's understandable, Homer. Especially when you consider all the stress you've been under," Marge says.

In my old copy of the outline, the word "sweet" is written over this dialogue. Sam instructed me not to play the scene for laughs. Someone suggested that maybe Marge could read a poem that she'd written for Homer as they lay in bed. I loved that idea.

The next scene was Homer saying goodbye to his kids and then heading downstairs. When we got to the second-to-last scene where Marge finds Homer's slumped body, Sam peered at his notes. "Wait, Jim has an idea for here."

I transcribed the pitch exactly as Sam read it: Marge touches his chin. "His drool is warm. He's alive. He's alive."

This is truly my favorite line in the entire episode. Hilarious and poignant, it's quintessential Jim Brooks.

Sam rejected the scene I'd added to explain why the poison-ous fugu hadn't killed Homer. He said nobody would question Homer's survival. (It still kind of bugs me.) I'd also added a tag that wrapped up all the story threads. Sam thought it worked well and approved it.

Writer's Draft

Armed with a very detailed outline, I strung a script together. There are always discoveries along the way. I added "Hang glid-ing" to Homer's bucket list.

> "Oh Homer," says Marge, "that's too dangerous."
> "Maybe at the end of the day," he concedes.

I took Sam's tonal note to be sweeter. In addition to writing a poem for Marge, I put in three quick beats of Homer stopping by each of his kids' bedrooms for one last look.

```
                    HOMER
     Goodbye, Maggie. Stay as sweet as you
     are.
                    (then)
     Goodbye, Lisa. I know you'll make me proud.
                    (then)
     Goodbye, Bart. I like your sheets.
```

Table Read Draft

As a freelancer, I didn't take part in the next stage where the staff "tables a script." This means going through page-by-page before the table read. Sometimes scripts are overhauled com-pletely and writers end up with a "Written by" credit on an episode they barely recognize. I was told that "One Fish, Two Fish . . ." changed about the same amount as a script by a writer on staff.

The changes made scenes punchier. Bart and Lisa singing "Mockingbird" became Bart and Lisa singing "Shaft," one of the most memorable sequences in the episode. At first, the FOX censors wouldn't approve the song because of the lyric: "He's a bad mother—Watch your mouth!" The producers pushed back. Sam sent over a tape of Isaac Hayes performing "Shaft" on the Oscars and the censors relented.

Only one revision bumped me. At one point, Homer offers Bart three phrases that will help get him through life. The table script read: "Number one, 'Cover for me.' Number two, 'Oh good idea, boss.' Number three, 'It was like that when I got here.'" Fans love that line, but I still prefer the original three pieces of advice: "Number one, you'll end up with a bad job, but if you kiss up, you can take a day off every now and then. Number two, find a woman who loves you, think twice about having kids. Number three, don't eat blowfish."

Production (or Shooting) Draft

George Takei was cast as Akira Kurosawa, the sushi waiter, and Larry King read the Bible passage, tacking on some sports picks at the end. Al and Mike shepherded the script through the production process. For animation that includes recording the actors, approving animatics (preliminary sketches), and adjusting the script and animation at every step. "One Fish" ran long and needed trimming. Sometimes it makes sense to omit an entire scene rather than making smaller trims throughout, which can lead to choppiness. Sadly, Homer seeking solace from Rev. Lovejoy didn't make it to air.

Produced Episode

"One Fish, Two Fish, Blowfish, Blue Fish" premiered on January 24, 1991. I watched with my sister Claire and brother-in-law Rob and was delighted to see the finished product. The biggest surprise came at the very end. I was expecting the tag that wrapped up all of Homer's actions, but it was slashed for time. Instead, Homer simply declares, "From now on, I will live life to the fullest!" This pronouncement is followed by a hard cut to Homer in his armchair, eating pork rinds while watching bowling on TV. There was no dialogue. Just the sound of a bowling commentator and crunching pork rinds. The new last scene—concocted by Al and Mike—was a gut punch. Homer had stared death in the face . . . and had learned absolutely nothing. In that moment, we all became Homer, staring at a cartoon character who's staring at bowling as our lives tick away.

The quality and quantity of material generated by the *Simpsons* writers was astonishing. I could have written three different versions of the same story. And even if Homer learned no lessons from his experience, I learned one from mine. At *Newhart,* I'd been instructed to write "Joke, joke, joke, joke." Working with Jim and Sam taught me there was another choice: to play a scene for real emotion. Here's a comparison of Marge's poem in my writer's draft (left) and the dialogue that aired.

MARGE	MARGE
The blackened clouds are forming	The blackened clouds are forming
Soon the rain will fall	Soon the rain will fall
My dear one is departing	My dear one is departing
But first please heed this call	But first please heed this call
That always will I love you	That always will I love you
Dah-dah-dah-dah-dah-dah dah	**My one, my love, my all.**
Sorry, I didn't have time to finish the couplet	

Sometimes sweet and sincere trumps snarky. I didn't understand that until I heard Julie Kavner's gravelly voice reading Marge's poem. When she got to the last line, I didn't laugh, but my eyes got misty. I suddenly cared deeply whether a cartoon character lived or died. And that's a far more complex and interesting response.

With the permission of *The Simpsons*, here's the lost tag from "One Fish, Two Fish, Blowfish, Blue Fish":

INT. SIMPSON HOUSE—LIVING ROOM—THAT AFTERNOON

HOMER IS ON THE COUCH, DRINKING A DUFF AND WATCHING ARM WRESTLING ON TV. HE LOOKS VERY CONTENT. MARGE APPROACHES CARRYING MAGGIE AND SEVERAL PINK MESSAGE SLIPS.

> **MARGE**
> Homer, the phone's been ringing off the hook. (HANDS HIM SLIPS) The police moved your court date . . .

> **HOMER**
> Ohhh.

> **MARGE**
> The towing company has your car . . .

> **HOMER**
> Barney!

> **MARGE**
> Your father says he wants to fly kites with you . . .

> **HOMER**
> Oh, yeah.

> **MARGE**
> And your boss wants to see you first thing in the morning.

> **HOMER**
> Oh, no.

BART STICKS HIS HEAD IN.

BART
Hey, Dad, Mr. Flanders says, and I quote, "Where the ding-dong-doodley are the steaks?"

HOMER
(THROUGH GRITTED TEETH) It's still great to be alive.

THE END

CHAPTER 7

Brush with Greatness: Working for Letterman

Top Ten Least Popular Summer Camps
10. Camp Tick in beautiful Lyme, Connecticut

—My first Top Ten joke, aired July 12, 1990

B Y JUNE 1990, IT WAS STARTING TO FEEL LIKE I BE-longed in Hollywood. I knew my way around the free-ways and I'd already had the obligatory threesome with Warren Beatty. Okay, that's an exaggeration. But I did have dinner with Warren and one other guy. Sadly, I can't confirm that Warren is a Grade A lover, but I can confirm that he's a Grade A wingman.

I met political pollster Pat Caddell at a party where we had a nice talk and he asked for my number using the oddest pickup line that I'd ever heard: "Maybe we could have dinner some night. I'll bring Warren Beatty."

Odd, but effective. We made a date for dinner at a dark

restaurant in Brentwood. Pat arrived, solo, and explained that Warren was tied up in post-production on *Dick Tracy*. Ah, the old bait and switch. It was fine. I could always talk politics with Pat, who made his name helping Jimmy Carter become president. Pat and I were halfway through dinner when suddenly . . . he walked into the party like he was walking onto a yacht.

Warren Beatty, in the flesh, made his way toward our table and sat down. He apologized for being late, and then did something that truly amazed me. Instead of launching into a monologue about his life, he started asking me questions about mine. He wanted to know all about *SPY* magazine. Were Kurt and Graydon good guys? He even asked follow-ups, which meant he was listening to my answers. No wonder women tumbled for him.

The next day, I called my mom. "Guess who I had dinner with last night?" I said, pausing for effect. "Warren Beatty!"

"Don't you sleep with him," my mother snapped in a tone I'd never heard before.

"Don't worry, Mom," I said. "It's not gonna happen."

My reasoning was less moral and more realistic. "He's currently dating Madonna," I added.

Not much was going on in my personal life around this time. A long-distance relationship with a nice guy in NYC had cratered during my time at *Newhart*. I thought about moving back east to try and jumpstart the romance. Impulsively, I sent some more material to Steve O'Donnell, the head writer at *Late Night with David Letterman*. I even included a small Japanese toy in my envelope, employing the same trick as charities that give you a nickel to get you to open their letters.

I didn't hear back so I took a job on a new sitcom called *Married People*. Created by Robert Sternin and Prudence Fraser, the series centered on three couples (newlyweds, new parents, and grandparents) who lived on different floors of a townhouse. I was just settling in when, at the start of the second week, Steve

O'Donnell called. He'd received my material and they had an opening. Could I come in and meet with Dave?

I was in shock. *Late Night* was known for being a frat house—a *Harvard Lampoon* frat house, but still. At that point, Merrill Markoe was the only woman who'd ever worked on the writing staff. Bitingly brilliant and inventive, Merrill served as head writer in the early years and is widely credited with co-creating the show.

"What's the difference between Johnny Carson and David Letterman?" Merrill once joked. "Me."

Merrill and Dave were also a couple, but after seven years and four Emmys, she walked away from both the job and the relationship. There'd been no female writer hired since. I called Gavin excited that I had a shot at joining the *Late Night* staff. He couldn't fathom why I'd even contemplate a leap from a prime-time sitcom to a late-night talk show.

"Everyone wants to go the other way," Gavin said.

"I know. But I want to write for the funniest man on television."

I took that Friday off from *Married People* and flew east. My first meeting was with Steve, whose office had papers piled on every surface and even spilling onto the floor. I'm not an organized person myself so the mess put me at ease. Also, Steve is one of the most affable and quick-witted people on earth. I spoke fondly of his equally clever twin brother, Mark, who drew cartoons for *SPY* (and wrote novels and plays including the Tony-award winning book for *Hairspray*). Steve walked me down the hall to Dave's office and handed me off to an assistant. That's when I realized that I'd be meeting with Dave alone.

I'd seen photos of Dave's office in magazines, so the first thing I did was look up to see the dangling pencils that he famously tossed into the acoustic tile ceiling. For the rest of the meeting, the pencils hovered above me like little swords of Damocles. Dave sat behind his desk, wearing sweats and clutching a football. I'd prepared some jokes, but my main task was to convey that I could fit in. I mentioned my sportswriting background. We talked about favorite teams while Dave tossed the football into the air. When an employee walked in, he threw the ball at her without warning. She caught it.

Before long, Dave signaled the interview was over.

"Thanks for stopping by," he said, standing up.

The meeting seemed to go well. I hadn't startled Dave by making any sudden moves. Later that day, Gavin called. He sounded angry.

"Congratulations. You got the job. Now turn it down."

I screamed with happiness.

Gavin told me I was nuts. The job was a 75 percent pay cut for me, and, by extension, for him. I told him that this was my dream job. He reminded me that I already had a job and a two-year contract that my bosses might not let me break. I returned to LA and talked to the *Married People* showrunners. I told them that I had a chance to write for Letterman, and they gave me the reaction that my agent hadn't.

"You have to take it!" they both exclaimed.

I moved back to my rental studio on Fifty-Seventh and Eighth, walking distance from the *Late Night* offices at 30 Rock. The night before my first day, I opened my closet to figure out what to wear. After trying on a dozen outfits, I decided to go with Levi's, a monochromatic shirt, and shiny patent-leather Oxfords from Fiorucci. People say, "Dress for the job you want," and since I wanted a job that guys had, I dressed like a guy.

On the walk to work the next morning, I felt a combination of excitement and pride. Only later would I learn what journalist Alexandra Petri perfectly expressed in this tweet: "wish I could shake younger me and tell her 'if you are the only girl in the room it doesn't mean you're better. it means something is wrong.'"

I now understand some of the factors that helped me slip through the gates. Studies show that men are promoted based on potential and women on experience. For most of the male writers, *Late Night* was their first TV job. I had already racked up credits on five TV series, including *The Simpsons*. I had proved myself to the point that *Late Night* was willing to take "a chance" on me. Second, I was a good "culture fit"—a popular and flawed hiring strategy that considers a candidate's background in addition to their skills. A good culture fit allows a new employee to slide into an existing team. It's also a great way to keep out the weirdos. The *Late Night* writers' room was filled with college-educated, white, cisgendered men who liked sports and were always up for pizza. I rifled through my credentials. Harvard degree? Check. Hetero? Check. Sports fan? Check. Up for pizza? Check. Penis? Well, I'd had my share.

There's no doubt that my privileged background and skin color helped get me the job. Years later, I worked on a short-lived sitcom with the stunningly talented Larry Wilmore. One day, Larry and I got into a friendly argument about who had it tougher in TV writers' rooms: women or African Americans. You can probably guess who took which side. Larry and I argued our cases to a stalemate. We did, however, agree on one thing: African American women had it the hardest.

Today, I would concede to Larry that, at least at *Letterman*, it was preferable to be a white woman. The show ran from 1982 to 2015, and the writers' room never included a person of color.

That first morning, I got to work early and settled into my office, which was located on the main hallway, across from the copy room. A stack of papers was sitting on the desk—*New York Times, Daily News, New York Post*—the tools of a topical joke writer. Other writers started streaming past my door. Most waved and kept going. One stopped to introduce himself and chat about mutual friends. It all seemed friendly until just before he exited when he made an offbeat prediction.

"Before this is over," he said, pointedly, "I will see a tampon fall out of your purse."

I felt strangely shaken as he walked away. Over the years, when I've repeated this story, friends usually react confused.

"Why would he have said that?"

I had no idea . . . until about twenty years later when I was working on *Lean In* and learned about "stereotype threat." It turns out that when members of a group are made aware of a negative stereotype, they are more likely to conform to that stereotype. For example, our culture perpetuates the myth that girls don't excel at math so when asked to check off a box marked M or F before a math test, girls perform worse. Simply reminding girls that they're girls creates anxiety which disrupts cognitive processing. Our culture also perpetuates the myth that women aren't funny. Perhaps this explains why that male writer went out of his way to remind me of my gender that first day. If he were simply trying to shock, he could've said, "Before this is over, I will hear you fart." It's the same joke construction (i.e., in the future, some bodily function will embarrass you) but nongender specific. I don't think he acted consciously, but by mentioning a tampon, he singled me out by what set me apart.

In a more hospitable gesture, someone on the production

Late Night 8th season baseball shirt

staff stopped by my office to give me a welcome gift: an old-timey, pinstriped *Late Night* baseball shirt made of scratchy white wool flannel. The shirt had an "8" on the front and back commemorating the eighth season. I tried it on and it fell to mid-thigh. Most show jackets and t-shirts billow on me. They always give me a "small" but it's often a "men's small."

Dave also paused at my door to greet me. Actually, I caught a glimpse of the boss almost every day when he passed my office at about 10:50 a.m. Dave walked briskly, like a guy hurrying home in a rainstorm. In those days, Dave rarely set foot in the writers' room and preferred to hear pitches over the car phone on his drive home. The writers would generate ideas during the day, then we'd break for that night's taping. After the show, Dave would return to the office for a postmortem. We'd wait until we saw him hustling past the writers' room, head fixed straight ahead to avoid any eye contact. About seven minutes later, Steve would gather his papers and say, "Well, I guess I'll go call Dave."

Even this minimal interaction was reduced when the show switched networks in 1993 and relocated to the Ed Sullivan Theater. In the new offices, Dave and the writers were no longer on the same floor. At first, a glass security door to the executive suite required a card swipe, but supposedly Dave kept forgetting his ID so they switched to a thumbprint recognition system. At CBS, relations between the host and the writers grew even more strained. A former intern told me that Dave once dispatched him to hand back pitches for the top ten list to the writers with the message, "Like this. Only funny."

Despite Dave's bullying tactics, everyone in the office was eager to please him. It was practically built into the job description, which boiled down to "make Dave happy." When you're working that hard to please one person, it starts to feel like infatuation and the women—and men—who worked on the show routinely fell in love with the boss.

Since retiring, Dave has grown a long white beard and looks like his home address is a deserted island. But back in the day, he made sneering sexy. Dave combined a Midwest "aw-shuckness" with a New York City "fuck-youness" and the result was irresistible. Movie stars threw themselves at him. Julia Roberts and Drew Barrymore openly flirted with him onscreen. Behind the scenes, a stunning, Emmy-award winning blond actress once complained to a *Late Night* producer, "Why won't Dave fuck me?"

Dave was catnip to nonfamous, brainy women, too. A book editor friend pleaded with me to get her a date with my then-boss.

"He seems so miserable on the show," she told me. "But I think I could make him happy. We'd have fun!"

My friend's complete confidence that she could soothe Dave's anxieties led me to coin a proverb: "A woman who thinks it would be fun to date David Letterman is a woman who knows nothing about show business."

Show business attracts performers driven by the need for attention, the need for praise, the need for approval . . . the need . . . the need . . . See the through line? The creative process is often wrapped up in bottomless anxiety and when the world applauds the result, it lessens the anxiety. Briefly. Then the need returns and even intensifies. Dave's superpower was being able to cling to his neurotic insecurity in the face of staggering success. It made no sense to me. He was consistently funny and the best interviewer in late night. Yet his perception seemed to be that every joke tanked and every show was lame. One Friday, Dave finished taping what I thought was a fine and entertaining hour of television—a perfect kickoff to a weekend. A few minutes later, I heard Dave storming from the elevator to his office.

"You know what I'm gonna do?" he blared. "I'm gonna go to Connecticut, shut all the doors and windows, and pump my house full of snot!"

Another time, Dave was so distressed that during the show's postmortem, he made a group of producers and staffers line up. He stood at the head of the line and announced that he wanted each of them to take a swing at him. Nobody wanted to hit their boss, but apparently, he insisted. He moved down the row, stopping in front of each staffer and encouraging them, "Harder.

No, harder!" as they delivered uncertain punches to his shoulder. This story perfectly captures Dave's unique spin on the power dynamic: he's the bully who makes you punch *him*.

Truth is often the best basis for comedy, so I embraced the "Dave is a bully" conceit for many of my sketches. In one viewer mail bit, I had Dave hold a magnifying glass over a tiny sunbather in the miniature NYC cityscape until the sunbather exploded in flames. Another letter asked, "How many pairs of glasses does Paul Shaffer own?" Dave answers that Paul actually wears a new pair of glasses every night. Dave tries to badger Paul into telling the audience why, but Paul is reluctant to explain. Dave tells Hal Gurnee (the director) to roll some "bogus" explanatory videotape. We cut to a pre-taped segment of Paul exiting into a hallway where Dave is waiting, his jacket slung over his shoulder.

"Well, well, well, look who we have here. If it isn't Paul Shaffer," Dave says menacingly.

Dave proceeds to shake Paul down for money. Paul swears he doesn't have any so Dave roughs him up, shoving Paul face-first into a wall. When Paul turns around, his glasses are mangled. Dave looks on and laughs as Paul shakes his head and mutters, "Every day we seem to go through this."

Although Dave played a convincing tormentor on TV, he was always nice to me. Sometimes while racing to his office in the morning, he'd break his stride and pause outside my door.

"Hey, how's it going. Do you need anything? Would you like some soup?"

Once Dave dropped in to let me know that one of my Top Ten pitches surprised him. I looked forward to the occasions when he stopped by, until one day in the writers' room, we landed on a timely idea. Some of the writers wanted Steve to pitch it to Dave immediately so we could run with the premise that night. Steve seemed reluctant. He preferred to wait and call Dave in his car.

"Or," he said, "perhaps Nell could pitch it to Dave the next time he's in her office."

I was mortified at being singled out. It was just an offhand comment, but I took it as an insinuation that I was forming a less-than-professional relationship with the boss. My response was to start shutting my door at 10:30 so that when Dave strode down the hall, there'd be no reason for him to pause.

My hyper-sensitivity probably stemmed from my experience with Stafford. I had a deep distaste for colleagues blurring the line between personal and professional, and lines were being blurred like crazy at *Late Night*. To me, the office resembled Versailles. It was a culture of palace intrigue with whisper campaigns, shifting alliances, and sexual liaisons. Dave reigned supreme, enjoying the rights and privileges of the monarch. It was admirable of me to shut my office door to remove any appearance of impropriety. It was also incredibly stupid. I cut myself off from having direct access to the king.

Like many, I tried to ignore the intrigue and focus on the work. That had its own frustrations. Writers would submit sketches by slipping them under Steve's door, which explained the papers I'd seen on the floor of his office. Months would go by without a reaction. I joined the show in July and my first week there, I wrote a script for an elaborate pre-taped trailer for a summer blockbuster *Late Night: The Movie*. The bit featured Dave as an action star being chased by fireballs down the halls of 30 Rock while tossing out his catch phrase: "Aw, man, would you look at this?" The trailer also starred Michael Douglas as "Morty," Denzel Washington as "bandleader Paul Shaffer," and Glenn Close as "the lovely assistant Rose who betrayed them all." I never got any response, yes or no. Summer turned into fall and an action movie trailer no longer made sense.

I contributed in every way available. For immediate gratification, there was always the "Top Ten List." A bigger thrill was when

Dave included jokes I wrote in his monologue. One gag started with Dave complaining that his mom was cleaning out the attic and had tossed a bunch of his things even though there was "some valuable stuff in there." The audience imagined Dave pining over his Golden Age comic books or baseball cards, and then he delivered the punchline, "I said, 'Mom, Mom, did you have to throw out my collection of Krugerrands?'"

Prop from Viewer Mail

Thursdays were my favorite because we tackled Viewer Mail. One week, a viewer noted that Dave seemed to have "an extra air of giddiness" about him. I created a new cologne for Dave to hawk: "Uncork the bottle and release the giggly schoolgirl inside you! Dave Letterman's "Giddiness"—available at all fine perfume counters. By Prince Matchabelli."

A more elaborate sketch involved a pre-tape of Paul at the "People's Choice Awards," winning in the category, "The Celebrity You'd Least Like To Have Dinner With." I got to sit behind Paul in my only on-camera appearance for *Late Night.*

Me, top left-hand corner, appearing in a
Viewer Mail bit, featuring Paul Shaffer.

In October, Steve let me know that the show was picking up my option for the next cycle. Unlike at *Newhart,* I hadn't been worried. The increased job security meant I could upgrade from the studio I'd been living in since my divorce. I found a one-bedroom rental in the back of an Art Deco building on Central Park West and signed a two-year lease.

That night, I couldn't sleep. The thought of spending more time at *Late Night* made me uncomfortable. I couldn't quite pin-point the problem, but the show's creative process was wildly inefficient and the overall mood was unhappy. This wasn't just my perception. Years later, Dave greeted a new writer by saying, "This is a terrible job, but it will look good on your résumé."

I'd been so concerned about whether I would suit *Late Night* that I hadn't contemplated whether *Late Night* would suit me.

Samples from Two Submissions for Top Ten Lists

Top Ten Ways You Know You Have a Bad Doctor
10/25/1990

- He bets you five bucks that it's two livers and one kidney

- Combination diploma/cab driver's license

- As he writes out prescriptions, he says, "One for you and one for me . . ."

- He wears a rubber glove on his head (Oh sorry, that's the way you know a bad comedian)

- When you mispronounce his name and he tells you it's a hard *g* in "Mengele"

- He makes you do your own pelvic exam while he watches

- When she giggles she was a stewardess before she met her husband, Dean of Yale Medical School

- He insists on holding the specimen cup

Lots of talented people—male and female—managed to become long-time denizens of what one producer dubbed "Crazytown," but I just couldn't see me thriving there. Roughly five months after I got my dream job, I decided to quit. I only wish I'd come to this realization before I signed a new apartment lease.

After I gave notice, I was summoned to Dave's office.

"I hear you're moving on," Dave said. "Seems like you just got here, so I was wondering why."

I considered pouring out my frustrations, but didn't see an upside. Only an idiot would complain to the owner of a donut shop that donuts are unhealthy. Also, Dave's office door was open and his assistant, one of his rumored mistresses, was sit-

Top Ten Ways McDonald's Is Getting Healthier
7/25/1990

- Fresher salads, fewer snipers

- Reducing radiation emitted by Golden Arches

- Fired all lepers on staff

- Less horse tallow in the beef tallow

- Ended tie-in promotion with *Henry: Portrait of a Serial Killer*

- Special sauce now used for original purpose of killing bugs

- Customers instructed to remove cardboard from hot apple pie *before* eating

- Employees encouraged to use Kleenex instead of hamburger buns

ting within earshot. I figured any complaints I voiced would be repeated and used against me.

"I just miss LA," I shrugged.

"You're welcome back any time," Dave said.

I glowed. Like everyone else, I wanted the approval of the king.

And I don't even hold the record for that show's fastest-quitting writer. Another writer got so frustrated that he left before his first cycle was up. Unlike me, he supposedly didn't hold back and told Dave off before he left. Later, he and Dave patched things up and Louis C.K. returned to the show.

The *Late Night* culture fit me about as well as that too-big, scratchy baseball shirt they handed me on day one. I once brought the shirt into a tailor to see if it could be hemmed. The tailor shook his head and informed me that "the thick fabric did not lend itself to alteration." Now it hangs in my closet, a perfect metaphor.

On my last day at *Late Night*, I wrote my final top ten jokes and packed my entire office in a small box. There was just one last matter to bring everything full circle: As I was saying good-bye to some writers, a tampon fell out of my pocket. The writer who'd predicted this would happen on my first day was there to see it happen on my last. We looked at each other in amazement. Yep, he called it. And we laughed.

Maybe because I was already out the door, I didn't feel embarrassed. There was no denying that I was a woman. And if anything, being a woman meant I had to work harder and be tougher. As the saying goes: Ginger Rogers did everything Fred Astaire did, backwards and in heels . . . and while bleeding from her vagina five days each month.

CHAPTER 8

The Meet Cute

Sometimes I go into my own little world. It's okay, they know me there.

—Joel Hodgson

M OST ROMANTIC COMEDIES BEGIN WITH A MEET cute. At a coffee shop, a man and woman both reach for a latte marked "Alex" . . . and their eyes meet. In a vet's waiting room, a dog barks at a cat, forcing the owners to break up the fight . . . and their eyes meet. Meet cutes are cheesy, but sometimes life imitates cheesy art.

After quitting *Late Night*, I returned to LA for good. Gavin thought it might take a while to get back into sitcoms, but comedic genius Robin Schiff (who later scripted *Romy and Michelle's High School Reunion*) galloped in like a knight in shining armor. Robin had read my *Simpsons* script and brought me onboard for punch up during the January 1991 shooting of *Princesses*, a pilot she cowrote with Barry Kemp and Mark Ganzel. Three weeks of work turned into over two years after Barry offered me a co-producer job on the hit sitcom *Coach*, which he created solo and starred Craig T. Nelson as a beleaguered college football coach. The series followed *Roseanne* in the lineup and consistently finished in the top ten. *Married People*, the series I'd been working on before moving back east, lasted only eighteen episodes. Unintentionally, my detour into late night had landed me on a more successful track.

Coach star Craig T. Nelson, circa 1991

During my second year at *Coach*, my friend Pat Whitney invited me to a "fun party." Now to me, a "fun party" is an oxymoron. I know many share my fear of social interaction, but the difference is when others say, "I'm terrible at parties," their friends respond, "What? No! You're great." When I say, "I'm terrible at parties," my friends respond, "So, what TV shows are you watching these days?"

I fail at fun. I don't drink. I don't smoke. I don't like small talk. I also don't like loud music that drowns out small talk. I worry about forgetting names or committing a *faux pas*. When I do, it fills me with regret for days. So I keep to myself at parties and eat a lot of chips, which also fills me with regret for days. Still, I really wanted to see Pat, and he really wanted to go to this party, so I tagged along.

As soon as we entered the Hollywood loft, I knew this gathering was well above my play-grade. I recognized a bunch of cool, funny actors including Janeane Garofalo and our host Mark Fite. Pat was instantly engaged while I stood off to the side, eating chips. After consuming a regretful amount, I went looking for something to drink.

The tiny kitchen was empty. The fridge was filled with beer and I rummaged around for a soda. I found one in back and was just about to close the door when—

"Hey, do you see any beer in there?" a male voice drawled behind me.

"It's pretty much *all* beer in here," I said.

I moved aside and the guy maneuvered around me. He grabbed a beer, closed the fridge, turned around . . . and our eyes met. I felt a jolt. Ohmigod, I was having a meet cute! It wasn't dramatic like Sandra Bullock saving Peter Gallagher from being run over by a train in *While You Were Sleeping*. But on the bright side, the guy wasn't in a coma.

We stood in the kitchen making small talk, which I suddenly didn't mind so much. His Midwest drawl sounded familiar, but I couldn't quite place him.

"Hey, I'm Joel," he said, sticking out his hand.

It clicked. I was talking to Joel Hodgson, the creator and star of *Mystery Science Theater 3000*, a hilarious, Peabody Award–winning show. The premise of *MST3K* is two mad scientists kidnap a regular Joe (in a red jumpsuit) and send him into space where they force him to watch B-movies. To ease his loneliness, Joel builds a bunch of chatty robots from spare parts. The bulk of an episode featured Joel and two robots in silhouette watching bad movies while sliding in wisecracks. The result was an original, inexpensive show that had the highest joke-per-minute ratio on TV.

I expected Joel to return quickly to the cool kids in the living room, but instead he lingered and sipped his beer. He said he'd recently moved from Minneapolis. I frantically searched my brain for any personal connection to the Midwest and chimed in that I was working on a TV series *set* in Minnesota. Lame. But Joel turned out to be a *Coach* fan. Before he returned to the party, we exchanged numbers.

The next day, Joel called. *Before noon*. I already loved this guy for not making me sweat it out. We met for coffee at Du-par's later that day. We both lived in Studio City, and since geography is the greatest determinant of whether a friendship will last in Los Angeles, we sailed over our first hurdle.

Spending time with Joel was light and easy. Although our backgrounds were very different, we had similar interests. We'd sit side by side on his couch, flipping through his sketchbooks and talking about ideas for shows and movies. We'd go to The Magic Castle, the members-only Academy of Magical Arts' club where Joel sometimes performed. (I don't know what attracts me to magicians, but I admit it: I'm a "mag hag.") We'd go to the Silent Movie Theatre on Fairfax and then grab a late-night dinner at Canter's Deli. Our evenings seemed date-like, but nothing was developing between us physically, not even a tingly brush of the hand while reaching into a tub of popcorn. Joel never mentioned a girlfriend, but a few times, he did bring up an ex-girlfriend. I can't remember what he said because my brain was too busy shouting, "He's straight! He's straight!"

I tried to play it cool. I didn't want to press the matter because maybe Joel wanted to take it slow. Finally, late one night after a comedy show, Joel drove me home. I was renting a little house at the end of a dead-end street so he offered to walk me to my door. We climbed the stairs and then chatted on the doorstep as the tension built. Something was going to happen. Something physical. We both felt this was the moment.

"Well, good night," Joel said. Then he thrust his hand out for me to shake.

I was stunned. I didn't know what else to do so I shook his hand.

"Nice to meet you," I said.

My limited cool deserted me. I started babbling about how I was hoping this would be more than a friendship, but it didn't seem to be headed in that direction and was that even a possibility because I really thought he was amazing. In a romantic comedy, this would have been Joel's cue to stop my babbling with a kiss.

Instead, he said, "I need to talk to you about that."

Nothing good ever follows those words. It's never "I need to talk to you about that . . . because I want to spend the rest of my life with you!"

That night was no exception. Joel explained that he was dating a British comedian/actress and, for several reasons, they were keeping their relationship quiet. Given the long distance, he wasn't sure that things would work out, but they were both committed to trying.

"I want you to meet her," he said. "I think you two would like each other a lot."

I nodded. Since we'd already shaken hands, I offered a quick goodbye and slipped inside the house. It hurt to be rejected. I flashed back to my teenage self, sobbing to my best friend Lisa Cetlin, "But I *really* liked him." I also worried that my unabashed declaration of desire might ruin our friendship. Would spending time together now be awkward? I went to bed feeling alone and unhappy.

The next morning, the phone rang and I heard a familiar Midwestern lilt.

"Hey, Nell. It's Joel."

I was *so* happy to hear his voice. He asked if he could come by.

I said, of course. A little later, Joel walked through my door and handed me a manila envelope.

"Here," he said. "I made this for you."

I opened the envelope and pulled out a piece of art.

Art by Joel Hodgson

My heart melted. The colors have bled over the past twenty-five years, but Joel's sweet and colorful gesture of friendship still hangs framed in my office.

Joel asked if I wanted to grab some lunch. It was early but sure. (Joel was born in Wisconsin and still insists on eating lunch at noon like a dairy farmer.) Within twelve hours of my feeling rejected, we were back to normal. I quickly converted my crush into a sisterly devotion and shifted my sights to a different kind of partnership. From the start, it seemed like Joel would be fun to collaborate with. We have similar senses of humor, but different skill sets. Joel's a visual thinker—as much an artist as a writer—and his years of performing magic and standup gave him an incredible sense of timing.

In late 1991, Disney hired me to do a last-second punch up for the Emilio Estevez classic *The Mighty Ducks*. (Yes, *The Mighty Ducks was* punched up.)

When Disney approached me about another job, I pulled Joel in. Our first collaboration was *Honey, We Shrunk Ourselves,* the third installment of the franchise. A first draft had been written by the supremely talented Karey Kirkpatrick, but the studio wanted revisions and Karey was already committed to a new project. Joel and I got the nod.

Honey, We Shrunk Ourselves was perfectly suited to Joel's visual sense of humor and to my love of tiny, shrunken people. We bought model train HO scale figurines and placed them all over my living room furniture to generate ideas. I had two wicker chairs and we realized that wicker could be climbed like a ladder. We used this device to get Wayne (played by Rick Moranis), his wife, and their friends Patti and Gordon to a windowsill where they find themselves knee-deep in dust. From our script:

```
INT. WINDOWSILL — DAY
THEY START KICKING AND PLAYING IN THE DUST. IT'S A
WINTER WONDERLAND AS GORDON SCOOPS UP AN ARMFUL AND
THROWS IT AT PATTY.

                    PATTI
          (laughing; re: dust) What is this stuff
          anyway?
```

                     WAYNE
Things decomposing—skin, hair, bug parts.

PATTI SHUDDERS AND QUICKLY SHAKES THE DUST OUT
OF HER HAIR.

Storyboard artist's drawing of the scene of the shrunken adults playing in the
dust. The curled bridge in the foreground is a broken piece of wicker from the
chair.

    The wicker chair excursion made it into the movie but the
playing-in-the-dust scene was nixed by the producer. He said
the dust would have required extensive hair and makeup cleanup between takes. Directed by Dean Cundey, *Honey, We Shrunk
Ourselves* was released direct-to-video in 1997 and became Disney's third-highest grossing movie of that year.

    After *Honey*, Joel and I were asked to do a pass on the live-
action *George of the Jungle*. Our additions included the opening
animated sequence and fighting to make the character "Ape" (an
ape) talk. At first, the studio balked at the talking animal con-

ceit, but Joel and I convinced them it was essential to fans of the cartoon. We wrote the first pass of Ape's dialogue which Monty Python's John Cleese voiced to perfection.

Joel's rendering of Ape Mountain

George of the Jungle became a massive hit thanks in large part to the sparkling Leslie Mann in her first starring role. The writing credit on the movie went into arbitration, which meant a jury of Writers Guild members read each version of the script and determined who contributed what percentage of the material. First and last writers—Josh Olsen and Audrey Wells—were awarded onscreen credit. Joel and I fell short.

Next, Joel and I decided to write a movie on spec. He had an idea about garbage bags that come to life and smother people, which worked brilliantly as an allegory for how we're all drowning in our own packaging. Joel called the project "The Bags" and we wrote it quickly. The tone tried to capture the heightened dialogue of the B-movies that Joel had lampooned on *MST3K*. In the climax, a twenty-foot garbage bag designed by sculptor Claes Oldenburg comes "alive" and terrorizes the town. We even gave Claes a speaking part.

Joel drew an awesome cover and we sent the spec script to our agents. I was convinced there'd be a bidding war.

Script cover by Joel Hodgson

It never sold. Much like trash, Hollywood didn't care.

Joel and I had better luck when we pursued writing an episode of *Space Ghost Coast to Coast,* an animated TBS talk show hosted by intergalactic crime fighter Space Ghost and his bandleader-slash-nemesis Zorak. We pitched a story to the producers that parodied "Amok Time," the *Star Trek* episode where Mr. Spock is drawn back to his home planet Vulcan to mate. In our version, Zorak (a praying mantis) also feels the urge to return to his home planet and mate. A complication arises when Zorak learns that after mating, a female praying mantis devours the male's head.

"Afraid of commitment!" exclaims Space Ghost.

The producers approved our plot and sent us off to write. It was the most insane script Joel and I ever wrote . . . and we wrote a movie that featured a huge, homicidal garbage bag designed by Claes Oldenburg.

Space Ghost producer Matt Hannigan had given us a Thursday deadline. On Wednesday evening, we stuffed our pages in a FedEx envelope and sent them to Atlanta. Things were a little rushed at the end, but we figured we'd make fixes after we got notes.

We didn't hear anything from the producers on Thursday. We didn't hear anything from the producers on Friday. I started to worry. There are no insecurities like writers' insecurities.

Monday came and still no phone call. On Tuesday, I was at Joel's house and, with his permission, I called to "check in" with Matt Harrigan.

"Hey, Matt. I just wanted to make sure you got the script," I said, using that old ruse.

"Yeah, we got it," Matt responded.

"Good, so Joel and I were wondering when you'll be giving us notes."

Dead silence on the other end. Oh, no. They must have hated the script.

"Actually," said Matt, "we recorded it Friday afternoon. It's all done."

"What?"

"Yeah, and it read great. Thanks so much."

I hung up the phone, and turned to Joel.

"We should quit right now," I said. "We will never have a better experience than this."

Over the next few years, Joel and I supported each other's TV projects. He was *Sabrina*'s magic supervisor and I wrote on *The TV Wheel*, his sketch-comedy pilot for HBO. Eventually, we got pulled in different creative directions. We stayed friends but didn't work together again until 2017 when Joel revived *MST3K* and invited me to write on a couple of episodes. It was like getting a chance to play for the '75 Red Sox.

Writing with Joel was mostly a clever excuse to spend time with him. I think a lot of successful collaborations boil down to people who just enjoy being together. That's true for everyone I've teamed up with. Walking into a room and seeing A. Scott Berg, Doug Coupland, Ian Stokes, Rob Bragin, Tim Carvell, or my sister Claire makes me instantly happy.

Shifting between a duo and solo career has helped me appreciate both. It's great to have a brilliant partner who shares the burden of generating ideas and dialogue. And it's great to write without a partner and not have to litigate every fucking line.

With *Last Week Tonight* EP Tim Carvell in Vegas where Tim was reporting a story about Wayne Newton, 2003

Collaboration is like canoeing: both paddlers need to row at the same speed and in the same direction. In some collaborations, one paddler steers and sets the pace. In others, the paddlers are perfectly synchronized. If the partnership works, the canoe glides through the water. If it doesn't, the canoe goes in circles.

I get why so many writers are drawn to collaboration, especially at the start of their careers. When you're insecure, it helps to have a partner say, "That's funny. Put it in the script." The downside of a partnership is splitting a paycheck; the upside is easing the loneliness of writing, and imposing some discipline. Writers struggle to motivate themselves. If you don't believe me, I have three half-written feature scripts to show you. Having a partner who depends on you raises the stakes and forces you to deliver. No writer wants to let down someone they love and respect. But letting yourself down? That's just Tuesday.

Joel's and my meet cute turned out to be less "rom" and more "com." Still, those early days when I was falling in love made me realize that after years of focusing on my career, I craved having someone to come home to. Pickings were slim in LA. Director Mike Nichols used to say that every relationship needed "a gardener and a flower." I definitely wanted to be the flower. But how would I find a gardener in the desert?

CHAPTER 9

We're All Oompa Loompas

Ohmigod, you're working on The Muppets? *That show must be soooo much fun to write for!*

—People who don't work in Hollywood

YOU'RE PROBABLY FAMILIAR WITH PHYSICIST ERWIN Schrödinger's thought experiment involving a hypothetical box, some radioactive material, and a hapless cat. But you might not know that Schrödinger's cat also reveals two fundamental truths about Hollywood. First, Schrödinger's experiment suggests that the act of observing a dynamic changes the dynamic. The same is true for a writers' room. Sometimes a journalist will try to capture the experience of being a TV writer with an article entitled, "A Day in the [*fill in the show*] Room" or even "A Week in the [*fill in the show*] Room." But until you've spent "Eight Soul-Crushing Months in the [*fill in the show*] Room," you can't understand what it's like. An outsider isn't privy to the venting in the parking garage or a coworker pantomiming blowing his brains out in the snack room. A writers' room is like a family and we all know that families act differently when they have company.

Schrödinger's experiment also illustrates the absurdity of quantum mechanics because until the lid of the box is lifted, the cat inside is simultaneously dead and alive. This brings us to the second truth of the writers' room: Working on a TV show is simultaneously fun and not fun. When people conclude that it must be "soooo much fun" to work on *The Muppets*, it's like assuming the Oompa Loompas love every minute working at Willy Wonka's chocolate factory. To outsiders, it's all chocolate waterfalls and funny songs. But late at night, someone's got to clean up after all those nut-testing squirrels. And let's just say the nuts are very high in fiber.

On the plus side, I can't think of another workplace where job performance is tied to how hard you can make your coworkers laugh. Perks include high salaries, low risk of injury, sweet snacks, salty snacks, and the chance to hang out with pop culture icons like Mahna Mahna and his back-up singers, the Snowths.

With the Snowths

The ratio of fun versus not fun varies from show to show and depends on what I call the three P's: the people, the process, and the product. It's a rarity to work on a show where all three Ps are consistently satisfying. You're lucky if you get two out of three. More often, you settle for one.

The people, process, and product are the factors that determine any employee's happiness. Here's a breakdown of Hollywood's unique spin on office culture:

People

Every show starts off a delight. The first week is like a group date with writers sharing well-honed stories about former jobs, nightmare relationships, and bouts of diarrhea. Fathers talk openly about their children while mothers often downplay theirs. If asked whether I have kids, I usually reply: "I've got two sons, but I'm blanking on their names right now." As work gets more pressured, the ease of the early casual weeks falls away. Personalities clash, factions form, and every day feels like Thanksgiving with your dysfunctional family.

The showrunner sets the tone, which bakes a potential problem right into the free bagels. Most showrunners begin their careers as writers, spending a lot of time in their heads. As they move up the production ladder, writers expand their skill set, learning how to cast, edit, approve wardrobe, etc. At no point are writers taught how to manage people. Eventually, the writer who was good at ordering around characters in his head ends up in charge of actual human beings. The Writers Guild recognized this oversight and created a Showrunners' Training Program to help teach management techniques to members. But not all the necessary skills, like empathy and generosity, can be easily taught. Good luck trying to explain personal boundaries to a showrunner who starts a Monday morning meeting with,

"The weirdest thing happened this weekend. I had a wet dream and woke up with a load in my pants."

Now this showrunner has every right to share his touching story. That's not just my opinion, it's the ruling of the California Supreme Court. In 2006, a *Friends* writers' assistant charged that lewd talk in the room constituted sexual harassment. The *Friends* writing staff denied the charge and argued that lewd talk was often part of the creative process. The justices sided with the writers and dismissed the suit. Every TV writer breathed a sigh of relief. Writers need to feel safe and comfortable enough to push boundaries and find comedy. If someone wants to divulge that his father is a chronic masturbator, that's fine. The only risk that information should carry is when his father visits the office and shakes everyone's hand, there will be lots of Purell jokes.

Still, there's a difference between allowing people to share personal information and forcing them to. The same showrunner who talked about his wet dream once went around the table and asked all the writers to reveal the age at which they lost their virginity. I declined. The question wasn't relevant to the show and the context wasn't work-related. The lower-level writers all answered even though some seemed reluctant. Then the showrunner launched into his own tale which was more horrifying than amusing. That white, straight, male showrunner missed the irony that the discussion that made him feel safe and comfortable might make a more vulnerable person feel trapped and targeted.

Fortunately, I witnessed early on how a great showrunner operates. My *Coach* boss Barry Kemp displayed the five qualities that you hope to find in a leader in any field.

A great leader . . .

1. understands the mission better than anyone in the room and can communicate it.

2. is the hardest working person in the room.
3. is the most generous person in the room, not just with compensation, but also with praise and credit.
4. allows dissent and even invites it.
5. listens and learns.

Barry hit all these points while still being the funniest person in the room. He was also flawlessly polite. If a joke fell flat during a table read, Barry would make a small question mark in the margin. After the read, we'd return to the room and start the rewrite. When we got to the page with a "?" next to a joke, Barry would ask for new pitches. Sometimes, the writer would blame the actor for blowing the line and lobby for a second shot. Barry would nicely, but firmly say, "Let's try something new." This went on for months until one day I figured out the code: Barry's question mark meant, "No." But where most showrunners don't think twice about slashing a line through dialogue or "X"-ing an entire page, Barry even respected the work that goes into a failed joke.

Coach writing staff, Season 4: (back row) Scott Buck, Warren Bell (middle row) Bruce Ferber, Bob Bendetson, me (front row) Eric Horsted, Art Everett. Missing: Executive Producer Barry Kemp. Also missing: Any diversity of skin color.

Barry's decency and thoughtfulness made him an outstanding mentor. When I was running *Sabrina*, I struggled to find ways to keep the room energized so I sought Barry's advice on how to motivate a staff.

"I like to treat the writers' room like a cocktail party," he told me. "I start with a funny story and warm people up and then shift to work and they don't even notice."

Ohmigod, that's exactly what he did! I sat in his room for over two years and never noticed the elegant and sly manipulation. The only problem was that the cocktail party blueprint suited Barry, who is a natural raconteur. His advice wouldn't work for me so I sought out a second opinion from Korby Siamis, my equally wonderful boss at *Murphy Brown*. Korby had a slightly different take.

"You want to know the best way to keep writers motivated?" she said. "Tell them they're fucking lucky to have jobs."

Barry offered a carrot. Korby offered a stick. I ended up somewhere in the middle. (A carrot stick?)

Process

When writers who work on different series get together, their first question is always, "How are the hours?" Long hours are a sure way to make a fun job less fun. I enjoyed my three freelance assignments at *Monk* in part because showrunner Andy Breckman ran the room so efficiently. The detective show was shot in LA, but the writers' room was located near Andy's home in New Jersey. Arriving for the first time at the offices via PATH train, I thought I'd come to the wrong place. The building also housed a medical lab and I had to step over metal specimen containers to reach the elevator. Operating outside Hollywood's sphere gave *Monk* a different feel. No one was reading the trades and the small staff buckled down and stayed focused.

Andy also ran one of the funniest rooms that I've ever sat in. Once, the subject of time travel came up and Andy tossed out a perfect sci-fi story, "What if . . . what if I went back to kill Hitler in Germany but when I arrived, he was in the middle of a speech and I had to wait. And as I listened, I started thinking, *You know, he's making some good points. The Rhineland is pretty nice.* And next thing I know I'm goose-stepping with the army and saying 'Sieg Heil' and that's when I realize that the whole Third Reich is made up of time travelers who came back to kill Hitler and decided to join him instead."

I always enjoy tangents from funny storytellers, but some rooms spend so much time ordering lunch and watching videos that it's suddenly three o'clock and the script has barely been touched. And sometimes staying late has nothing to do with work at all. One showrunner, who was single, used to keep writers around so he had company while he watched *Letterman*. Even worse, this was back when Dave was on at 12:30 AM.

After inquiring about work hours, writers will inevitably ask each other: "And how's the network treating you?" Entire books are devoted to cataloguing ridiculous script notes from executives. When I assumed the helm at *Sabrina*, showrunner Eileen Heisler advised me to get good at nodding my head and saying, "I'll take a look at that."

"Don't argue with the network," Eileen warned. "You will never convince them that you're right and they're wrong."

She shared her trick for dealing with these situations.

"I just keep asking questions. 'Why do you think that? Where did the scene start feeling off to you?' Make them pinpoint the problem so you can solve it. Sometimes it's just one line that needs to change."

I've also worked with some insightful and inspiring network executives who make every project better. CBS's steady success over the past twenty years can be largely credited to longtime Entertainment President Nina Tassler. I've worked on several pilots with Nina, including a light drama, which was pitched to me as *Clueless* meets *CSI*. After reading my first draft, Nina called to give notes. Her voice sounded upbeat without a hint of disapproval. She had loved the A (main) story, but had problems with the B (secondary) story.

"It just didn't grab me as much," she said. "And I'd love for you to come up with something else because I just want the B story to be as good as the A."

"Of course," I said. "I totally get it."

We batted around some other ideas and after landing on one that Nina liked, I thanked her for the feedback and hung up the phone, smiling. A minute later it hit me: Nina had just tossed out my entire B-story. And I had thanked her. That's how good she is.

Stars are another major variable in the production process. At *Charmed*, the writers would watch dailies—scenes filmed the previous day—in shock as one actress openly insulted the writers with the cameras rolling.

"I'm not saying this line," one witch said. "It's stupid."

So first, had she seen the show? And second, creating a character works best as a symbiosis between actors and writers. When that relationship breaks down, the product suffers. Of course, writers can be tone-deaf with actors, too. At *NCIS*, I got called to set once when Mark Harmon had an issue with some dialogue I'd written. Mark is a consummate professional and that show is a massive success not just because of what he does onscreen, but because of what he does off. When I arrived on set, Mark (Lt. Gibbs) was holding his "sides"—the pages from the script being shot that day.

"Maybe you can help me," Mark said. "I'm stumbling over this scene, specifically this line."

He pointed and I peered. The director hovered, anxiously. This discussion was eating up precious shooting time. I asked Mark if I could hear him say the line. He gamely complied.

"That sounds fine," I said, genuinely not seeing the problem.

"Really?" Mark said. "It doesn't feel right to me. Sounds a little weak."

"I don't think it's weak," I said. "It's vulnerable. Gibbs even admits that he's 'puzzled.'"

Mark frowned a bit. The actress in the scene was a semi-regular and joined the conversation.

"I think it sounds fine," she said helpfully.

Mark glanced over at the director who was eager to roll camera. Mark came to a decision.

"All right," he said. "I'll give it a try."

I can still see Mark shaking his head slightly as he walked back into the set.

Now some actors will purposely tank a line to prove a writer wrong. Not Mark Harmon. He delivered the line as written and 100 percent made it work. Still, I look back on the way I acted that day and cringe. The same way Barry used to put a question mark that meant "no," Mark was being respectful. Without demanding a new line, he made it clear that's what he needed. I'm ashamed that I was too locked into my own intention and too worried about the time. I had listened to respond, not listened to understand.

Product

No TV writer ever admits to working on a bad show and will bend themselves into paperclips to justify their time and effort. "The show's dumb, but fun!" they'll say. Or "The first drafts are great but the network's noting us to death." Some even blame the space-time continuum: "I just don't think the audience is ready for this show yet."

I would like to break this pattern by admitting that I've worked on bad shows. Maybe even terrible ones. And yet despite their badness, some were very popular. You don't always get to work on shows that suit your personal taste, and the shows that *do* suit your taste, don't always work out.

I fell hard for *The War Next Door*, a sitcom created by Chris Viscardi and Will McRobb, Originally titled *Kill, Kill, Kill*, the show centered on a clean-cut CIA agent who retires to a quiet life in the suburbs until his arch-nemesis moves into the house next door. I'd met the showrunners at a one-day punch up session on their hit movie *Snow Day* and was thrilled when they asked me to write a freelance episode.

The War Next Door had an absurdist, *Get Smart* vibe. We broke the story in a group and I happily fleshed out scenes where grown men tried to strangle each other with garden hoses. That episode, "And Baby Makes Death," turned out well and Will and Chris asked me if I wanted to tackle the two-part season finale. I said yes, and poured my heart into the scripts. The episodes were cleverly produced, and I was truly proud to have my name on them.

USA cancelled the show before that two-parter ever aired.

I've had the opposite experience, too. In 2007, I was part of a three-writer tag-team working on an *NCIS* story about a killer car developed by DARPA. There are times that scripts are written quickly and turn out fine. This was not one of them. We all shared writing credit, but when the episode aired, I didn't alert my family or my agent. It seemed better to let that one pass unnoticed.

"Driven" turned out to be the highest-rated program on TV that week. In my entire career, it's the only time my name has appeared on the week's number one show.

All Together Now

Murphy Brown, starring the sublime Candice Bergen, was the only time in thirty years where all three Ps came together. When my contract at *Coach* was up, I wanted to jump to a new series, preferably one with more female voices onscreen and off. *Murphy* showrunners Gary Dontzig, Steve Peterman, and Korby Siamis read my material and called me in. When I walked into their airy office on the Warner Bros. lot, Korby was seated, her skinny legs casually flung over the side of the armchair. She waved hello but made no move to stand. Steve was behind the desk and Gary sat on the couch. The meeting was fun and relaxed. When I got up to leave, Korby stood to shake my hand and that's when I noticed she had a basketball under her shirt. Weird, I thought. Why would someone put a basketball under their shirt?

Korby noticed my confused expression because she gestured toward the basketball and said, "Oh, yeah. I'm pregnant."

Of course! My brain hadn't been able to make sense of the obvious. Korby explained the baby was due over hiatus so she'd be back in the room by the time the sixth season started. It was a life-changing moment for me. An Executive Producer was not just pregnant, she was *nonchalantly* pregnant.

"I want to be nonchalantly pregnant someday, too," I thought while getting into my car.

Murphy hired me as Supervising Producer. When I walked in the first day and saw three other women sitting at the table, my heart leapt. After years at *Coach* and *Late Night* and *Newhart* and *Smothers Brothers*, it felt so good to be on a staff where I didn't have the additional role of representing all women. I could just be me.

Murphy Brown writers' room (left to right) Eileen Heisler, Rob Bragin, Gary Dontzig, Korby Siamis, DeAnn Heline, Steve Peterman (seated) Bill Diamond, me, Adam Belanoff, Mike Saltzman aka (left to right) Blackie, Professor, Gary, Little Miss Can't Be Wrong, Blondie, Steve, Babyface, Noodles, Kid Mumbles, the Worm.

Like Mark Harmon, Candice Bergen set the tone on the stage. She was professional, generous, and respectful to all. At *Murphy*, scenes were automatically shot twice in front of an audience. One night, Candice nailed 95 percent of her dialogue on the first try, but fumbled one joke. I'd cowritten the episode with Rob Bragin and we were standing on set, trying to decide if it was worth mentioning the bobble to the director. Just then, Candice strode by.

"I blew that line," she said as she passed. "Watch me go get it."

She got it.

The high level of performance attracted high-level guest stars. I wrote an episode about a member of the original FYI news team—the fifth anchor—who was fired for being annoying. "Stuart Best" (a combination of Stuart Sutcliffe and Pete Best) returns for a reunion special and to figure out who got him shit-canned. (Spoiler alert: it was mostly Murphy.) The network wanted John Ratzenberger from *Cheers* to play the part, but the writers were all rooting for Wallace "Inconceivable!" Shawn. Ratzenberger fell out (or was he pushed?) and Wally stepped in to delight us all.

With Wallace Shawn. Photo was a gift
from fellow *Murphy* writer Mike Saltzman.

The Fourth P: Personal Life

My fond memories of *Murphy* are colored by a happy personal development that same year. At the last moment, the show needed a guest star to play a Howard Stern–type character and someone suggested Penn Jillette. I volunteered to contact him directly to see if he was available. He wasn't, but he invited me to hang out with him in Vegas that weekend. He and Teller were committed to moving west and Penn was flying in with his architect to look at some land.

I headed to Vegas on a Saturday morning and caught up with Penn and his—wow, he's really cute—architect, Colin Summers. Colin was a recent graduate of Cornell's College of Architecture and I'd seen him around the P & T offices where he doubled as Penn's "computer geek." Penn, Colin, and I fell into an instant rapport as we tramped around the desert. That night the three of us went to a Gentleman's Club to watch a performance by Penn's friend Venus DeLight. (Pretty sure that's not her real name.) As Venus slid around a gigantic martini glass, Colin and I got to know each other. Where romcom "meet cutes" had failed me, hardcore reality came through. Nothing in my past would have suggested that I'd fall in love in a strip club in Vegas, but that's what happened.

Colin and I made plans to meet early the next morning for a joint rollerblade (him) and run (me) along the Strip. He was faster so he'd circle back, gliding gracefully around me, while talking about architecture, music, and technology. My head was spinning.

Colin drove me to the airport that afternoon. The night before, we'd discovered that we both enjoyed the movie *True Romance*. When Colin dropped me off, I slipped a note into his bag that repeated what Patricia Arquette said over and over to Christian Slater: "You're so cool."

A few months later, Colin moved from NYC to Vegas to design Penn's house. On weekends, he'd ride his motorcycle to LA so we could be together. After six months, the subject of having kids came up. I was conflicted. At thirty-three, I wanted a family, but I didn't want to stop working. Then Colin said the sexiest thing I'd ever heard a man say.

"I'd be happy to stay home and take care of a baby for the first year."

"Seriously?"

"Seems fair. You carry the baby for the first nine months and I'll carry it for the second."

I was making good money, especially when compared to a budding architect so the arrangement made financial sense. Still, the best part of Colin's offer is that he didn't make it solely for financial reasons. He truly wanted to be the primary caregiver.

A year after meeting Colin, I got my wish and became "nonchalantly pregnant." I built a baby while Colin built a gorgeous house for Penn known as "The Slammer." About a month before I gave birth, Colin moved to LA full-time. Once Rudy arrived, Colin settled happily into his new role, returning to architecture when an interesting project cropped up. Pretty amazing, right? Unless you reverse the gender, and then it's what women who have the choice to stay home do 95 percent of the time.

Colin and I originally rejected the idea of getting married: our relationship, our rules. But by the time I became pregnant with our second son, we were living in Brentwood and owned a Volvo. You can't get more married than that, so we decided to make it official. Our wedding consisted of three people: the bride, the groom, and the magician who married us in our backyard.

Penn Jillette, Colin Summers, and me on our wedding day, November 12, 1997. Two things I love about this photo: (1) I'm standing on my tiptoes so I won't look so short; and (2) Rudy's little hand is in the left foreground. He was two.

Everything about that year on *Murphy Brown* was magical so of course it couldn't last. Steve, Gary, and Korby moved on at the end of the season, leaving the showrunner slot open. I secretly hoped that the three highest-ranking writers (which included me) would be promoted. Instead, Warner Bros. brought in an outsider. The studio gave me an opening to leave and I took it. Securing another job didn't worry me. I was solidly in the "Get me Nell Scovell" stage of my career. Plus, a year on *Murphy Brown* and finding Colin had helped build my self-esteem. I felt ready to create my own show.

CHAPTER 10

So You Want to Run a TV Show

INT. SABRINA'S BEDROOM—NIGHT

          SABRINA
Salem, do you think the Council will grant
the time reversal?

          SALEM THE CAT
I'm the wrong witch to ask. They weren't very
lenient to me. Sentenced to a hundred years
as a cat. And for what?

          SABRINA
I don't know. For what?

          SALEM THE CAT
Oh, like any young kid, I dreamed of world
domination. Of course, they really crack down
when you act on it.

          SABRINA
Wow. No wonder you're so possessive of the
sofa.

                    Sabrina the Teenage Witch, pilot

A S A FIRST-TIME SHOWRUNNER AND CREATOR, I felt strangely confident going into the table read of the pilot episode of *Sabrina the Teenage Witch*. I felt good about the script. I felt good about the cast. I felt good about the director. The only thing I did not feel good about was that I had to kick off the table read by giving a speech. Public speaking is hard for me. My heart starts to pound and my voice gets all quivery. It worried me that if I seemed nervous, it would set a bad tone. I considered delegating the speech to someone else, but no one knew better than I did what made *Sabrina* special. After all, how many shows had a talking cat? Then it hit me like a ton of sticks. I had a plan.

The day of the read, the crowd filed in. Viacom President Perry Simon patted me on the back and flashed me his impish smile. I waved to our director Robby Benson who most people know as the star of *One on One* (if male) or *Ice Castles* (if female) or both (if me). At a nearby table, an animatronic cat sat stiffly on a wooden plank. Crew members and writers milled around. Actors took seats and flipped through their scripts. Finally, the ABC contingent entered, led by newly named President of Entertainment Jamie Tarses and Head of Scheduling Jeff Bader. Jamie was the highest-ranking person in the room and when she took her seat, it was showtime. All eyes turned to me, then suddenly, the stiff cat came to life.

"Greetings, humans!" Salem called out.

Everyone lit up as the cat cranked his neck. The writers had composed a short, funny speech for "Salem" who was voiced by fellow writer Nick Bakay. The cat welcomed the group, then after a few lines, started to cough and hack trying to expel a hairball. With his last breath, Salem turned the table read over to me.

After Salem's funny intro, the pressure was off. I calmly thanked the network and studio for their support, the crew and writers for their work, and lastly, I thanked the actors.

"You're all amazing," I said. "I love this cast. But please know if you complain too much . . ."

My voice trailed off as I gestured toward the animatronic cat, which sprang to life again. The implication was that the actors could all be replaced by fancy puppets. People laughed.

I nodded to Robby who read the opening stage direction: "INTERIOR. SABRINA'S BEDROOM—NIGHT." We were off. About twenty-four minutes later, Robby read, "FADE OUT. END OF SHOW." Everyone applauded. They always do, so I didn't read anything into that.

The network executives huddled in a corner while the writers, production staff, and actors headed to stage. While I waited for notes, I thought about how far we'd come in only four months. It all started when my new agent Abby Adams called to ask if I'd been a fan of the *Sabrina the Teenage Witch* comic books as a kid. I had. Part of the Archie universe, *Sabrina* was created by George Gladir. Viacom Productions turned the premise into a cable movie written by a group led by Barney Cohen. That cable movie was edited into a four-minute presentation that Viacom shopped to networks. Ted Harbert, then-President of ABC, saw *Sabrina* as a good fit for the family-friendly TGIF lineup and ordered thirteen episodes. Easy!

Not so fast. Jonathan Schmock, a gifted writer and artist, wrote a pilot script. He was slated to run the show as soon as he wrapped up his job on the already-cancelled *Brotherly Love*. Then in a surprise move, the fledgling WB picked up his show and Jonathan was no longer available.

After *Murphy*, I had jumped into an overall deal at 20th Century Fox Studios. Peter Roth, one of the nicest and most successful executives around, signed me to an eighteen-month contract to create sitcoms. The studio paired me with novelist Doug Coupland to develop his book *Microserfs* into a TV show set in the tech world. We pitched our concept to the head of the FOX network who listened intently.

"This is the most thought-out pitch I've ever heard," he told us. "And I didn't understand a word of it."

Microserfs crashed. I rebounded and sold a concept to the WB about two high school besties with a cable show. *Prudy and Judy* was picked up to pilot and we cast two phenomenal sixteen-year-old actresses: Jackie Tohn and Laura Bell Bundy, who later originated the role of Elle Woods in the musical *Legally Blonde*. Barry Kemp directed and Alan Thicke played Laura Bell's father. The WB passed on the series, which made me sad, but also freed me up to meet on *Sabrina*.

As the new *Sabrina* showrunner, I was given leeway to rewrite Jonathan's pilot script, which centered on Sabrina screwing up her driver's test. I refocused the story on Sabrina discovering her magical powers and worrying about her social status.

"I don't want to be special," Sabrina insists to her warlock father. "I want to be normal."

"I understand," her dad responds. "But that ship has sailed."

On her first day at school, Sabrina makes a series of mistakes. She gets hit in the head by a football in front of the boy she likes. She fails a pop quiz. Finally, she loses her temper in the cafeteria and uses her magic irresponsibly. The second act opens in the Spellman kitchen. Sabrina enters, panicked, holding a pineapple.

<pre>
                    SABRINA
        I hate being a witch. I just turned the most
        popular girl in school into a pineapple.

                    HILDA
        Chill. I can fix this. (TAKES A CLEAVER OUT)
        Chunks or rings?

                    ZELDA
        Hilda, there are other ways.
</pre>

                    HILDA

Wedges?

Aunt Zelda turns the cheerleader Libby (named after my niece) back into her human form. Libby isn't sure what just went down.

"You did something to me," she says. "You sent me somewhere. It was small and smelled like Hawaii."

Expertly played by Jenna Leigh Green, Libby storms out, promising to destroy Sabrina's reputation. And she has the power to do it. "She's a cheerleader," says Sabrina. "No one has more credibility." Desperate to undo the disastrous day, Sabrina petitions the Witches Council to turn back time. Jonathan had written a similar scene although in his version, the aunts and Salem accompanied Sabrina. I felt Sabrina should have to plead her case alone. I cast magicians Penn and Teller as Council members Drell and Skippy, respectively. In a set inspired by surrealist art, Sabrina argues for a second chance. This scene set up the metaphor of the entire series: being a teenager means coming into your powers, but being an adult means learning to control them.

Left: With Penn, who played Drell, head of the Witches Council; Right: Teller, who originated the role of Skippy the witch, in a Magritte-style bowler hat with a fish wrapped in pearls behind him.

The Council turns down the request. Sabrina has no choice but to go back to school and face Libby's ridicule.

"Fine. I surrender," Sabrina says as she heads off the next morning. "I guess every school needs a weird kid. Might as well be me."

"I was the weird kid!" Hilda calls after her, cheerfully.

It made my heart beat faster to hear Caroline Rhea deliver this line in such a chipper voice. I was the weird kid, too. *Sabrina* was my attempt to create a show that my teenage self would have watched.

In the final scenes, Aunt Hilda confronts Drell and forces him to give her niece a do-over. Sabrina makes the most of her second chance. She catches the football, aces the pop quiz, and *doesn't* turn the cheerleader into a pineapple. At the end of the school day, Sabrina races home, triumphant.

"Yay! I'm normal!" she declares. "Gotta go tell the cat!"

Viacom execs Steve Gordon and Chris Sanagustin were true partners and helped shape my early drafts. The biggest argument we had concerned a character who's not even in the pilot: Sabrina's mom. Jonathan's script had Sabrina say, "I never knew my mom" implying Mom had died in childbirth. The studio thought this was a fine way to explain Mom's absence, but I didn't see any reason to kill her off. The tradition of matricide in "family" movies from *Bambi* to *Finding Nemo* has always rankled me. I presented my case to Steve and Chris.

"Why can't we just give the mom a job that keeps her far away?"

"Like what?"

"What if she's an archeologist on a long dig in Peru?" I said.

"And she just abandoned her kid?"

"Sabrina's *not* abandoned," I said. "She's living in a nice home with her two loving aunts. I mean, her dad's not with her and you're okay with that. You're not insisting we kill him off."

"No."

"So why is it different with a mom?"

Sabrina's mom got a stay of execution. Still, Steve and Chris asked me to make it clear that Mom keeping her distance wasn't a choice. I added a line of dialogue that explains if Sabrina sets eyes on her mortal mother in the first two years after becoming a witch, her mom will turn into a ball of wax. Sabrina's dad adds this policy is how the Council discourages marriage between witches and mortals.

Back at the pilot table read, the ABC huddle broke. The group rejoined the Viacom folks and me. As president of the network, Jamie Tarses delivered the notes. She opened by saying she enjoyed all the performances. She liked the animatronic cat. She thought the story worked fine. She did, however, have one "fairly major note." I tensed. Jamie felt there wasn't enough conflict between the two aunts. She asked me to describe each one.

"Zelda's the straight man: logical, restrained, and stable," I said. "Hilda's the wild card: emotional, blunt, and an incurable romantic."

Jamie thought we needed to push the contrast more, especially in the aunts' attitudes toward their niece. She pitched an idea: What if one of the aunts didn't want Sabrina living with them? What if Hilda's attitude was more like, "Our lives were so much better before our niece came to live here. She's ruining everything!"

Jamie's pitch definitely created more conflict, but it felt off to me. I'd been primed to nod and say, "Let me look at that," but I couldn't see doing any version of this pitch.

"That just seems sad to me," I said. "Sabrina's a teenager. If she's not with one of her parents and the aunts she's living with don't want her there, how can we laugh?"

Jamie and I went back and forth. I kept hoping someone from Viacom would back me up, but arguing against a network president is a lonely task. We reached an impasse. I sensed it was my cue to say, "Okay, I'll try it that way," but before I got the words out, network VP Jeff Bader jumped in and uttered the four most beautiful words in the English language: "I agree with Nell."

Most networks present as a monolith so Jeff offering an independent opinion was completely unexpected. His speaking up broke the deadlock.

"Fine," Jamie said, ready to move on. "Leave it."

I will always be grateful to Jeff for his creative support at such a crucial moment. From that moment on, the pilot shoot went smoothly, thanks in large part to Robby Benson's creativity, preparation, and expertise. Robby even did double-duty when he agreed to play Sabrina's dad and had to direct himself.

The only small disappointment for me came during the Witches Council scene. Penn and Teller had flown in from Vegas and were prepared for their parts. Debbie Harry (lead singer of Blondie) flew in from Europe and was a bit bleary, but quickly got up to speed on her lines. The fourth member of the Council, Mr. X, had no lines . . . because Mr. X was only six months old. I wrote the part with a specific baby in mind. From the moment he was born, our son Rudy had a sunny disposition. As Mr. X, all he had to do was sit and look cute. Rudy got the part.

The day of the shoot, Colin brought Rudy to wardrobe where they dressed him in a custom, purple velvet onesie. Mr. X arrived on set, looking positively regal. The crew was still lighting the set when out of nowhere:

"Wah."

Colin and I exchanged a look. Rudy rarely fussed.

"Is the outfit bothering him?" I wondered.

Colin checked the onesie's high neckline. "Seems fine."

"Wah."

"Does he feel hot to you?" Colin asked.

I pressed my lips to Rudy's forehead. He *was* warm. We assumed the polyester onesie was to blame so we stripped it off him. That didn't help. Rudy was running the first fever of his life. I looked over at Robby Benson who was reviewing shots with the camera crew. The scene had multiple speaking parts, special effects, and mechanical props. Adding one more uncontrollable variable would stress the shoot. As Executive Producer, I made the hard choice to do what was best for the production. I cut my own flesh and blood from the scene. Colin took Rudy straight home.

Six months later, around his first birthday, Rudy made his network debut, appearing as Cupid at the end of the opening credits sequence for our Valentine's Day show. The double meaning of "Created By" is kind of awesome.

Sabrina holds Cupid (aka Rudy Summers, age one)

After the pilot, the writers started breaking the next twelve episodes in our offices on the Universal lot. The *Sabrina* writers' room was underneath a parking structure and every time a car drove in or out, the whole room shook like there was an earthquake. We used to joke that if "the big one" ever hit, we'd all shrug and figure, "Eh, it's just a truck" right before the ceiling collapsed and crushed us to death.

Closing in on our September 27, 1996, premiere, *Sabrina* was

My Three Favorite Reviews for Sabrina the Teenage Witch

Perfectly respectable family fare, yet not so perfectly respectable that it's drippy, *Sabrina the Teenage Witch* made a bright and sprightly addition to ABC's Friday night.

           —Tom Shales, *The Washington Post*

Not just TGIF fare, but TV good enough for any night.

           —David Wild, *Rolling Stone*

Sabrina is a series with two levels. Its unabashed silliness designed for a young audience, its nuanced satire something that adults also may find a kick.

           —Howard Rosenberg, *Los Angeles Times*

flying under the radar as ABC focused its promotional efforts on *Clueless,* a TV adaptation of Amy Heckerling's perfect movie. I worried that TV reviewers who were, and still are, mostly male might not appreciate our series and its three female leads. Some reviewers did dismiss the show, calling it "daft" and "borderline funny-dopey." But a few heavy hitters, like Pulitzer-prize winner Tom Shales, were charmed.

Sabrina premiered on a Friday night and the next morning at exactly nine a.m., I stood in my kitchen, dialing into the ABC "Overnight Ratings Hotline." TGIF shows typically received a ten to fourteen share (percentage) of the audience. I listened as the monotone voice on the hotline droned through the eight o'clock shows. My heart was pounding as he announced, "Eighty-thirty. ABC. *Sabrina the Teenage Witch*, premiere. Twenty share."

I screamed. Over the weekend, I dialed that number over and

over and never got tired of hearing that monotone "twenty share," which translated to over 18 million viewers. Within weeks, my hero and ABC scheduling guru Jeff Bader was telling *Entertainment Weekly,* "*Sabrina* is the little show that could."

The network flipped our timeslot with *Clueless.* We stayed in the nine o'clock slot and finished 30th out of 155 shows for the 1996–1997 TV season. More importantly, the Valentine's Day episode fulfilled a dream of mine to get mentioned in *TV Guide*'s "CHEERS & JEERS" column. Even better, it wasn't a "Jeers."

CHEERS to sharp gamesmanship. A recent episode of ABC's *Sabrina* found our favorite teenage witch (**Melissa Joan Hart**) undergoing a ritual to test her affection for her boyfriend, Harvey (**Nate Richert**). The first hurdle involved her becoming a contestant on the "True Love Game Show." But wait a minute—those loud flower-bedecked curtains, that tacky theme music, the silly questions ("Harvey #2, if you were a condiment, what would you be?")—it was a fastidious and funny recreation of that TV trifle from the '60s, *The Dating Game.* (Filling in admirably for host **Jim Lange** was **Peter Marshall**, who earned his game-show stripes on *Hollywood Squares*.) The campy spell cast by *Sabrina* was enchanting.

TV GUIDE MARCH 8, 1997

As showrunner, I got to build the writing staff and hired Co-Executive Producer Norma Vela and Supervising Producers Carrie Honigblum and Renee Phillips. I'd never worked on a show with so many high-level women. Still, I should have been more inclusive. The *Sabrina* room had some diversity—a disabled writer, a writer married to a Latino, a Stanford grad—but we didn't have any writers of color. I'm aware of all the excuses I could make to justify the homogeneity because they've all been made against me on male-centric shows. I had the opportunity to include more voices and I didn't make enough of an effort. That was a mistake. It would have made the show funnier.

The cast was all-white, too. Early in the pilot process, my CAA agents pitched Cicely Tyson for the part of Aunt Zelda. Tyson is a Tony Award– and Emmy Award–winning actress and I should have jumped at the suggestion. Instead, I said that we were already zeroing in on Caroline Rhea and it wouldn't make sense for the two to be sisters.

"It's a world of magic. Maybe one sister is black," my agent said.

It would have been an interesting and bold move, but I didn't pursue the idea.

The rest of the writing staff included Salem's alter-ego Nick Bakay who was indispensable and went on to a stellar career in both TV and movies. (You can thank Nick for *Paul Blart: Mall Cop*.) Frank Conniff was better known as "TV's Frank" from *MST3K*. Rachel Lipman had written a classic *Rugrats* episode. I leaned heavily on Co-Producer Jon Sherman, who went on to become an Executive Producer of *Frasier*. Jon and I cracked each other up with smart/dumb jokes like, "Oh good, there's a lecture at MIT on the Heisenberg Uncertainty Principle. It's either at eight or at ten o'clock."

On set, Paul Feig was hysterical as Sabrina's biology teacher Mr. Pool (first name Gene). Watching Gary Halvorson direct six episodes was a master class in how to run a set. Editor Stu Bass made every show funnier. (Hey, I never got to make an Emmy speech so I'm doing it here.)

The show's tone tended to be my favorite mixture of grounded and absurd. Sabrina's high school football team was nicknamed "The Fighting Scallions," a misprint of "Stallions" that the school couldn't afford to correct. We wrote in a giant flan and a lint monster that leapt out of the dryer because we could. We hired guest stars that we wanted to work with like Bryan Cranston, Henry Gibson, and Donald Faison. Raquel Welch played Sabrina's fun-loving, thigh-high leather boot wearing Aunt Vesta and helped deliver the show's highest-rated episode. Raquel was a total pro and all-around good sport, who was as enchanting offscreen as on. During breaks, I peppered her with questions.

"Who's the biggest flirt you've ever worked with?" I asked.

"Richard Burton," she said without hesitation. "He was the best." Then her eyes twinkled as she confided lustily, "I mean . . . in a closet in a minute."

A giant flan—was it a dream or real?   Linty, the lint monster.

Beth Broderick and Caroline Rhea made a fantastic team as Aunts Zelda and Hilda. Beth anchored the plots and accepted the necessary task of laying out exposition. Caroline took the show to comedic heights. Caroline's friendly, upbeat delivery allowed her to say the most insane lines with complete conviction. When Hilda and Drell started a relationship, she explains that if he breaks a date, he always sends a pot roast which magically appears in the oven.

"Flowers wilt," Hilda says. "Say it with beef."

It made *perfect* sense coming out of Caroline's mouth. In another episode, a backfiring spell causes Hilda to grow a thick luxurious beard. I worried the beard might make Caroline self-conscious, but it had the opposite effect. Caroline sauntered onto the set in a tight shirt, little skirt, and full bushy beard. I swear she never looked sexier.

With Caroline Rhea before her morning shave.

The original order for thirteen *Sabrina* episodes expanded to twenty-two and then the network added two more. We had some turnover in the writers' room and with five shows left, I hired my friend Barry Marx as a staff writer. Barry had never written for TV, but he'd worked on a video game with Penn & Teller and I knew he could do the job. Barry moved from New Jersey to the west coast for a couple of months, subletting an apartment near the Hollywood sign.

By the final two episodes, I was exhausted. New shows are a lot of work and having a green staff meant a lot of rewriting. Executive Producer Liz Friedman once summed up the experience: "Running a show is like being beaten to death by your own dream."

My contract had been for a season and Viacom offered me a generous, but not perfect, deal to extend for another. I was on the fence about returning for a variety of reasons and I didn't have the psychic energy to sort it out while still in production. My goal was to finish strong. The penultimate episode was built around Sabrina and her classmates visiting Salem, Massachusetts. I'd written a detailed outline that the studio and network approved on a Friday. That was the good news. The bad news was the table read was on Monday, which meant I had to write the script over the weekend.

That Friday evening around seven, I sent the writers home. It had been a tough day filled with drama so most people bolted from the room. One writer lingered.

"Is there anything I can do to help?" Barry asked.

"Thanks," I said. "I'll be fine."

Barry flashed me a sweet, kindhearted smile. We said good night and I returned to the set, where we shot for another couple of hours. When the set wrapped, I headed home to Colin. We were already in bed at eleven when the phone rang. It was Penn in Vegas. Barry's girlfriend in NYC had just called. She'd been talking to Barry on the phone when he suddenly exclaimed, "Ow, that really hurts!" and then cut out. She tried calling back but the line was busy. She didn't know how to call 9-1-1 from out of state so she called Penn who was calling Barry's friends in LA. Another friend, Rich Nathanson, had already reported the emergency. Colin and I jumped in the car. All indications pointed to awful news. Barry was not the type to let anyone worry. Colin drove too fast. I wailed.

Police cars were outside the apartment complex when we arrived. Rich was standing on the lawn, his face contorted. We cried as coroners carried a heavy body bag to the van.

"There goes our friend," Rich wept.

A policeman informed us that Barry had died of natural causes. We later learned that he'd suffered a rupture in his aorta, a congenital defect. He was forty.

That was Friday night. I spent Saturday with friends and my family. On Sunday, Jon Sherman came to my house and together we turned the Salem witch trial outline into a script. I was so grateful to have Jon's talent and friendship.

The table read was a blur. Barry was so new to the show, most of the crew and actors had no attachment to him. He was like a real-life *Star Trek* redshirt. (That may seem cruel, but the reference would've made Barry laugh.) Later that afternoon, I stumbled through a phone call with Barry's parents, telling them how sorry I was and how much we would miss him. I felt guilty that the job had moved him three thousand miles away. I couldn't imagine their pain.

That same week, my lawyer called to say Viacom was pushing for an answer on their latest offer. I asked if we could hold off until the season wrapped. Viacom's business affairs department said no. And this is what I learned: If you're on the fence about signing up for an all-consuming project and that same week you watch a friend carried out in a body bag, you will determine that life is too short. You will make the choice that allows you to spend precious time with the people you love most. I walked away from *Sabrina*.

There are days when I regret that decision. There were compelling creative and financial reasons to stay. There were also unpleasant aspects of the job that may not have been fixable. Mitch Hurwitz, creator of *Arrested Development*, once compared running a show to "piloting an airplane while the passengers throw rocks at your head." I know that feeling well. You want to turn around and shout, "Hey! If I go down, we *all* go down."

My friend Miriam Trogdon took over as *Sabrina* showrunner

Colin and Rudy during *Sabrina* days

and I appreciated that Viacom hadn't replaced me with a male writer. (Eventually, that happened.) Miriam called me to check in and offered some helpful advice.

"Here's my recommendation," Miriam said. "Never watch the show again."

I took her advice, although once while switching channels on a plane, I caught a scene from a much-later season. Sabrina and her aunts were arguing in the Spellman kitchen and the characters' attitudes were unrecognizable to me. The only things that felt familiar were the little teacup handles on the kitchen cabinets that I had picked out with the set decorator for the pilot.

Sabrina continued for three more years on ABC and two on the WB. Ratings were never as high as that first season, but they remained strong enough for the show to sell into syndication.

In 2016, the show celebrated its twentieth anniversary and a reporter reached out to women who'd grown up watching. Lena Dunham was ten when the show premiered and shared this: "*Sabrina the Teenage Witch* was truly formative for me on every level—it was subtly radical feminist storytelling, never denying the power of sisterhood or the magic of a teenage girl. Sabrina had agency, she had spunk, and it took the form of magic. It makes me laugh to this day. I feel lucky it was on TV for girls like me."

Lena's words made me think back to the table read where I fought to keep the aunts welcoming of their niece. "Never denying the power of sisterhood" turned out to be a key to our success.

As a science fiction fan, there are times I fantasize about visiting a parallel universe where I'd stayed on as *Sabrina*'s showrunner. I'd like to meet alt-Nell and ask if it was worth navigating the obstacles to create bigger flans and lintier monsters. But mostly I want to go to that parallel universe and spend time with alt-Barry Marx who is still alive and well and flashing his sweet, kindhearted smile.

Barry Marx holding Rudy

Assorted Guest Cast Who You Might Not Have Known Appeared on *Sabrina, the Teenage Witch*

GUEST STAR	EPISODE	BEST KNOWN FOR	WHAT THEY PLAYED	HIGHLIGHT
Bryan Cranston	The Troll Bride	*Breaking Bad*	Lawyer from the other realm	Wore a tailored 4-piece suit, including jacket, pants, vest, and boxers
Henry Gibson	Cat Show	*Laugh In*	Judge Samuels	I got to tell him how much I loved his performance as Haven Hamilton in Robert Altman's *Nashville*
Raquel Welch	Third Aunt from the Sun	Sex symbol, movie star	Vesta, Sabrina's third aunt	"Shake your whammy fanny funky song, funky song"
Dana Gould	A Girl and her Cat	Brilliant stand up	Monty	"Monty" was best described as a Paul Lynde–like character . . . only gayer
Chris Elliott	Mars Attacks	*Late Night with David Letterman*	Warren, a spy impersonating an insurance salesman	Chris and I hadn't overlapped at *Letterman* so this was our first time meeting.
Brady Anderson	Sabrina Through the Looking Glass	Baltimore Orioles, 50 HR in a season	Himself—and struggled to do that	Everyone on the set had a crush on him—including me.
Milo Ventimiglia	Terrible Things	*Gilmore Girls, Heroes, This is Us*	Football player	Votes for Libby as class president based on her platform of "more pizza at lunch"
Donald Faison	Magic Joel	*Scrubs*	Justin	Auditions to be Magic Joel's assistant
Brian Austin Green	Dream Date	"David Silver" on *Beverly Hills 90210*	Sabrina's dream date made from Man Dough	He seemed to have second thoughts about appearing, but delivered a great performance with over-the-top enthusiasm

Stage Three

GET ME
A YOUNGER,
CHEAPER
NELL SCOVELL!

CHAPTER 11

Poetry Is in the Doing

"Welcome the felicitous accident."

—Arthur Penn on directing movies

IN DECEMBER 2002, COLIN AND I ATTENDED THE LA Film Critics Association gala dinner at the elegant Hotel Casa del Mar. We were penthousing—or whatever the opposite of slumming is. From our primo table, I was close enough to rub Daniel Day-Lewis's shaved head. I could hear Julianne Moore snapping her gum. I could feel the glare of Jack Nicholson's grin as he presided over the *About Schmidt* table. And directly across from me sat our friend Arthur Penn who was receiving a lifetime achievement award for a body of work that included *Bonnie and Clyde, Little Big Man,* and *Penn and Teller Get Killed*. That last one wasn't Arthur's best-known film, but it's the reason we met. I'd interviewed Arthur for *Rolling Stone* in 1986 and kept our interview going for the next twenty-five years.

The other seats at our table filled up with Arthur's friends and my heroes: *Tootsie* writer and *M*A*S*H* creator Larry Gelbart, Mel Brooks and his wife, Anne Bancroft. Arthur directed Anne in *The Miracle Worker* on Broadway and they both won Tony Awards. He also directed her in the film version and both were nominated for Academy Awards. Anne took home the Oscar that year, but Arthur lost to David Lean and *Lawrence of Arabia*. (Talk about a category killer.)

The Film Critics gala was a true celebration of cinema. As one winner noted: "It's lovely to receive an award from people who actually saw the movies." Spanish director Pedro Almodóvar kept coming over to our table to hug Arthur. Later, Almodóvar observed in his charming, accented English, "You are the nicest people I ever have dinner with. For an orgy, I don't know. I have to look around. But for dinner, very nice."

Toward the end of the program, Anne Bancroft rose from her seat and headed to the stage to present Arthur with his award. As soon as she arrived at the podium, a voice rang out from our table.

"Mention me!" Mel Brooks shouted.

"I'm not gonna!" Anne shouted back in her native Brooklyn accent. The entire room cracked up.

Anne lavished praise on Arthur to the point that he started turning red, then he joined her on the stage. Arthur spoke about his life in the theater and movies, and the importance of his friends, his wife, and his children, Matt and Molly. There were two standing ovations that night. One was for Arthur Penn. And the other was for Arthur Penn.

The gala was a once-in-a-lifetime evening, but I was just as happy sitting alone with Arthur in his Central Park West apartment and listening to him tell stories. Arthur knew an astonishing number of artists, literally starting from birth since his older brother was celebrated photographer Irving Penn. At Black Mountain College, Arthur studied with Buckminster Fuller. Before Mike Nichols became a renowned director, he asked Arthur to direct "An Evening with Mike Nichols and Elaine May." Arthur even knew Dorothy Parker.

"It was horrible how drinking destroyed her," he once told me, shaking his head.

Arthur and I spent a lot of time talking about directing. It's what he loved and he'd revolutionized the form. Now it's a trope to shoot violence realistically and in slow motion, but Arthur pioneered that style with the ambush that ends *Bonnie and Clyde*. When I got my first directing assignment in 1998, one of my first emails went to Arthur with the subject line "Help." I realize that asking Arthur to mentor someone making a Showtime Family movie was a little like asking Michael Phelps to teach your five-year-old how to swim. But if Phelps is willing, why not?

Oddly, what inspired me to become a director was not greatness, but mediocrity. In the years that I'd been writing and producing sitcoms, I'd worked with a hundred directors. Many were thoughtful and skilled, but a few bumbled their way through, barely knowing the script or planning the blocking. I drew my inspiration from their incompetence. As a director, I wasn't gunning for visionary genius like Arthur, but I figured I could clear the bar of solidly mediocre.

After *Sabrina*, Viacom Productions wanted to find a new project for us to work on together. They asked if I had a movie premise that could later be turned into a TV series. Watching the young actors on *Sabrina* had sparked an idea: What if a washed-up has-been sixteen-year-old former child star had to go to high school for the first time? For her, it would be weird to be normal. Viacom liked the idea and made a deal for me to write the script. My one request: I wanted to direct.

We pitched *Hayley Wagner, Star* to Showtime executive Dominique Telson. She bought it and approved me as a first-time director. I don't believe it's a coincidence that I owe my big break to an African American female executive. My timing was good to expand into a traditionally male field. During the 1990s, women were securing more leadership positions. Ruth Bader Ginsburg joined Sandra Day O'Connor on the Supreme Court. Ann Richards became Governor of Texas. Madeleine Albright was named Secretary of State. Like Sally Ride, the women's movement was racing toward equality at mach speeds . . . until 1998 when President Bill Clinton's dick brought it all to a screeching halt. (For more on this, please read my book *Just the Swollen Parts*.)

The technical aspects of directing scared me the most. Stu Bass, the editor on *Sabrina*, and I spent countless hours discussing blocking and camera placement. To me, preparation was the key, but Arthur cautioned me not to lock into all my shots before stepping on set.

"Welcome the felicitous accident," he said.

Arthur urged me to resist the urge to shout "Cut!" when a fly bothers an actor or an actress struggles to walk in high heels. An itchy nose, an unstable gait can all lend a moment of tension or verisimilitude. Arthur also recommended that I get options. Once I had the take that I was looking for, he encouraged me to get the take that I hadn't been looking for.

"Wait for the moment," Arthur advised me.

"What moment?"

"The one you're waiting for," he said with a smile.

The film would shoot in Vancouver where the American dollar stretched further. I hated the thought of being away from home for six weeks. One consolation was that since leaving *Sabrina*, I hadn't been working crazy-long hours. I'd taken a development deal with Brillstein-Grey and consulted on a few shows. Currently, I was working three days a week on the medical show *Providence*. As always, it helped knowing that Colin was capable of taking care of three-year-old Rudy and not-yet-one-year-old Dexter.

Vancouver was gorgeous and I quickly fell in love with its waterfront parks and cheap sushi. I lucked out that Viacom hired Richard Davis, a delightful, white-bearded Australian to produce the movie. Richard had decades of experience and was supportive without being coddling. He felt like a partner from the start. Still, I worried about being accepted by the rest of the crew.

"There are three things that Canadian crews dislike," a friend in LA had warned. He ticked them off on his fingers. "One: American directors. Two: First-time directors. Three: Female directors."

Triple threat, baby.

From the moment I stepped on set, I felt some pushback. The director of photography (DP) who's in charge of the Camera Department, would sometimes roll his eyes at my choices for framing a shot. In one scene, Hayley was auditioning for a part in the school play. The DP thought the shot should be tight, focusing on actress Bethany Richards' face. I asked for a looser shot starting at Bethany's waist to catch her funny body language and fabulous outfit styled by Elizabeth Stewart. The DP kept pushing for tighter. When I finally insisted on the looser shot, he literally threw up his hands.

"That's what she wants, so give it to her," he informed the cameraman, then walked to the other side of the set.

Stephen Gaghan, screenwriter of *Traffic* and director of *Syriana,* once sat next to me at a Guild meeting and boiled down the experience of being a director. "You think you'll get to be the dictator on the set," Stephen said, "but really you're the center that always has to give—the space that finds harmony."

I struggled to find harmony that day, and I beat myself up

that night. I knew it was a mistake to piss off the DP who has tremendous influence on the production. Fearing that I'd lost his crucial support, I emailed Arthur and asked for advice. He wrote back:

> *On my first Hollywood film, the crew drove me nuts with "this is the way WE do it" slowly and meticulously and phony. Implied "not like you TV parvenus who have no tradition, and just slop it." I asked the DP to shoot with two cameras. He resisted. I insisted. He wrote on the clapboard slate for camera 2 "shot under protest." The battle lines were drawn.*

It was comforting to know that even Arthur, an experienced man, had wrestled with the same situation. I stopped beating myself up for insisting on a shot. That was my job. Still, I knew the movie would turn out better if those "battle lines" were erased. I wanted to get the crew more on my side, but how? Then I welcomed "a felicitous accident."

Early in our second week, we were shooting near a pond when the skies opened up. Most of the crew headed back to the trucks to stay dry, but I decided to stay close to the set so I could jump back in as soon as the rain stopped. A small tarp had been set up nearby—not to shield humans but to protect the expensive equipment. I headed over, wrapping my purple Patagonia raincoat tightly around me. As soon as I ducked under the tarp, I realized I wasn't alone. Harvey LaRocque, the A-camera operator, had stayed with his camera, watching over it like the captain of a ship. We exchanged nods as we'd done since the project started, never speaking at any length. But as the rain pounded away, I felt pressure to make conversation.

"Where are you from, Harvey?" I asked.

"A small town in Ontario," he responded. "Parry Sound."

"Bobby Orr's hometown!"

Harvey reacted, startled.

"How'd you know that?"

"I'm from Boston. I grew up watching the Bruins."

"I don't believe it," he said.

It was more an expression of surprise than a challenge, but since we had nothing better to do, I decided to rattle off the names of the Bruin players from that era. "Bobby Orr, Phil Esposito, Johnny Bucyk, Wayne Cashman, Kenny Hodge, Gerry Cheevers, John McKenzie, Derek Sanderson."

When I got to Dallas Smith, Harvey held up his hand.

"Okay! I believe you," he said.

We both smiled. The sun didn't break out at that moment (although in the movie version, it will), and from that moment on, Harvey became my secret weapon on the set. When the DP and I hit an impasse, Harvey would try to bridge the gap, sauntering in to the set to offer an adjustment that brokered a compromise. Instead of a showdown, the process became collaborative, which is always better.

Connecting with Harvey helped, but I still felt like an outsider. Once, I saw a small group of crew members off to the side of the set, laughing. I headed over and as I neared, they clammed up.

"Sorry," I said. "I didn't mean to interrupt."

"It was nothing," said a cameraman.

"Well, it looked like you were laughing about *something*," I said.

A crew member pointed at another. "He was just telling a dirty joke."

"Ooh, I want to hear," I said.

"Not in front of a lady," he demurred.

So I told the group a joke so disgusting that I can't even repeat it here. From then on, the crew included me in their huddles. Once at craft services, a gaffer sidled up to me. "Have you

Alyson Hannigan, Penn Jillette, and standup Paul Provenza, who dropped by the set. Note how bundled up I am compared to Alyson. It was so cold, but she toughed it out.

heard this one?" he asked. "What's the difference between a refrigerator and a woman?"

I had no idea.

"A refrigerator doesn't fart when you take the meat out."

It was a gross joke but a sweet moment.

The *Hayley Wagner, Star* set found harmony thanks to a hard-working crew, strong producer, supportive studio, and focused cast that included Priscilla Presley, Meghan Ory, and Pam Grier. Even our dreaded night shoot turned out fine. It helped that I cast Penn Jillette to play the director of the zombie movie within the movie. Seeing an old friend's face made a long night easier. Alyson Hannigan flew up during a *Buffy the Vampire Slayer* hiatus to play the star of the zombie movie. Channeling a self-centered diva was a stretch for Alyson who was anything but. Still, she seemed to have a certain actress in mind while playing the part.

I returned to LA to edit and happily reunite with my family. Our early-rising one-year-old was thrilled to have more alert company in the mornings. (I'm more of a morning person than Colin.) And no parent enjoyed driving their three-year-old to preschool more than I did that first week back.

Hayley Wagner, Star scored solid ratings when it aired in 1999 and Bethany Richards earned a well-deserved nomination for a Young Artist award. Viacom cut a trailer and the WB ordered a TV pilot. Sadly, the network wouldn't approve me as the director. I turned again to Robby Benson who'd done such a stellar job on *Sabrina*.

Lightning didn't strike twice and *Hayley Wagner, Star* didn't make it to series. The success of *Hannah Montana* six years later made me think we were in the right ballpark on the wrong day.

The learning curve of directing was steep and I wanted to keep the momentum going. I met with my agents and shared my intention to find another opportunity right away.

"I'll take any meeting," I told the three guys in suits. "I'm open to anything. I just want to direct."

The agents exchanged looks. I felt the chill in the room.

"You know, Nell," one agent said. "The *second* movie is the hard one to get."

That made *no* sense. The *first* was the hard one because I needed to find someone to take a chance. Now I'd made a film—a well-received, on-budget film. I had experience. We could build off that.

"How can that be?" I challenged.

The agents shrugged. "That's just the way it is."

I walked away, demoralized. Those agents never got me a single meeting for directing. Not one. Sometimes I blame myself for not being more aggressive and seeking out opportunities on my own. But directing is exhausting and to have to push to do it felt like being forced to run a marathon before you're allowed to climb Mt. Everest.

In 2016, I wrote an Op-Ed for the *New York Times* about the lack of progress that female directors have made since the eighties. Despite all the programs to develop talent and mentor women and people of color, the percentage of diverse directors wasn't rising. People insist it's a pipeline problem. Instead, I dubbed it, "a broken doorbell" problem. Competent and talented women are right there on the doorstep, leaning on the buzzer, but no one is answering the door.

This fault lies in our culture's misperceptions. Studies show that employers routinely perceive men as more competent than women even when the data doesn't support the claim. For example, software code written by women is routinely rated as higher quality by male engineers . . . unless the raters know who wrote it. Once gender is identified, the raters devalue the female-generated work. Men applying for jobs also benefit from being able to openly acknowledge their success. Too often women are taught to downplay their success with statements like, "I got lucky" or "I had help." Guess what? The men got lucky and had help, too. These double standards make it harder for women to be seen as capable of helming a blockbuster. The massive success of Patty Jenkins's *Wonder Woman* may move the needle. Or not. The year after Kathryn Bigelow won an Oscar for Best Director, the percentage of women directing features actually dipped.

When employers hesitate to hire a female director, they claim it's rooted in an aversion to risk. I see it as a surrender to bias. My agents' warning about the second movie being harder to get became a self-fulfilling prophesy. It took eight years for me to get my next assignment.

Joey Plager is the kind of dogged producer that every writer dreams about. Long ago, Joey optioned *Betrayals*, a script I co-wrote with my sister Claire in the eighties. A cross between *Sex and the City* and Agatha Christie's *And Then There Were None*, *Betrayals* revolved around five female college roommates who gather for their tenth reunion. Each roommate reveals a dirty secret that they've never told anyone, like committing adultery, going to rehab, insider trading. After the confessions, they hug and feel closer than ever. But when the five roommates return home, each receives a blackmail note. It's clearly an inside job, but which of the five is the blackmailer?

After over a decade of dust gathered on the script, Joey swept it off and pitched the low-budget project to Susanne Daniels who was President of Entertainment at Lifetime. Susanne approved me as the director. I don't believe it's a coincidence that a female executive gave me my second break. Still, there was a catch. There's always a catch. The movie needed to go into production immediately, which conflicted with my current job as Consulting Producer on *NCIS*. We had two episodes left on the season, but my bosses let me bow out early. It cost me more money than I'd make as a director, but I was so excited to be getting another shot.

Production would take place in Vancouver (again) and the reality of low-budget movie-making hit hard. The French production company that was co-financing the project sent along their request that I shoot the movie "to look like Hitchcock." The shower scene alone in *Psycho* took seven days to film. We had seventeen days *total* for the entire movie. I said I would try, but unfortunately, the *Betrayals* crew would have frustrated Ed Wood. There were normal mishaps and mistakes, like when the locations manager forgot to make sure the sauna we were shooting in had been turned off the night before. That morning, we opened the cedar door and felt a blast of heat. The DP declared, "It's like a sauna in here."

The heat fogged the camera lens so we cut the breaker and brought in fans. It took over an hour to cool down the set. Even then, it remained toasty. At one point, the makeup person had to wipe real sweat off the actresses before spritzing them with fake sweat. We wanted a lovely glow not a literal hot mess.

Before the shoot began, I worried that having five female co-stars would generate a lot of drama. That notion was sexist. The actresses were professional and completely supportive of each other. We had no rehearsal time, so they arranged to get together on their own and run lines. When we didn't have stand-ins to help the DP light scenes, the actresses would pull double duty and remain on set so that shots would look better.

The six of us formed a tight-knit group in part because we felt under siege.

Kira Clavell, Elisa Donovan, Sarah Joy Brown, Jordan Ladd, Marissa Jaret Winokur, me.

The DP was tight with the Canadian producer who dealt with the money and hired the crew. Together, they repeatedly tried to box me out. They asked for my storyboards—blueprints for how I planned to block and shoot each scene. When I shared them, they immediately started re-blocking the cameras, addressing each other while ignoring me. When I called the two on it, they laughed.

"We're just so used to working with each other," the producer said. "We've got a shorthand."

At a loss, I shot another emergency email to Arthur. He responded immediately:

> Nell . . . Close the gap right away. Don't let them get control
> IN YOUR PRESENCE. You know, certainly, they will
> talk behind your back. That's a given. But in your presence:
> you take charge. Don't be stunned by these guys. Expect
> venality.
>
> Second point. A storyboard is a license for all to direct. I hate
> them. It's an open invitation to all the power wielders to beat

you to the punch. If you must have it, keep it minimal, bare bones.

Third: Close down the field of discussion. Keep it specific. "Your concern is the sufficiency of EXT. Shots? OK let's review those." "Walk me through the movie." Reframe that. Don't let it be about shots. Talk tone, mood, atmosphere, the ineffable that distinguishes you, THE DIRECTOR. Sorry if this sounds paternalistic. Not my intention. The director's role is mysterious, personal, and must not be reduced only to hardware and its function. There's a quotient of poetry that is not describable. It's in the doing. Love you, Nell.

This note still makes me tear up. I'm sharing Arthur's words so that others can see how the best mentors go beyond offering practical advice. They also break down the psychology of the dynamic, which is usually only understood after years of painful experience. Finally, the best mentors inspire. "There's a quotient of poetry that is not describable. It's in the doing." Nothing could have made me want to fight for my vision more than Arthur's definition of the director's role.

In my first movie, the crew warmed to me by the end. In my second, relations grew colder. The third to last day, we had a killer schedule with ten pages to shoot. I came in with all my blocking and approached the DP to discuss. He refused to talk to me. I pressed him to tell me what was wrong.

Obligatory director sitting on a crane shot. Nine years later . . . same purple Patagonia jacket.

"The actresses broke my heart," he said. "I no longer care about this movie."

And they say women are emotional.

I had no idea what the DP meant by his statement, but I couldn't question him further because he walked off the set. We were on the clock so I went over my shot list with a cameraman, who was inexperienced but present. The actresses came in fully prepared and ready to work. Miraculously, we made it through six pages before lunch.

I returned from our break to block a shorter scene in the same set. Suddenly, the DP reappeared in an upbeat, chatty mood.

"I have an idea for how you should shoot this next scene," he said, then launched into his suggestion.

His method seemed complicated.

"Let's stick with what I've got," I said. "It worked this morning."

"This will be faster," he said.

I was skeptical. The DP called the producer over and pitched him the plan.

"It would take three hours. Tops," the DP said.

The producer turned and looked me straight in the eye.

"That's the way you should shoot that scene," he said.

I ignored Arthur's advice and let them take control. It was a disaster. Four and a half hours later, the two-and-a-half-page scene still wasn't complete. We were grabbing closeups when the producer returned to set.

"You're done. This scene's over," he announced. "Moving on."

"But we don't have all the pieces," I said.

"Too bad," he said, then added, "You did this to yourself!"

I bit my tongue a lot on that shoot but not this time.

"You *know* I didn't design these shots. And you *know* you're the one who approved them," I said.

"Don't play the blame game!" he screamed.

That was the day I ended up sobbing on the floor of a coat

closet on the phone with my friend Jesse Dylan. I was so lucky he was available. Jesse's advice to "Go down fighting" snapped me out of my tailspin. I returned to set and, in the last three hours, I got what I needed. Sort of.

Back in LA, Stu Bass took the footage and performed his editing magic, teasing out both the comedy and the suspense. The actresses turned in superb performances under trying conditions and the friendships they formed shone through onscreen. Lifetime changed the title and the film premiered on November 11, 2007, the same week that I turned forty-seven. The previous week, Hollywood was shut down by a Writers Guild strike which lasted through February.

Once again, I hoped to build momentum, but as it turns out, the *third* movie is the hard one to get. Since then, I've only had the opportunity to shoot one half-hour episode of the MTV show *Awkward*. It's hard to know if I could have become a decent director. A person supposedly needs 10,000 hours of deliberate practice to master proficiency in a skill. I'm currently about 9,500 hours short.

In 2009, I visited Arthur and his wife Peggy at their home in NYC. In his eighties, Arthur had recently suffered a medical setback. We went for a short walk over to Central Park, then returned to the apartment. Over tea, I mentioned that I'd just seen an article about the fiftieth anniversary of the Broadway debut of *The Miracle Worker*.

"I re-watched the movie recently," I said. "And it's a very different experience as a parent. I cried so much harder at the beginning."

Arthur nodded. He had grown quiet. Maybe he was knocked out by our walk so I continued talking.

"When was the last time you watched *The Miracle Worker*? You know, I've never seen either of the movies that I directed since they aired. It's too painful when you know the difficulties behind every scene, but then I've only made low-budget cable movies. You've made beautiful movies, nominated for Oscars. You must be able to watch and enjoy them, right?"

Arthur shook his head.

"You always remember the compromises," he said. "It's a bargain with the devil."

CHAPTER 12

The Ones That Got Away

Anosmia: an·os·mi·a

1. the loss of the sense of smell, either total or partial.

2. a great name for an *X-Files* episode

D O YOU ENJOY DISAPPOINTMENT? YOU DO? THEN I have the perfect industry for you.

Hollywood disappointment comes in all shapes and sizes. There's the bittersweet early disappointment that can still make you smile at your own naïveté. There's the late-in-your-career disappointment where you're surprised to learn that you still care enough to feel let down. There's even the inexplicable disappointment where you feel bad about not getting offered a job that you didn't want.

I've had a wide variety of disappointments, but if I had to choose, these are the top five projects that I wish had turned out differently:

The X-Files

In the spring of 1995, I signed an overall deal with 20th Century Fox that included an assistant and a corner office. On my first day, the operations manager walked me over to a warehouse filled with furniture. Since my title was Executive Producer, he ushered me over to "the good stuff" and told me to pick out whatever pieces I wanted. Using Post-it notes, I tagged a desk and a lamp, then searched for a sofa. Most were black or brown leather and looked like they'd light up one of those *CSI* DNA semen detection tests. Then a couch covered in a pink-and-green floral chintz pattern caught my eye. It was positively girly.

"Is that one available?" I asked, pointing to the flowery couch.

"Yeah," the operations guy said. "It belonged to Lucie Salhany."

"Seriously?" I said. "That will make my power naps feel more powerful."

Lucie Salhany may not be a household name, but her influence on our culture is enormous. In the eighties, Lucie helped launch four syndicated shows that hit almost every demographic: *Entertainment Tonight, The Arsenio Hall Show, Star Trek: The Next Generation,* and *Hard Copy.* In the nineties, Rupert Murdoch brought her in to be Chairman of FOX, making her the first woman to run a major broadcast network. She had an extraordinary first year, overseeing the network's expansion from four nights of programming to seven and leading the negotiations to secure NFL game rights. The third year, Murdoch reportedly breeched a guarantee in Lucie's contract. She lawyered up and resigned.

"The reason I left was very complicated," she told me on the phone in 2017. "Rupert and I never really got along. He didn't like the fact that I didn't check in with him all the time or go to his house on Saturday, and he lied to me. He was a bully, distrustful, and discriminated against me, as he did with most women."

Lucie is fearless and funny. We only recently connected when I called to confirm that we had shared the same chintz-y couch.

"Yes!" she said. "That was mine."

I told her my theory about the other leather couches being covered in genetic material.

"There was no semen on my couch," she assured me. "Just a lot of blueberry, yogurt, and pineapple smoothies."

I thanked her for that, and for something else. While Chairman at FOX, Lucie greenlit *The X-Files*, one of my all-time, favorite TV shows. From my FOX office window, I could see creator Chris Carter's bungalow. Even better, I knew one of the writers, Howard Gordon, who went on to help shape the cult TV trifecta of *The X-Files*, *Buffy the Vampire Slayer*, and *24*. Occasionally, I'd stop by Howard's office to chat. One day, I worked up the courage to ask him if I could pitch some story ideas. They only had one freelance script left, but Howard said he'd check with Chris. To my amazement, Chris said he'd be happy to hear my pitches.

I knew moving to the next stage was a long shot. As a female writer, the odds of writing an episode for *The X-Files* were slightly worse than surviving *The Hunger Games*. This is not an exaggeration. During the show's original run, only seven of two hundred episodes (3.5 percent) were written by women. Meanwhile, one out of twenty-four survived *The Hunger Games* (4.2 percent). Katniss had it easy.

The morning of my pitch, I got out of bed and almost threw up. That was partially because I was nervous about meeting Chris, but also because I was twelve weeks pregnant. My condition made me self-conscious. *The X-Files* was—and still is—a boys' club, and boys don't get pregnant. To cover up my puffy abdomen, I dressed in an oversized button-down shirt and tied a sweater around my hips. When I entered the bungalow, Chris greeted me warmly and I sat down quickly. I pitched three stories and both Howard and Chris sparked to one called, "Anosmia."

The story kicks off with a kooky cat lady who contacts the FBI after her cats go missing from her Florida apartment complex. Agent Mulder investigates and finds that tensions are running high between the mixed-race tenants. Mulder gets a whiff of what's wrong: the government is releasing an alien scent through the apartment ventilation system. The scent drove the animals away. The humans weren't as smart. Soon, tenants start dying off under strange circumstances—as one does in Florida.

I told Chris and Howard that smell was the first sense to develop and it was so successful that, in time, the small lump of olfactory tissue on top of the nerve cord evolved into a brain. Our cerebral hemispheres were originally buds from the olfactory stalks.

"We think because we smell," I said.

Chris suggested that in addition to the alien scent affecting behavior, there should be something in the environment that triggers a "hate response." One of us suggested that watching TV news could be that trigger. FOX News was only two years old and fairly mild so we had the idea first. The meeting wrapped up. Chris said they'd discuss my ideas and get back to me.

Howard called the next day with good news. Chris dug "Anosmia" and because my pitch was so detailed, I was approved to go to outline. I'd snagged the last freelance *X-Files* episode of the fifth season. I did a happy dance around Lucie Salhany's couch.

I'd never written an outline for a drama, but I'd seen every *X-Files* episode and knew the show's rhythm. My teaser opened on a twelve-year-old African American boy swimming in a courtyard pool. His mom runs upstairs to get a towel, figuring the boy will be safe because he's surrounded by neighbors. Bad plan in Florida. A watch falls from a balcony into the water. The boy dives down to retrieve it and the watch mysteriously pulls *him* down. When the mom returns, her son is floating in the pool, face up. Drowned.

Scully immediately knows something is wrong since a drowned body would be facing down. During the autopsy, she lifts the boy's eyelids and discovers that the whites of his pupils have turned yellow. The boy's system appears to have been flooded with bile. Scully explains that long ago, scientists believed that bile was the seat of bitterness.

"So what killed the boy?" asks Mulder.

"Medieval 'doctors' would have determined that his cause of death was hate," says Scully.

With each act, the body count rose. The not-so-subtle message of the episode was that humans had not yet evolved to the point where we could co-exist with alien species. In fact, we could barely co-exist with each other. This was the final paragraph of the outline:

> Mulder runs back downstairs to help Scully. As they try to revive Kathleen, Mulder finishes his voice over: "There are many kinds of evil on earth, so it's easy to forget that evil is not only the thing that destroys but also the thing that allows evil to destroy. It's easy to recognize evil when it's obvious and cruel, but ignorance and apathy can kill as swiftly and as sure." As the camera floats back to Mrs. Bryant watching TV, we fade out. END OF ACT FOUR

It took me a week to finish the outline. As a freelancer, it's hard to know all the rules of a show so I figured I'd get a lot of notes. A few days later, Chris's assistant called my office and asked me to hold for her boss. My heart started racing. I really wanted Chris to love the outline. He picked up and sounded cheerful. Good sign!

"I have an update," Chris said. "The show has some exciting news that hasn't been made public yet."

"Really? What's that?" I asked.

"It turns out Stephen King is a big fan and he just reached out to us. He wants to write an episode."

"That's amazing!" I said.

"Yeah, the problem is we only have the one freelance assignment left . . ."

Oh. Chris wasn't calling to give me notes. He was calling to let me know that I was getting replaced by Stephen King. I went from sixty to zero in five seconds.

"We'll definitely pay you for the outline," Chris said. "And maybe next season, we can talk again."

I hung up the phone. My office had gotten eerily quiet, like abandoned-hotel quiet. I'd been so excited and now I didn't know what to feel. No writer could be angry about getting bumped by the Master of Horror. It's like learning that Picasso wants to paint over your mural. "Have at it, Pablo."

King and Chris ended up cowriting "Chinga" which featured an antique doll who makes people tear out their eyes. I couldn't bear to watch so I know how the victims felt.

Since then, I've thought about how so many of King's novels revolve around everyday folks whose lives are upended by an agent of chaos like the rabid dog in *Cujo* or the Clown in *It*. These Stephen King monsters come out of nowhere and wreak havoc on unsuspecting rubes. And it occurred to me that the Stephen King monster in my life was Stephen King.

Robert Altman

In 1976, my father took me to see Robert Altman's *Nashville* and it blew my teenage mind. Altman wove together story lines for over a dozen oddball characters and brought them all together for a shocking climax. Driving home afterwards, my dad and I talked about the themes of politics, motherhood, fame, and violence in the film. It was my first grown-up movie discussion and Altman became my favorite director.

In the late eighties, I watched every episode of his HBO mini-series, *Tanner '88*, which was set on the presidential campaign trail and blurred the lines between fiction and reality. *Tanner '88* was a success and a year later, Altman started pulling together a similar project that would be set in the world of entertainment and star Carol Burnett. When my agent told me that Altman was interested in meeting with me to discuss the project, I thought, "Seriously? Why me?" But I said, "I would love that."

"The premise is simple," Altman explained as we sat in his New York City hotel suite. "Carol is touring the south, for real, and her concerts provide the backdrop for backstage drama, all fictional. We surround her with a cast of characters—assistant, hairstylist, family members, agent. We'll develop story lines, and because of Carol's skills, we want the actors to improv a lot. But we're also looking for a writer to sit on set and throw out lines. Does that interest you?"

I nodded vigorously.

"And you're familiar with Carol Burnett?"

I *worshipped* Carol Burnett. As a kid, I watched her variety series religiously and bowed down to her performance as Winifred the Woebegone in *Once Upon a Mattress*. Winifred belting out "Shy" was my kind of princess.

Altman and I brainstormed ideas for ancillary characters: a driver selling secrets to the tabloids, a hairdresser hiding that he's straight, an *All About Eve*–type assistant who has no talent. We laughed a lot and he offered me the job on the spot.

"We're moving quickly," he said. "Could you pack this weekend and meet me and Carol in Atlanta next week?"

"If a family member were on life support, I'd pull the plug so I'd have nothing to keep me from leaving town," I said.

"Great," he said. "We'll be in touch soon."

I floated home to 57th Street. It was a Friday afternoon and my agent promised to get into the deal with the network first thing Monday morning. She cautioned me that the pay would be low. *Really* low. That answered the question, "Why me?"

Over the weekend, I called my dad with the news.

"Wow," he said. "You're in the big leagues."

Monday came and I hung out at home, waiting for the call while cleaning my apartment in case I needed to bolt. Early afternoon, the phone rang. I heard a brusque male voice.

"Nell, it's Bob."

I was confused.

"Bob who?" I said.

"Bob Altman."

Oh. Right. Bob is a nickname for Robert.

"The deal's off. CBS is screwing around so it's not gonna happen. Okay, I gotta go."

And with a click, that dream job would forever remain a dream.

Pre–*Daily Show* Jon Stewart

Jon Stewart has so many Emmy awards that he could leave one at every exit on the New Jersey Turnpike and still have a couple left over. But before he landed at *The Daily Show* (created by Lizz Winstead and Madeleine Smithberg) in 1999, Jon sought out potential partners to develop his own show that would shoot in NYC. I'd just come back from directing my first movie when my agent asked if I wanted to meet him. I called Becky Hartman, a mutual friend and comedy writer, to ask what she thought.

"Yes!" she declared. "You will love Jon."

Jon and I got together in LA and we talked about ways to

shake up the talk show genre. We were dissecting the format when I pinpointed what I perceived as a dead spot on every late-night talk show. After the host finishes his monologue, he heads back to his desk, which forces him to turn his back on the audience. To cover this staging faux pas, the host typically throws focus to the bandleader. Letterman always introduced "Our good friend Paul Shaffer." The camera would then cut away to Paul wearing a new pair of zany glasses while Dave scurried to the desk. It felt like filler because it *was* filler.

Jon nodded. "So what would you do instead?"

"Well, what if . . ." I said. "What if you wore a pair of *So Fine* jeans?"

"*So Fine* jeans?" he said.

"You know like from the Ryan O'Neal movie."

So Fine was an early eighties Andrew Bergman film about a business man who needs money and launches a new fashion craze: buttless pants.

The poster for *So Fine*. What can I say?
The eighties were weird.

"Are you serious?" Jon asked.

I wasn't really, but on the drive over to the meeting, I realized that a move to New York didn't make sense. My husband liked LA and we had two kids under four. Since I didn't want the job, I had nothing to lose. I doubled-down on the joke.

"Yes, I'm serious. I mean, you wouldn't wear the *So Fine* jeans every night. The idea is to build up anticipation as you near the end of the monologue, so the audience can't wait for you to turn around and head to the desk: 'Will he be wearing the *So Fine* jeans or not?!' And when you do, they'll go nuts."

Our meeting wrapped up quickly. There was no callback.

Jon and I have bumped into each other a few times since. I've never had the nerve to ask if he remembered my ludicrous pitch. My guess is he erased it from his memory, which means . . .

The *So Fine* jeans idea is still up for grabs. *James Corden, call me!*

Marshall Brickman

On May 25, 1997, I emailed a friend, gushing like a teenager: "I spent two hours on the phone with Marshall Brickman this morning. There's a chance we'll work together on a TV show!"

I have a huge comedy crush on Marshall who was the co-screenwriter of Woody Allen's funniest movies. Here's mathematical proof:

Woody Allen + Marshall Brickman = *Annie Hall, Sleeper, Manhattan*
Woody Allen − Marshall Brickman = *Scoop, Folly's Friends, Whatever Works*

Okay, I made up *Folly's Friends,* but if you didn't immediately realize that, I've made my point. Marshall worked in TV early in his career, writing for *Candid Camera* and *The Tonight Show with Johnny Carson*. Thirty years later, he was looking to make a return. He'd written a hilarious pilot script, *Norman of the Future*, about—wait for it—a guy named Norman who lived in the future. NBC bought the project and Marshall was interviewing TV writers with recent sitcom experience to executive produce the series with him.

I had just left *Sabrina* and loved his idea with all my heart. We spoke over the phone about how the future and magic overlap. I quoted Arthur C. Clarke's third law: *Any sufficiently advanced technology is indistinguishable from magic.* He thought I'd be a fine addition to the creative team and told the network. NBC refused to approve me. They wouldn't even meet with me to discuss the project. I was devastated. I felt like I'd proven myself as a showrunner. Did *Sabrina* not count because it was a TGIF show? Did my gender factor into the equation? Marshall was a complete class act and went to bat for me. The network refused to budge.

In this case, my disappointment goes beyond the personal. Marshall's unique brand of smart/silly comedy never made it to air. *Norman of the Future* had no future.

Seinfeld

Seinfeld was wrapping up their second season when my agent Abby Adams submitted me to be a low-level writer. The show wasn't a hit yet, but I'd been a fan back when it was called *The Seinfeld Chronicles*. The first step to meeting with co-creators Jerry Seinfeld and Larry David was to get the approval of Castle Rock executive Glenn Padnick. Abby sent my scripts over and Glenn responded with this letter:

February 7, 1991

Ms. Abby Adams
Creative Artists Agency, Inc.
9830 Wilshire Boulevard
Beverly Hills, California 90212-1825

                    Re: **Nell Scovell**

Dear Abby:

Thank you for letting me read the enclosed "NEWHART", "GARRY
SHANDLING" and "SIMPSONS" scripts by Nell Scovell. As I said on
the phone the other day, I really enjoyed them. Yesterday, I
gave copies of the "SIMPSONS" script to Jerry Seinfeld and Larry
David with my recommendation that they consider her for next
season. As you know, the bigger issue is whether we have a next
season. If we do, I hope Ms. Scovell will be available to work
with us.

Very truly yours,

Glenn Padnick

GAP/srg

Enclosures

Here's the key sentence: *"As you know, the bigger issue is whether
we have a next season."*

Seinfeld was on the bubble. It scraped by for two more seasons
before breaking into the Nielsen Top 30. A meeting never happened, but I held on to the Castle Rock letter because it offered
encouragement early in my career. Now it hangs in my office as a
reminder of how the greatest success story in the history of television came close to getting cancelled.

I did eventually get a chance to work with Larry David. In
2007, *Curb Your Enthusiasm* threw out a net, soliciting ideas for
the upcoming season. I typed up a few notions, including one

where "Larry" needs to bring flowers for a hostess gift and decides to steal them from a roadside memorial. Larry bought the
concept and turned it into season six's "*The Ida Funkhouser Roadside Memorial.*" The show didn't give me onscreen credit, but
they paid me two thousand dollars. Larry also gave me his word
that the show would pay writers better in the coming season.

With that incentive, I pitched some additional story areas.
Larry seemed interested in one concept, but it didn't move forward. A year or so later, we both attended a book party. Our mutual friend, Kimberly Brooks, introduced us.

"Larry, do you know Nell?"

"Nell! Of course, I know Nell," Larry said. "In fact, I was just
talking about you today."

Whoa. Larry David was talking about me? That felt good.

"Really? How come?" I asked.

"Well, one of the producers said that you'd sold us two ideas
for episodes, but I insisted it was just one. We argued about it, and
now here you are. You can solve the mystery!"

"Oh," I said, a little disappointed. "It was just one."

"Yes!" said Larry, happy to have been right.

"But you did like another idea of mine," I added quickly, trying to save face.

"Which one?"

"The one about the pee drinker."

Larry looked confused. I re-pitched the idea.

"Larry's at a party with a guy who won't stop talking about
all his thrilling adventures. The guy goes hiking in the Hima-
layas . . . helicopter snowboarding . . . sailing around Tierra
del Fuego. And in every story, he runs into complications and
recounts how, in order to survive, he was forced to drink his own
pee. Later, Larry sees the thrill-seeker go into the bathroom with
a near-empty bottle of beer and when he comes out, the bottle is
filled to the brim. Larry watches as the guy takes swigs from the

"beer" bottle and becomes convinced that the guy is drinking his own urine. The great adventures are just a cover! The truth is the guy is *purposely* putting himself into life-or-death situations because it's the only socially acceptable way to drink your own pee!"

I didn't say "ta da" at the end of the pitch, but it was implied. I looked at Larry expectantly.

He shook his head and offered one long, drawn-out syllable: "Nooooo."

Cue the *Curb Your Enthusiasm* theme mandolin and tuba.

CHAPTER 13

You Sexy Motherwriter

I believe the children are our future . . .
    meals.

—Shorter Jonathan Swift

AT THE EXACT AGE OF TWENTY-NINE, I OPENED *THE New York Times Book Review* and thought, "How nice! Kurt Vonnegut, one of my favorite novelists, wrote an essay." One paragraph later, I felt sucker-punched. Here's what Vonnegut wrote:

> If Lloyds of London offered policies promising to compensate comical writers for losses of senses of humor, its actuaries could count in such a loss occurring on average at 63 for men, and for women at 29, say.

Say what?

My comedy career was just taking off and now someone I respected was predicting that I'd lose my sense of humor—the source of my livelihood—at any moment. And why did men get thirty-four more years of being funny than me?

While the ages seemed off, Vonnegut did identify a truth. In comedy, growing old is an occupational hazard. In 2010, TV and screenwriters were awarded $70 million to resolve a class action suit that charged networks, studios, and talent agencies with age discrimination. The cutoff age for participating in the suit was not sixty. Or fifty. It was *forty*. Forty is when doctors, lawyers, and accountants start hitting their stride. Sadly, writers line up more with strippers: after forty, everything's downhill and nobody wants to talk about what's really going on in the back room.

Because of age bias, looking young in Hollywood becomes important even for writers. Both men and women are affected although not everyone buys in.

"I just try to come across as the kooky aunt," the phenomenally successful Paula Pell told me.

I wish I could adopt Paula's attitude. It's ridiculous to spend time and money on superficial appearance. Yet, I've done it. I started experimenting with Botox in 2002 as part of "research" for a Botox party scene for a script. Still, I haven't gone full Real Housewife. When one dermatologist suggested fillers for the laugh lines around my mouth, I passed. My mom had the same lines and when I look in the mirror, they remind me of her. Also, if my coworkers and I do our jobs right, the lines are concealed by actual laughter.

Along with youth, it often helps for writers to exude sex appeal. Sadly, this doesn't come in a syringe. I once left a pitch meeting where I'd been the only female and as soon as the elevator doors closed, my agent snapped at me.

"Why don't you flirt a little, Nell?" he said, peeved. "You could get away with it."

I had no idea what he was talking about. Clearly, I had missed some subtext. Those words stuck with me. I don't know of many jobs where it's detrimental to act *too* professional. And not everyone does.

"I just texted a photo of my boobs to my boyfriend!" a female writer once declared to the room after a bathroom break.

The straight men responded with hoots and applause. I stopped myself from adding, "And I just texted my husband a photo of me rolling my eyes."

It was hard to avoid sexual innuendo in that particular writers' room. Once, our director doubled over on the set in pain and required an emergency appendectomy. The next day, we were speculating on his recovery time. Since I'd had abdominal surgery, I decided to chime in.

"It's not that bad," I said. "I've had two C-sections and if you don't twist . . ."

Before I could finish my sentence, a male writer interrupted.

"Wait—so you're still tight?"

I looked at him hard.

"Yes, that was the point of my story," I deadpanned. This was one of the rare times that I brought up giving birth in the room so it was disheartening that my colleague turned it into confirmation that I could still sexually satisfy a man. Years later, this same colleague was accused by nineteen coworkers of "inappropriate behavior." He denied the charges, insisting that while he had made comments about coworkers' looks, those comments "were not sexualized." I guess he meant that I was "tight" in the nautical sense.

Stereotypically female topics often get short shrift in the room. Two male writers used to give detailed updates on their fantasy football teams at the start of almost every workday. Then while trying to break an episode about a wedding, a female writer shared a story about her disastrous honeymoon. She didn't race through, but told the story beautifully, letting it build to a funny climax. The moment she stopped talking, one of the two football fans jumped in.

"Thanks for telling the story of your weeklong honeymoon *in real time*," he said.

The storyteller's head dropped and she let her hair dangle over her face.

"I just thought . . ." she muttered, then her voice trailed off.

I wanted to lunge across the table, grab the writer by his collar and say, "I've listened to your endless fantasy football discussions and never made you feel like you were wasting my time. So fuck—and might I add—you!"

Women are rewarded for talking about sex in the room, but talking about marriage or motherhood often brings a room down. Some view motherhood as the antithesis of funny since moms are associated with nurturing, gentleness, and safety while comedy wants to be twisted, dangerous, and mean. For example, Mother Teresa spoke at my college graduation and didn't crack a single joke. She did explain to all the graduating women that "the greatest gift you can give your husband is your virginity." My roommates and I laughed really hard, but I don't think that counts.

The entertainment business is not the only field where motherhood is a disadvantage. A 2017 report showed that if a man and a woman work identical hours at identical levels, the woman's income will drop four percent after she delivers or adopts a child while the man's income will rise six percent after he becomes a dad.

"The motherhood penalty is not a disputed finding," sociologist Marianne Cooper told me. "Oh, it's real."

She then described a study that discovered a woman's chances of getting hired nosedives if four words appear on her résumé: *Parent-Teacher Association Coordinator.*

"The assumptions are that mothers aren't committed to their careers," Marianne explained. "And this is a huge problem since seventy percent of moms work."

"Is there anything moms can do to offset this?" I asked. "Can't we just work even harder?"

"That can help in some cases. But then those hard-driving women get dinged because people think they aren't good mothers and are *cold*," she said. "You really can't win."

I didn't need any studies to prove the "motherhood penalty" existed. Instinctively, I kept my pregnancies hidden for as long as I could. My first pregnancy was complication-free, which made it easier. My first delivery went less smoothly, which leads me to a story I would never feel comfortable telling in the writers' room.

At my thirty-nine-week checkup, my obstetrician measured the baby and concluded that I should be induced on my due date. A week later, Colin and I drove to Cedar Sinai in the dark and by six a.m., the Pitocin was flowing. Contractions started and my OB stopped by around eight to cheerfully observe, "You're having a baby today!"

Not so fast. The hours ticked by and the baby wasn't descending into the birth canal. I started to run a fever so a second IV was added filled with an antibiotic. I had monitors everywhere—and I mean, *everywhere*. Seventeen hours later, my OB informed me that the baby's head was too big to pass through my hips. The situation required an emergency C-section.

"We'll get you in as soon as possible," he said, moving toward the door. "I already called for the backup surgeon. Any questions?"

I phrased my question in the form of an emotional breakdown and burst into tears. The OB stopped. He returned to my side and took my hand.

"It doesn't make you any less of a woman," he said, sympathetically.

If I'd had the strength, I would have slugged him. Not for a moment did I think I was "less of a woman." I was exhausted and scared and concerned about my baby.

Rudy made it out safely and I was lucky not to suffer any postpartum depression. I continued to push myself professionally. Two weeks after giving birth, I was in casting sessions for my pilot,

Prudy and Judy. And two months later, I teamed up with Joel to do a pass on *George of the Jungle.* Joel was cool about me taking breaks to pump milk and often clowned around with Rudy.

CRAZY UNCA JOEL

Joel inscribed the Polaroid himself.

After turning in our *George* rewrite, Joel and I got called in for a notes meeting at Disney. We were waiting for the top executive to arrive when I felt a sudden, painful stab in my left breast. I knew from experience that it was a blocked milk duct, and the key with a blocked milk duct is to unblock it fast. I excused myself and ran into the hall, sprinting past the centrally located women's room to look for a more remote restroom. When I found one, I checked under the stalls to make sure I was alone, then I whipped out my left breast, and started working with my hands to express the milk into the sink. It was excruciating—the kind of pain that radiates down your spine. I kept my head lowered so I wouldn't catch a glimpse of myself in the mirror. No Disney Imagineer would have imagined this. After ten minutes, the pain began to subside and the milk streamed more easily. The dam had broken.

I turned on the faucets and washed the milk down the drain, splashing handfuls of water against the sides of the sink. I ran back to the conference room and rejoined the meeting just as it was starting. It was one of the few times I was grateful that movie executives are always tardy. I sat through the notes, which turned out to be more painful than a blocked milk duct.

Oh, and please tell me again how mothers aren't dedicated to their jobs.

During my second pregnancy, I again kept a low profile, writing mostly at home. Then, exactly two weeks before my due date, just when some cultures send their women into a hut to squat until it's over, I got a call from my agent. Joss Whedon and David Greenwalt were taking meetings for a job opening at *Buffy the Vampire Slayer*. My agent knew how much I loved the show and even though I had no hour-long credits, with my *Sabrina* background, she thought she could get me a meeting. The timing was terrible. At thirty-eight weeks, every inch of me was bloated. My belly was so distended that I could rest my folded elbows on it like a shelf. But Joss and David were making staff decisions right away so I couldn't push it off.

Before the interview, I brainstormed ideas for episodes, including one where Zander, Oz, and Giles all become magically pregnant. I found a shirt that wasn't completely stained from pregnancy-induced clumsiness and drove to the meeting. I described my reception in an email to a friend.

> *April 22, 1998 11:06 AM*
> *I am 38 weeks pregnant. I went in to meet with Joss Whedon, creator of "Buffy the Vampire Slayer" (my favorite show on television) on Monday. He took one look at me and said, "Boy, are you fat." I laughed so hard, I thought I was going to have the baby. Co-Executive Producer David Greenwalt followed up by asking, "Should I put down a tarp?"*

They didn't hire me. On a happier note, I gave birth to a healthy baby two weeks later with the cool, geeky birthday of May the Fourth aka *Star Wars* Day. ("May the Fourth be with you.")

"Nell, you're a terrible mother," Penn Jillette once told me. "But you're the world's greatest dad." His words stung at first until I realized he was making an astute observation about cultural stereotypes. Now I find Penn's comment comforting. Comparing myself to stay-at-home moms, I fell short. But comparing myself to working dads, I held my own or even excelled. Did other dads have to unblock a milk duct before a meeting? Factually, they did not.

And I did have *some* stereotypical Mom skills. My mother made a home-cooked meal for our family every night and dinner was the one time each day when all seven of us would be together. Since I often worked late, I shifted the concept of family dinner to family breakfast. I'd wake up early and make popovers and buttermilk pancakes from scratch. One day a week, I made crepes, customizing each order. Colin likes his crepes filled with Nutella, bananas, and freshly toasted pecans. Rudy likes Nutella and pecans. Dexter likes Nutella and marshmallows and prefers his crepe folded in half like an omelet. Eventually, the tradition codified into "Crepes Thursday," the holiest day of the week.

Colin was a patient and loving dad, and it helped that Rudy and Dexter were best friends. Oddly, my kids' personalities turned out to be similar to the aunts in *Sabrina*. Rudy is enthusiastic and warm like Hilda. At eight years old, he even invented his own emotion. On Christmas, 2004, Rudy suddenly announced, "Mom, I just discovered a new feeling. It's called 'perpy.' It's when you're excited and cheerful and have no doubts about the world."

"So it's better than happy?" I asked.

"Yeah. When you're perpy, it's like the love is unstoppable." He smiled broadly and said, "I just feel so perpy!"

Dexter is more like Aunt Zelda, pragmatic and shrewd. When

he was seven, we were walking in Washington, DC and Dexter spotted a penny on the sidewalk. He reached down and grabbed it.

"Mom, I found a lucky penny," he said. "I want you to have it."

"Aw, thanks," I said.

"But I get to keep the luck."

The kids and Colin have always been understanding about my missing occasional milestones because of work. Still, when the production schedule for *Hayley Wagner, Star* came out and I saw that Dexter's first birthday fell on the second day of the Vancouver shoot, it tore me up. But what could I do? I couldn't fly home in the middle of the movie.

Colin came up with a solution. He got himself and two children under the age of four onto a plane to Canada, through customs, and onto the set so I could kiss Dexter on his first birthday.

The family in Vancouver, May 1999

My decision to be the breadwinner suited our family, but everyone who has a choice needs to make their own decision. If a woman decides to leave her job and raise her kids full time, I think she's amazing and brave. And if after a few years, she wants to return to work, I think she's amazing and brave to do that, too. Men should have the same options as women. We need to free ourselves from the cultural belief that mothers are better at raising children than fathers. In the deepest way possible, I can tell you that is not true.

Fortunately, attitudes about mothers having a place in comedy are evolving. I cheered in 2009 when a *very*-pregnant Amy Poehler rapped a boisterous tribute to Sarah Palin on Weekend Update. Ali Wong filmed her 2016 standup special *Baby Cobra* while seven months pregnant. Samantha Bee did stellar work as a correspondent for *The Daily Show* while pregnant and, in a *New York* magazine interview, urged others to try.

"It'll add to your comedy in ways that you never expected," Bee said.

All these women are hilarious and tough, or what I call, "maternal."

Why Two Serial Killers Have the Same Names as My Children

Naming characters, or children, is hard. Certain names carry certain associations. This explains why there aren't many girls named Squeaky. We thought we'd given our kids fine names—Rudy and Dexter—until 2006 when "Dexter," a series about a serial killer debuted with huge, blood-splattered billboards all over LA. Oh, well, there was nothing we could do.

Then one day, my old *Charmed* colleague Daniel Cerone called. Daniel was one of the *Dexter* showrunners and he had a question.

"I'm working on an episode where we meet Dexter's brother and he needs an alias," Daniel said. "I was thinking—if you're okay with it—I'd name him 'Rudy.' But you should know that Rudy is also a killer so—"

"I love it!" I said.

"I knew it!" Daniel said. "I knew you'd be the one friend excited by this."

And that's why in the season one finale, "Dexter" and his brother "Rudy" are reunited until—spoiler alert—Dexter slashes Rudy's throat.

CHAPTER 14

The Decade-Long Roller-Coaster Ride

A young man sits on a park bench reading a book when an old man sits next to him. Thirty seconds later, the old man announces, "Oy, am I thirsty." The young man tries to concentrate, but thirty seconds later, the old man repeats, "Oy, am I thirsty." This continues every thirty seconds until finally the young man gets up, buys a water, and hands it to the old man. "Thank you," says the old man and he takes a long sip. The young man sits back down to read his book. Thirty seconds later, the old man says, "Oy, was I thirsty."

—old Jewish joke

THIRTEEN YEARS AFTER I BROKE INTO TV, I'D RISEN to the level of creator and showrunner. I'd written and directed my own movie. My career expectations were high, but as supermodel Paulina Porizkova once wrote, "The

American woman is told she can do anything and then is knocked down the moment she proves it."

That's how I felt. And it's not just supermodels and me. A 2014 study revealed that "by the age of thirty-nine, college-educated women working full-time stop getting raises and see their salaries peak." Meanwhile, college-educated men get an additional nine years of wage increases, peaking at forty-eight. It's important to note that this happens to women working *full time*. Women are not necessarily pulling back. Sometimes, they get pushed back. (Also, there should be a German word for the joy you feel when a study proves that a bias you've experienced is real and you weren't just paranoid. Wharton professor and psychologist Adam Grant suggests this emotion be called *vindicatzinstudie.*)

In my twenties and thirties, I converted almost every meeting into a job. In my forties, I struck out a lot. By then I'd worked in so many genres—late-night, variety, animation, sitcoms, dramas, and features. I thought this range would make me a utility player. Instead, jumping around genres seemed to confuse the market. I heard more than once that comedy executives considered me a drama writer and drama executives considered me a comedy writer. I was a pigeon without a hole.

It didn't help that I was no longer a mid-level writer. Rising to a leadership position and being a woman led to wariness about my character. (See chart on facing page.)

Years later, I learned about a Columbia Business School professor who divided a class in two and assigned each section to read about a successful venture capitalist. The case studies were identical except for one detail—the entrepreneur was identified as "Howard" for half the students and as "Heidi" for the other half. The next day, the students were asked to give their impressions of the "two" entrepreneurs. Both Howard and Heidi were deemed competent, but they weren't both judged as likeable. Howard received only favorable responses. Students described him as "the

HOW MALE AND FEMALE SHOWRUNNERS ARE PERCEIVED DIFFERENTLY (AN UNSCIENTIFIC CHART)

	Men	Women
Arguing a point	Thoughtful	Crazy
Defending a joke	Perfectionist	Difficult
Missing deadlines	Creative	Crazy
Holding back on sharing an outline	Protective	Difficult
Crying at work	Sensitive	Crazy
Suggesting a character be less sexist/racist	Progressive	Difficult
Throwing objects (phones, scripts)	Passionate	Crazy
Refusing to delegate	Commanding	Difficult
Hiring friends	Loyal	Crazy
Negotiating for more money	Savvy	Difficult
Massive drug habit	Struggling	Crazy and difficult

type of person you would want to hire or work for." Heidi, however, was perceived to be "selfish" and "out for herself."

"Women are expected to be nice, warm, friendly, and nurturing," my patient sociologist friend Marianne said, interpreting yet another study for me. "If a woman acts assertively or competitively, if she exhibits decisive and forceful leadership, she is deviating from the social script. We are deeply uncomfortable with powerful women. In fact, we often don't really like them."

I felt the industry and even my own agents chill toward me. Fine, I thought. If Hollywood didn't consider me a showrunner, there was only one thing to do—I lowered my expectations. I convinced myself that I didn't want to run a show. "I'd rather be the Co-Executive Producer," my brain rationalized. "Then I don't have all the responsibility and won't have to deal with all the politics."

Like many women—some out of choice and some out of necessity—I leaned out. I shifted my career goals away from securing power and creative control and toward simply continuing to work. The aughts were a roller coaster for me professionally and I was lucky to have a supportive family and friends. Colin and my sister Claire listened to me vent constantly. I didn't want to complain but "Oy, was I thirsty."

Daily phone calls with my friend Rob Bragin were cheaper than therapy and a lot funnier. Once Rob emailed me, "This just in . . . NOTHING."

We stayed optimistic for each other. Rob would repeat his motivating mantra, "You eat what you kill."

For a decade, I accepted every job that was offered to me. A reboot of *McCloud* for Brett Butler on USA? Sure. A pilot loosely based on *Sliding Doors* for Lifetime? Sounds great. An hour-long dramedy about female inmates for FOX? Absolutely! Actually, I had a great time writing *Behind Bars* for Executive Producer Mike Darnell and we were both disappointed when the script didn't move forward. Would a series about women in prison have worked? I guess we'll never know.

I wish I'd enjoyed the down time more. Unfortunately, when you're in a dry spell, there's no way to know if it will rain tomorrow or if it's the start of a hundred-year drought. I still loved writing for TV and hoped someone would keep paying me to do that. I wasn't looking for fireworks. I just wanted to find a nice show and settle down. But like a good man, a good TV show was hard to find.

Looks Good on Paper (2001)

When the hit WB show *Charmed*, created by Constance Burge, hired me as a Co-Executive Producer, it seemed like a perfect match. I wanted to transition from writing half hours to hours and was well-versed in witchiness. The *Charmed* room was filled with gifted writers and had a fifty-fifty gender split.

"This is too good to be true," I thought.

And it was. The cracks showed early. The on-camera message of the "magical power of sisterhood" did not extend offscreen. By the time I joined the staff, all the *Charmed* Executive Producers were male. Out of 178 episodes, only eight were directed by women and series star Shannen Doherty was the only woman to direct more than once.

Figurines of shrunken Halliwell sisters from my episode, "Size Matters," which guest-starred Robert Englund aka Freddy Krueger. (left to right) Alyssa Milano, Rose McGowan, Holly Marie Combs

In the middle of my second season, the showrunner began to negotiate a new contract for himself. The studio approached my agents to float the idea of me taking over if those negotiations fell through.

"Oh, no," I told my agents. "I won't discuss that until the showrunner decides what he's doing."

I'd been in the business long enough to know that being competent enough to do your boss's job makes you an asset, but being competent enough to *replace* your boss makes you a threat. I prayed that he hadn't gotten wind of the phone call. This story makes me think he might have.

A month earlier, the showrunner had asked me to cowrite a sweeps week episode with him. We divided the work by acts. I penned the teaser, act one and act two. He penned acts three and four. We put our work together and the network and studio approved the script, which went into production. On the morning of the table read, I walked into the conference room, grabbed a coffee, a freshly printed script, and took a seat next to my boss and cowriter. He leaned over.

"I made a few small changes last night," he said.

"Okay."

That was his prerogative. Besides, last-minute tweaks are easy to spot because once a script is locked for production, any change is marked by an asterisk in the right-hand margin. I opened my script. My face dropped.

Every single line on the first page had an asterisk next to it.

I inhaled sharply and turned to the second page. Same thing. I started flipping through the script, like Shelley Duvall rifling through reams of "All work and no play makes Jack a dull boy" in *The Shining*. Every page of the teaser, act one and act two, was littered with asterisks. His acts—three and four—were totally clean. I looked closer at the actual changes. They were mostly minor, involving punctuation and word choices—just enough to trigger an asterisk, but by no means the major rewrite that those asterisks suggested. I felt humiliated. It would appear to the actors and execs at the table that my half had been a mess. I wanted to walk out, but worried it would look like I was upset at having been so heavily rewritten. I stayed. That was the last script I wrote that season. The showrunner refused to assign me another episode.

When my contract was up at *Charmed*, I left a Nell-shaped hole in the wall on my way out. I would miss the other writers. I'd even grown fond of actresses Alyssa Milano, Holly Marie

Combs, and Rose McGowan. And there was one other perk specific to that job that I enjoyed. At the wrap of each season, the costume department sold the production's used wardrobe. One of the actresses and I wore the same size jeans so not only did I get cheap high-end clothing, but I could brag about getting in a TV star's pants.

We're Just Not That into You (2002)

As a failed pre-med major, writing on medical shows always appealed to me. After *Charmed*, CBS executives encouraged me to join *Presidio Med*, a new medical drama set mainly in a neonatal unit. The show had a spectacular cast and Emmy Award–winning producers. The tone was a little somber, and the network hoped that I would help provide some lightness.

The series got off to a rocky start in the ratings and as we neared the holidays, the staff was jittery about whether we'd be picked up beyond the initial twelve-episode order. In late November, I was sitting in my office on a Friday afternoon reading a script that had just been turned in. The story had some problems so when an assistant stopped by to say the showrunner wanted to see me, I assumed it was to ask me to do a pass over the weekend. The thought didn't make me happy. I walked slowly down the hall to the showrunner's big corner office, trying to delay the inevitable.

"Have a seat," the showrunner said.

I sat.

"So the network wants more changes to the show. And given the new direction, we're going to have to let you go."

Wait, what?!

I felt psychological whiplash. My arms and hands went numb, as my body went into mild shock. I'd never been fired before and had no idea how to react. The showrunner noticed my stricken face.

"I'm sorry," she said. Her tone was calm and professional.

It seemed like my turn to say something so I blurted out the first question that popped into my head.

"If someone asks you about me, what will you say?"

"I'll say that you weren't right for the show," she replied. "And that I enjoyed working with you."

"Okay," I said. "Because I also enjoyed working with—"

I couldn't finish the sentence. Tears started streaming down my face. I struggled to breathe as emotion overwhelmed me. Apparently, my reaction to being fired was to cry sloppily.

"I'm sorry," I said and exited her office.

I walked quickly back to my office and closed the door. I phoned Colin.

"I just got fired," I said.

"Good," he said without hesitation. "You weren't happy on the show and now you're done."

Colin was right. I hadn't been able to lighten the tone. If anything, the show had become more serious. I'd even started joking with my comedy friends that the *Presidio Med* tagline should be: "Winning America's heart . . . one dead baby at a time."

After Colin calmed me down, I went into the hall to share the news with my coworkers. The mood was already gloomy. Another writer had also been axed. I recently asked Howard A. Rodman, President of the Writers Guild of America, West, from 2015–2017 if he knew the statistics of how many writers get fired at some point in their careers.

"I don't think we've even asked that in our survey," Howard messaged me. "I'd say a hundred percent, but what do I know?"

He was joking, but getting fired (or not having your option picked up) happens to almost everyone. As a manager once told me, "Show me someone with a long career and I'll show you someone who's had ups and downs."

I gathered my personal items from my office and threw them

in the trunk of my car. Then I paused. I didn't want to seem bitter and since the crying had stopped, I decided to go back to the showrunner's office and make a more professional exit.

Her door was open.

"Got a sec?" I asked, calmly.

"Of course," she said.

I stepped in just past the door jamb.

"I just wanted to say that I really do appreciate having the chance to work with so many talented—"

I couldn't finish the sentence because the tears started flowing again. I simply couldn't control them. This time, it struck me as funny so I said goodbye, crying and laughing simultaneously.

Unrequited Crush (2003)

I was back on the market. My agent asked me to come to the office so we could look at the shows that were hiring. As we went down a list, several times the agent noted, "They've already got two women on staff, so they won't be looking to hire another."

There was no sense that this remark dismissed my skills and reduced me to my gender. It also suggested there was a quota system that limited the number of female writers on staffs. I first encountered this casual attitude toward restricting the numbers of women in 1987 when *The Wilton North Report* was cancelled and some of the writers gathered to discuss our futures.

"Well, you're lucky," one of the writers said, jerking his head in my direction.

"Why am I lucky?" I asked.

"Because every show is looking for a woman," he said.

"*A* woman . . . and *nine* guys. How does that make me lucky?"

Thirty years later, there are still too many shows looking for "a" female writer and "a" minority writer. Some don't even do that.

24 premiered in the fall of 2001 and I watched every second of the first season. The second season was even more exciting. Creators Joel Surnow and Robert Cochran had found a new way to tell a story on TV with fresh characters like Mary Lynn Rajskub's darkly-funny Chloe.

Before the start of the third season, I had a general meeting at 20th Century FOX, which produced the show.

"We're big fans of yours," the executive said. "Are there any shows you'd like to work on?"

"Yes," I said. "*24*. It's the best show—not just on FOX but on any network."

"*24* won't hire a woman," he replied matter-of-factly. "They had one and it didn't work out. Any other shows?"

Yes, an officer of a publicly traded company said I couldn't even get an interview for a job because of my gender. And since I'm not sitting on piles of money, I obviously let the comment slide. Every year after that, I asked my agent to check with *24* to see if I could meet about working on the show. The answer every year was no.

A friend who worked on the show insisted it was for the best.

"You'd be miserable in that room," he told me. "Really, you're lucky."

Opposites Attract (2006)

On my first day as a Consulting Producer on *NCIS*, I was walking to my office when I heard a voice boom down the hall.

"Since when do we have pretty little girls working on this show?"

"What an odd thing to say," I thought, and kept walking.

The voice boomed out again. This time louder.

"Since when do we have pretty little girls working on this show."

Ohmigod, I realized. He's talking to *me*.

I turned and saw *NCIS* showrunner Don Bellisario. I waved and smiled. He smiled back.

Don is a TV legend. He created (or co-created) a long list of brograms including *Magnum P.I.*, *Airwolf*, *Quantum Leap*, *JAG*, and *NCIS*. In his seventies, Don was gruff, volatile, and had a twisted sense of humor. We hit it off during my interview and he added me to the small *NCIS* staff for the show's fourth season.

The military-based forensics show wasn't an obvious fit. The day after I turned in the first draft of my first script, Don called me into his office. He was furious. He'd only read up to page fifteen, but he had a major problem with a line I'd given to the lead character, Gibbs, played by Mark Harmon. Don shook his script at me.

"You have Gibbs say, 'I want to see the gun,'" Don shouted. "How did you get it so wrong?"

I was baffled.

"*What* did I get wrong?"

"Don't you know anything?" he bellowed. "Gibbs would never say 'I want to see the gun.' No military man would. He'd say 'weapon' not 'gun.' And you should know that!"

Don was intimidating, but for some reason, his rage struck me as comical. I opened my arms in bewilderment.

"What made you think I would?"

Whatever Don expected my reaction would be—apologies, cowering, tears—he did not expect me to throw it back at him. His anger dissipated.

"Just don't do it again," he warned.

I assured him I wouldn't. And believe me, I didn't.

Don taught me a lot. When hearing a story pitch, his first question was always, "Who do I care about in this story? And it can't be the victim!" This advice still rings in my ears whenever I brainstorm ideas for dramas.

After finishing a draft of my second *NCIS*, I asked my co-worker Shane Brennan to go over the dialogue with me. Seeking out a mentor paid off. The day after I turned in "Dead Man Walking," I got called into Don's office again. It was a relief to walk in and see he wasn't scowling.

"Good job," he said. "I love everything in the teaser, and acts one, two, and three. But I don't like act four. Give me a new one."

Again, I was confused. I had carefully plotted the story with setups that paid off in act four.

"So you want me to re-break the story?" I asked.

"No," he said, annoyed. "Don't change anything in the first three acts. Just give me a different killer."

"Okay, I can do that, Don," I said. "But all the clues are gonna point to someone else."

He dismissed me with a wave.

I had my marching orders and came up with a new ending. After the episode aired, I read the fan boards. Viewers *liked* that the ending was completely unexpected.

"I didn't see it coming," wrote one fan.

"That's because it came out of nowhere," I thought.

Don's secret formula for keeping a whodunit unpredictable was to change "who done it" at the last minute. "Dead Man Walking" taught me a lesson. As a writer, I want all the plot points to add up, but most viewers don't want to do the math. They're along for the ride and happy wherever it takes them.

On my last day at the show, Don pulled me aside in the hall.

"I want to tell you something," he said. "'Dead Man Walking' was the best episode we made this year."

I admit, I did not see that ending coming.

My One-Night Stand with a Movie Star (2009)

The *81st Annual Academy Awards Red Carpet preshow* reunited me with Gabe Doppelt, my *Vogue* editor in the late eighties. Gabe brought me on board to help write intros and questions for the hosts while she produced the fashion segments. It was a short, low-paying gig with great perks like sitting in the third row of a near-empty theater while Hugh Jackman and Beyoncé rehearsed the opening number directed by Baz Luhrmann.

On show night, I got to stand on the red carpet right where it bends to head into the Kodak Theatre. My duties were to stay close to host Robin Roberts and help her if she needed it. (She didn't.) Mostly I gawked. I watched Sean Penn (*Milk*) sneak a cigarette. I saw Meryl Streep (*Doubt*) wrestling with the train of her dress. I sighed as Brad Pitt and Angelina Jolie passed by, in love and glowing.

I had one other task that afternoon. In a production meeting, I'd thrown out an idea for how to kick off the half-hour special.

"Since there are so many stars on the red carpet, why not recruit a couple of them to be announcers?" I pitched. "The show could start with 'I'm Brad Pitt and *this* is the Oscars!'"

"That's a terrible idea," Executive Producer Robert "Morty" Morton said. "It adds a level of complication and who knows if the stars will agree to do it."

He had a point. The *Red Carpet* special is taped live and begins airing while the end of the special is still being edited in a van. I was ready to drop the idea when the show's veteran stage manager John Stewart spoke up.

"I can get them to do it," John said.

John is a renowned stage manager—the guy who stays calm in the middle of a tornado. He's also actress Kristen Stewart's father, which gave him access to the younger crowd.

"If you think they'll do it, give it a try," said Morty.

The plan got off to a great start when Taraji P. Henson, nominated for Best Supporting Actress in *The Curious Case of Benjamin Button*, agreed to play along. She looked stunning and delivered

the line with gusto: "Hi. This is Taraji P. Henson and *this* is the Oscars."

One star wasn't enough. We needed to build a package, except publicist after publicist torpedoed the idea. I started to think the Executive Producer's first reaction had been correct. Suddenly, through a swirl of tuxes, I saw John beckoning to me.

"Come. Mickey Rourke says he'll do it. He's in!"

This was a coup. Mickey Rourke was the comeback story of the year with his nomination for Best Actor (*The Wrestler*). I followed John to where Mickey stood in a small clearing, holding a mic. The cameras were rolling and John gave him a hand signal: "And action."

Mickey smiled broadly.

"I'm Mickey Rourke," he said. "And THIS is the fuckin' Oscars."

John and I exchanged a look of panic.

"Mickey, it's for TV," John said. "You can't swear."

Mickey nodded. "Oh, right, right, right. Let's go again."

John gave him a hand signal. "And action."

"I'm Mickey Rourke and THIS is the Oscars . . . *motherfuckers!*"

Laughing, Mickey handed the mic back to John and walked off. He'd been messing with us. I ran to the editing van and asked if they could trim off the word "motherfuckers." An editor tried but the cut was too abrupt and there was no time to massage the frames. I headed back to the Red Carpet, feeling disheartened that my idea had flopped.

Amazingly, as promised, John Stewart came through.

The 2009 Oscar Red Carpet preshow opened with one of Hollywood's most glamorous couples welcoming the audience with an enthusiastic "This is the Oscars!" It wasn't Brad and Angelina, but Vanessa Hudgens and Zac Efron looked adorable. Taraji P. Henson followed and sold the bit.

Later that night, Mickey lost the Best Actor award to Sean Penn. Sorry about that . . . *motherfucker.*

Finding Mr. Right (2009)

With my forty-ninth birthday approaching, I started to think "Old TV writers never die: they just FADE OUT." I started to think I might never staff again. Once my agent called to say there was a high-level opening on a kids' sitcom. The money was low, but the creators were eager to have a female writer on staff.

"Do you think they'd let me direct?" I said.

"You can ask," said my agent.

The creators and I grabbed lunch. They were smart and nice and I left thinking they'd be fun to work with. They seemed to want to work with me, too, but an offer never materialized. Instead, they hired a male with less experience. Years later, I reached out to one and, out of curiosity, asked why they'd passed.

"I loved your writing and you were an absolute delight," he wrote back. "But my partner was put off that you wanted to direct." At the end of his note, he added: "P.S. When I say he was 'put off' I meant he thought that your request to direct meant your heart wasn't really in writing for a kids' show."

Do men get hired based on their hearts or their abilities?

I didn't realize it at the time but female executives kept me afloat during my forties. Nina Tassler and Susanne Daniels continued to hire me when so many men were "put off." Chris Sanagustin, my favorite *Sabrina* executive, also came through. She reached out to me in 2009.

"Hey, Nell. There's a show I think you'd be good for," she said on the phone. "You probably won't want to work on it, but I thought I'd ask."

Was she kidding? I was *desperate* to work on any show. I tried to keep it cool.

"What show?"

"*Warehouse 13*. Have you seen it?"

"Nope."

"Well, you know at the end of *Raiders* when they put the Ark of the Covenant into a government warehouse? This is a show about the agents who work in that warehouse and collect powerful artifacts."

That sounded *fantastic*.

Chris arranged for me to meet with showrunner Jack Kenny. He was hilarious and full of great ideas. Everything fell into place the way it does when you find the right partner. The show combined all the genres I loved—mystery, science fiction, and character comedy. I made a two-year deal to become one of *Warehouse 13*'s Co-Executive Producers.

Warehouse 13 was the Syfy channel's highest-rated show. No one would confuse its viewership with *NCIS*, but I didn't care. I was thrilled to be working with smart funny people on a clever show with decent hours.

And just when I made peace with settling down and drifting into obscurity, I decided to step into the spotlight. *(Musical sting.)*

Stage Four

WHO IS NELL SCOVELL?

CHAPTER 15

"Fame Whore"

Staffer? I didn't even know her!

—the obvious joke

ON OCTOBER 2, 2009, DAVID LETTERMAN SAT AT HIS desk and informed his TV audience that he'd been the victim of a blackmail attempt. The crowd thought it was a joke and laughed. Dave continued, dead serious. He explained that "a guy" had threatened to expose him for doing "terrible, terrible things" and also "some creepy stuff."

"And the creepy stuff," Dave elaborated, "was that I have had sex with women who work for me on this show. My response to that is yes, I have."

The audience applauded wildly.

No one who worked on the show was surprised by this news, although we were shocked that Dave publicly admitted what we'd been whispering about for decades.

The details of the blackmail attempt trickled out. A package containing a letter and a synopsis of a screenplay had been left in Dave's limo by news producer Robert "Joe" Halderman. The two men were connected through Halderman's live-in girlfriend Stephanie Birkitt who worked as Dave's assistant. Actually, Dave had about five assistants and each had a function. One made his meals. One operated his charity. One answered the phone. Stephanie, a law school graduate, ran miscellaneous errands and shopped for Dave's entertainment, selecting books and films that she thought he might enjoy. Stephanie also kept a journal that revealed part of the entertainment she provided to Dave involved them getting naked. Halderman found his girlfriend's journal and threatened to write a screenplay that exposed the illicit relationship unless Dave paid him two million dollars.

Now this plan had a couple of problems. First, unless Halderman surrounded Dave with X-Men, he probably couldn't get that screenplay read. Second, Dave had access to a brilliant crisis management and legal team. Under the auspices of the Manhattan District Attorney's office, Dave's lawyer met with Halderman and handed him a phony check. When Halderman deposited the money, he was arrested and later pled guilty to attempted grand larceny in the second degree. Halderman received a six-month jail sentence.

Dave's openness about the plot earned him lots of sympathy and it should have. Blackmail *is* such an ugly word and Halderman committed a criminal act. At the same time, Dave pretty much got a pass for his own underlying misconduct. No one seemed to think that the "terrible things" he'd done were terrible at all. On *The View*, fellow TV host Barbara Walters staunchly defended Dave's decision to have sex with staffers.

"He's a very attractive man," Walters said on October 5, 2009. "Where do you meet people? In the workplace."

Cohost Joy Behar took a tougher stance, arguing that Dave's behavior might have created an uncomfortable workplace, especially "if you're one of the girls who works there and you're just doing your job and suddenly this other chick is getting the airtime and the AFTRA checks . . ." (Starting in 1996, Birkitt appeared on the show over 250 times. Around then, union (AF-TRA) minimum for an appearance on *Late Show* was about $700.)

Walters brushed off Joy's point. "Well, maybe you're annoyed today, but that's not necessarily sexual harassment. It isn't sexual harassment," she repeated for good measure.

"That's not necessarily true," countered Joy. "I think the definition also includes creating an atmosphere that's uncomfortable."

Joy was right. You don't have to be touched or propositioned to be a victim of sexual harassment. Sensing a teachable moment, the National Organization of Women (NOW) put out a statement: "As the boss, [Letterman] is responsible for setting the tone for his entire workplace—and he did that with sex. In any work environment, this places all employees—including employees who happen to be women—in an awkward, confusing and demoralizing situation."

I stared at the sentence. An "awkward, confusing and demoralizing situation" perfectly summed up my stint at *Late Night*. When I'd quit nineteen years earlier, I couldn't pinpoint what bothered me so much about the place. Now I realized my discomfort had a name: "Sexual Favoritism."

Sexual favoritism acknowledges that when employees *get* special favors by *giving* special favors, it affects more than just those involved. At work, most of us want to be judged by our professional performance, so when colleagues receive power and perks for satisfying their managers in ways that are not part of the job description, it's an affront. Women can end up feeling demeaned and both men and women can experience a "hostile work environment."

Awkward, Confusing, or Demoralizing?

Can You Match the Situation with the Employee Reaction?

    A. Awkward

    B. Confusing

    C. Demoralizing

1. While playing first base at a company softball game, Dave leans over to a young, male Production Assistant (PA) as a buxom batter steps to the plate.

    "I hope she gets a hit," Dave says. "I like to watch her run."

    The list of Worldwide Pants Inc.'s "Prohibited Conduct of a Sexual Nature" includes: "Making unwelcome comments about the appearance or anatomy of another." Now, Dave didn't make the comment to the woman directly and he's from a generation that thinks nothing of a little "locker room talk." The PA tenses but isn't about to call out his boss for being inappropriate. Instead, the PA forces a laugh.

2. A woman is being considered for a job on the writing staff when one of Dave's assistants—and rumored bed buddies—blocks the hire. Why would she deny another woman an opportunity? Did she feel threatened? And why is an executive assistant determining who sits in the writers' room?

3. Dave takes a shine to a PA fresh out of college. He passes her funny little notes at meetings and asks her opinion on important show matters. She's barely twenty-two and she's already making production decisions.

    One night, her phone rings at home. It's her boss.

    "I'm in a hotel room, all alone, eating French fries," Dave says.

He might just be making conversation . . . or he might be fishing to see if she offers to join him. She changes the subject. The next day, she encounters a chilly reception at work. The funny little notes from the boss stop and she's no longer asked to offer her opinion.

"Did I do something wrong?" she wonders.

Solution: All of them are all three.

The same week that the Letterman blackmail scandal broke, Nancy Franklin published an article about *The Jay Leno Show* in *The New Yorker*. Near the end, Nancy noted, "Leno has no women writers on his show. Neither does David Letterman, and neither does Conan O'Brien. Come *on*."

I stared at that sentence, too. Nancy's observation shocked me more than Dave's confession. Zero female writers? I went to IMDb and looked up the last female writer at *Late Show*. Meredith Scardino had left in 2005. For four years, they'd had an all-male staff. When it came to gender diversity, *Late Show* literally couldn't do worse. Even tokenism was dead. And then came insult to injury.

Rob Burnett, one of *Late Show*'s many Executive Producers and the head of Dave's production company Worldwide Pants, Inc., decided to push back against the criticism from NOW. He issued his own statement, which included this claim:

As an employee of David Letterman's since 1985, I have personally found the work environment on his shows to be fair, professional and entirely merit-based at all times.

My soul did a spit take.

Professional? Dave had just admitted on air that he was sexually involved with staffers. Plus, I'd heard rumors that other high-level male producers enjoyed their own "intern sleepover parties." Still, what chafed the most was Burnett calling the work environment "fair" and "entirely merit-based." "Fair" implied women had the same opportunities as men and "entirely merit-based" meant in the past four years, not a single female writer who had applied to the show was funnier than the least-funny male on staff. I personally knew one hilarious female writer who had submitted to the show with recommendations from two hugely respected comedy performers who had worked with her. She never even got a response on her submission.

By 2009, we'd elected an African American to occupy the Oval Office, but not one person of color had ever broken into the *Letterman* writers' room. If the show was "entirely merit-based" then Burnett's statement implied that since 1985, not a single African American, Asian, East Asian, or Hispanic writer—male or female—merited a spot on that staff. As Nancy Franklin would say, *"Come on."*

A switch inside me flipped that day. Someone needed to call out this ludicrous statement and stand up for funny women and minorities. And I knew the perfect writer to do it: a serious white male journalist named Nick Kristof.

Nick and I were college classmates and I'd recently heard him give a book talk in LA about *Half the Sky,* which he cowrote with Sheryl WuDunn. Nick had a huge platform at the *New York Times* and I trusted him completely. I emailed him and he called me back from an airport. I pitched him the story. He listened, then paused.

"Okay, my first question is this," he said. "Why aren't you writing the article, Nell?"

"Because you write about women and people will listen to you," I said.

What I didn't say was, "Because I'm scared to death." I knew speaking up would bring me both attention and criticism. It felt safer to hide behind Nick.

He wouldn't let me. "It's your story," Nick said. "There's no one who will tell it better."

I didn't want to. I even emailed a friend who worked on the show to say that I wasn't going to write anything. It was like announcing to my family that I was no longer going to eat refined sugar.

That night, I couldn't put the thought out of my head. When I exited the show, I had kept my mouth shut because I was young and professionally vulnerable. Now I was in a different place. Dave's admission had triggered a full-blown existential crisis. In the four stages joke, the final "Who is Nell Scovell?" is asked by studio executives who no longer recognize the name. Now I turned the question on myself: Who was I? What did I stand for?

It's hard to describe but I felt a compulsion to speak out. I considered the downsides. Dave was a towering figure in television and I might never work for CBS—or any network—again. It helped that I'd just signed a two-year contract at *Warehouse 13*, which gave me a little job security. I was reminded of a great line attributed to TV writer Tom Palmer: "I don't have 'fuck you' money, but I do have 'I don't like your tone of voice' money."

My note to my friend on the show turned out to be as effective as my declarations not to eat refined sugar. The next morning, I grabbed a glazed chocolate donut and started crunching data. The numbers would prove that the gender disparity in 2009 was not a fluke but a pattern. In twenty-seven years, *Late Night/ Late Show* had hired only seven female writers compared to over one hundred male writers. And the men stayed longer. There were individual white male writers who had worked on the show for a decade longer than all the women's tenures combined. I later learned that female standups were also under-represented on the show. From 2005–2010, *The Late Show* booked approximately ninety-six standup performances; women only appeared five times.

Sexual favoritism is an important subject, but my article pivoted to the lack of diversity in the writers' room. Our country boasted three female Supreme Court Justices while Letterman, Leno, and Conan couldn't find a single woman good enough for their staffs? Burnett and other male head writers have suggested that women and people of color just don't apply for these jobs. That's victim-blaming. The real problem was the hiring process often relied on current (white male) writers recommending their funny (white male) friends to be future (white male) writers. And I knew from personal experience that when women did apply, they were often ignored.

Nine months before the blackmail scandal broke, I heard *Late Night* was looking for monologue writers who could work remotely. Recalling Dave's words that I was "always welcome back," I submitted four pages of jokes. The submission got sucked into a black hole. Soon after, I sold a pilot to ABC and got busy with that. Still, the show's silence suggested that they were happier complaining about the lack of female applicants than actually responding to them.

I finished a draft of my article and ran it by many wise and funny friends, including Susanne Daniels, Amy Hohn, J.J. Jamieson, Kurt Andersen, Anne Kreamer, and Tim Carvell. They all offered helpful advice and encouragement. Finally, I sought approval from one more person.

The previous summer, our eleven-year-old son had gone to a one-week camp at a local school. After the first day, Dexter came back raving about a funny camper named Jake. I pressed him to get Jake's last name so we could make a playdate. Dexter came back two days later.

"Jake's last name is Brooks and his dad's a director," he said. "Alfred Brooks."

"Wait—do you mean *Albert* Brooks?"

"Yeah, that's it."

Oh, we made a playdate. By that October, I felt comfortable enough to share the draft with Albert and his wildly talented writer/artist wife Kimberly. I told them that I was still on the fence about speaking out publicly.

"Oh, you have to publish this," Kimberly said after she read the piece.

Albert looked more pensive.

"No one can argue with what you've written," he said deliberately. "It's been my experience that a fairer sampling of humanity will always produce better comedy."

I felt chills. "Albert, that's *perfect*. Can I use that line?"

"Sure."

Albert understood that shows should hire female writers not just because it's the right or fair thing to do, but because *it would make these shows funnier*. And he practiced what he preached. Albert wrote *Defending Your Life* by himself, but other times, he teamed up with Monica Johnson. Together, they cowrote *Modern Romance* and *Lost in America*. Both these films have female characters who are flawed and funny. Julie Hagerty gambling away the nest egg is something Monica might have done herself.

To be clear, I don't believe only women can write women and only men can write men. The craft for any writer is getting inside a character's head and understanding their fears, their joys, and their motivations. Emotions are universal but experiences are not. At *Warehouse 13*, I wrote an episode where Myka, the female lead, becomes magically pregnant. I included a beat in the outline about Myka's sense of smell becoming acute. On the notes call, an executive questioned the detail.

"I don't get the smelling," he said. "Is that like a thing?"

"Yes," I said. Then it struck me that of the seven people on the call, I was the only one who'd ever been pregnant.

Different backgrounds generate different experiences. A room that shuts out half the population as well as people of color and the LGBTQ community will have less material to work with.

I added Albert's line and after a final pass from my invaluable editor Mike Hogan, the piece was scheduled to post. I contacted my soon-to-be boss Jack Kenny and my agent Jill Gillette to let them know that "Letterman and Me" would go live the next day. Jack and Jill were both supportive, which helped tremendously.

The next morning, I opened my laptop. My inbox was flooded. I closed my laptop. I made breakfast for the kids and walked them to school. As soon as I returned home, the phone rang.

"Hi. Is this Nell? I'm a producer at *The Today Show*. We read your article and want you to come on the show tomorrow."

"Um," I said, unprepared for the call.

"We'll fly you to New York and you'd appear in studio with Matt Lauer himself."

TV morning news loves a sex scandal and even though my article didn't offer any juicy details, it would serve to keep the story alive.

"I need to think about that," I said.

My next call was to check in with Mike Hogan at *Vanity Fair*. There were other offers to appear on news and talks shows and we discussed how it could be good to get more exposure. Still, I worried about losing control of the narrative. Mike said I should do what made me comfortable. I called the *Today* producer back.

"I'm sorry," I said. "I'm gonna pass."

I opened my laptop and saw that my article had been picked up by several websites. All my friends had warned me not to read the comments. I ignored them. Some commenters dismissed me as a "fame whore" and "not funny." (Ah, the classics.) Someone else linked to an article by Rachel Sklar with the promising headline: "Nell Scovell Is My New Hero."

"Is Scovell as funny as any guy? Presumably, given her record," Rachel wrote. "So this isn't some screed borne of years of pent-up frustration—it's measured and thoughtful and matter-of-factly assesses the situation."

Rachel Sklar was *my* new hero. Men were angry but women got it. Mostly. An east coast friend emailed that they had just discussed me on *The View,* and Barbara Walters had accused me of setting women back by quitting. That stung. My phone rang.

"Nell? Hi. This is Matt Lauer. My producer tells me that you don't want to come on the show and I was hoping to change your mind."

Matt was smooth and charming. He walked me through why I should accept his offer to tell my side of the story.

"The problem," I explained, "is that people want to hear about interns in the bedroom and I want to talk about gender in the writers' room."

"We can talk about anything you want," Matt said.

"So, you're okay if I don't discuss Dave sleeping with interns?"

"Hey, I couldn't be held to that high a standard," Matt said with a chuckle.

Matt's "joke" made me queasy. With apologies, I passed a second time.

The only show I agreed to appear on was *The Joy Behar Show* since Joy had stuck up for me on *The View*. Before heading to the

LA studio, I called Lawrence O'Donnell, who I knew through Penn Jillette, and asked for some TV interview tips.

"Figure out the three points you want to make," Lawrence said. "And if you're lucky, you'll get to make one of them."

Joy was smart and sympathetic. Before the cameras rolled, she mentioned that she'd been trying to get booked to do standup on *Late Show* for years without success. The segment sped by so quickly that I can't remember if I made my one point or not.

Nell,

Thank You So Much For A Great Interview.

The Sisterhood Must Stick Together!

Love,
Joy

Note sent to me with flowers from Joy Behar.

The afternoon that my article came out, the *Vanity Fair* PR department received an email from legendary *New York Daily News* gossip columnist George Rush. He was publishing an exclusive item the next day and looking for a comment. Rush's scoop quoted an anonymous "longtime male *Late Show* staffer" who said my article had been "greeted with grumbling." Then the brave anonymous staffer slimed me, claiming that during my tenure, I didn't get any jokes on the air and that I quit because I was going to be fired.

I forwarded the quote to Steve O'Donnell, the head writer from my era, and asked if he remembered it that way. He emailed me back, "I know that you got picked up at the end of that first stretch, so you obviously were satisfactory, and as I recall you had only just started that second stretch when you gave notice."

It struck me as ironic that after describing how I felt demeaned by the show in 1990, the show's kneejerk response was to demean me again. In a way, their lies proved my point better than I could. I kept my response to George Rush short: "The *Late Show* can say anything they want about me; just hire more women."

When the *Daily News* item ran the next day, the *Vanity Fair* lawyer sent a letter, pointing out the claim that I'd left before I got fired was false and slanderous. That sentence was removed from the online version.

Late Show female staffers still working in the Ed Sullivan Theater wrote me on the sly to say they hoped the piece would trigger a confidential, external investigation. It didn't. Worldwide Pants conducted their own internal review and—surprise!— found no wrongdoing. Other employees, former and current, sent me nightmare stories of hostile treatment and I encouraged them to speak out. None felt secure enough to do so.

"What makes me sad is that so many women in Hollywood don't want to talk about these issues because they're afraid of seeming like pains in the ass," a funny female friend emailed me. "I went to a recent panel discussion for women TV writers, and someone asked the question about whether it was harder to be a woman in this business—and one of the four panelists actually said she thought it was easier. The rest soft-pedaled about whether it made a difference. It felt like Stockholm syndrome to me—an ingrained eagerness to appease/appeal to the system that keeps us down. I know that we don't want to feel like victims, and it's important not to dwell on the negative. And perhaps these women's experiences have been different. But . . . really?"

I know that instinct to gloss over the bad. A week after the article posted, I ran into a woman at a party who'd worked on the production side in the early days of *Jimmy Kimmel Live!*. She described at length how she dreaded going into the office.

"No matter how I dressed, my coworkers commented on my body," she said. "I felt sexually harassed *every single day.*"

The environment stressed her out tremendously and she told me that the second she got another job offer, she took it. Suddenly, she caught herself sounding negative and pivoted hard.

"But I'm really grateful for the opportunity they gave me," she added quickly.

Because women are so often excluded from these boys'
clubs, it's still perceived as a favor when one is allowed in. And
no matter how dreadful the conditions are, women are expected
to be grateful. I think this explains why several *Late Show* writers reacted with so much anger toward me. Not a single male
writer has disputed the validity of my criticisms. They simply
believe that by pointing out the show's flaws, I didn't demon-
strate the proper gratitude for the exceptional opportunity be-
stowed on me.

The buzz over the article died down quickly. I even attended
a meeting where an executive brought it up and didn't know that
I'd written it: "Who is Nell Scovell?" in action.

The *Warehouse 13* writers' room started up in early November and that was a welcome diversion. I was happy—and grateful—to go to work each day. I was the sole woman on the writing
staff that season, but what else was new?

Most of my coworkers had read the article. Some thought
it was cool, especially story editor Ian Stokes who told me he'd
heard them discussing me on *The Howard Stern Show*.

"Artie Lange said he'd 'do' you," Ian told me, excitedly.

As a longtime Stern listener, I felt honored.

Other coworkers seemed a bit wary. Once, someone made a
sexist comment in the room and another writer cautioned him,
"Be careful or Nell will write an exposé about you."

"Oh, yeah," I said. "Nineteen years from now, you are gonna
be *so* sorry you said that."

There did seem to be a hint of feminism in the air that season. While trying to figure out who the big bad villain might be,
David Simkins suggested a time-traveling H. G. Wells. We all
oohed at his idea. Then Jack Kenny looked at me with a sparkle
in his eye.

"And what if H. G. Wells was a woman?" Jack said.

"Yes!" I replied.

Jack's idea was inspired and Helena G. Wells anchored the second season.

Warehouse 13 set with Joanne Kelly (Myka) and Jaime Murray (H. G. Wells) on the left, and with CCH Pounder (Warehouse boss Mrs. Frederic) on the right.

Criticizing late-night TV blew up some old friendships and sparked some new ones. For me, there remained a lingering question: Had Dave read the article? I doubted it since he was busy with a court case, mending his marriage, and still appearing nightly on TV. Still, if he had read the piece, what was his reaction? Was he furious? My job at *Late Night* had been to make Dave happy, so making him unhappy still felt wrong.

I had a fantasy. One day, my phone rings. I answer it.

"Hold for Dave," says one of Dave's eighty-three assistants.

I brace myself for Dave to start yelling (because even in my own fantasy, people are mad at me) but instead, he thanks me. We have a long overdue conversation about including women and people of color in the writers' room. Dave agrees with everything I say and we're joking and having a great time until I have to run because my dead mother is calling on the other line.

Both those phone calls had the same odds of happening.

I resigned myself to never having a clue about Dave's reaction. At this point, he was so isolated from the staff that a producer told me, "We only knew Dave was in the office when we saw him on the show."

The *Daily News* item had included a quote from the anonymous male staffer stating, "Right now, there's almost an affirmative action policy [at the *Late Show*]. Most likely, the next job will go to a woman." The key word in that male staffer's sentence turned out to be "almost." The next hire was another white male. When I heard the news, I slumped. My speaking up had no impact. It reminded me of this old Jewish joke:

> Life in the shtetl is good until one day, there's a pogrom, and every man is lined up against a wall for the firing squad. The Cossacks aim their rifles and the head Cossack says, "Before we open fire, does anyone have any last requests?" Schlomo raises his hand timidly and says, "As a matter of fact, I have a request." Then Hymie leans over and whispers, "Shh! Don't make trouble!"

Maybe I should have listened to Hymie and kept my mouth shut. I didn't want to make trouble; I just wanted to make progress.

CHAPTER 16

The One I'd Been Waiting For

MAN AT *LEAN IN* BOOK PARTY: So you're the woman behind
Sheryl Sandberg.

ME: Yes, I'm behind Sheryl Sandberg and running as fast
as I can to keep up.

I FIRST LAID EYES ON SHERYL SANDBERG WHEN FRIENDS
started emailing me the link to her 2010 TED Talk with
subject lines like, *"You have to watch this!!!"* Or *"Have you
seen???"*

I assumed her talk advised women to use multiple punctuation marks.

The talk, "Why We Have Too Few Women Leaders," opened
with Sheryl telling a story about attending a boardroom meeting
where several women took seats on the side of the room until she
waved them over to join her at the table. I flashed back to my first
Newhart table read and how I, too, chose a chair on the periphery.

I had believed this instinct stemmed from my natural timidity, but Sheryl made me realize that choice was instilled by our culture. Then she explained why it mattered.

"Boy, it matters a lot," Sheryl said. "Because no one gets to the corner office by sitting on the side, not at the table, and no one gets the promotion if they don't think they deserve their success, or they don't even understand their own success."

I was captivated. As the head of Online Sales & Operations at Google and then Chief Operating Officer at Facebook, Sheryl had hired over ten thousand employees, which gave her a broad perspective. Her talk zoomed from the big picture to minute details, offering hard data and studies to support Sheryl's own conclusions. Sheryl connected the historical sweep of gender bias with individual decisions and then offered a way forward. Everything she said rang true.

Over time, I had learned to sit at the table, literally and figuratively, but getting the corner office had brought a new set of obstacles. Sheryl unpacked the unsettling feelings I'd encountered when trying to lead:

> *What the data shows, above all else, is that success and likeability are positively correlated for men and negatively correlated for women. And everyone's nodding, because we all know this to be true.*

How did she know I was nodding? This stranger was in my head.

When I finished listening to Sheryl's video, I felt odd. Normally a discussion about women in the workplace leaves me feeling agitated. Every few years, I used to get together for brunch with a group of upper-level female TV writer/producers and we'd unload stories about the unfairness we'd encountered. I'd tell my story about the time I was renegotiating to stay on a show and the Executive Producer stopped by my office to check on the deal.

"Did your agents call business affairs?" he asked.

"Yep, they're on it."

"And you don't care about money, right?"

I looked at my boss, incredulous.

"Yeah, I'm just here for the salty snacks," I said.

My favorite stories are ones where the sexism is blatant. As Co-EP on a show, I was asked to rewrite the script of a low-level writer. I did a big pass over the weekend and then sent the new draft to the EP on Sunday night for a polish. The next morning, the EP pulled me aside.

"Great job, Nell," he said. "But if you don't mind, I think it's better if I tell Mike that I did the rewrite. I don't want him to feel emasculated."

The women at the brunch would gasp at these stories before telling their own gasp-inducing tales. And the stories would keep coming. And coming. By the time the frittata was served, the relief of realizing the bias wasn't personal was replaced by the horror of knowing it was *so* pervasive. I'd always leave the brunch feeling worse than when I arrived. But Sheryl's talk made me feel calmer. In fourteen minutes, she had given me deep insight into my twenty-five-year career without a single carb. I forwarded the video to other friends with my own multiple punctuation marks. I also sent Sheryl a friend request on Facebook.

Around the time that I discovered Sheryl's talk, I started hearing some positive news about late night staffing. Leno added a female writer to *The Tonight Show* staff and *Late Show with David Letterman* added one, too. And while there'd been hundreds of dads writing comedy for late night, I believe Laurie Kilmartin holds the distinction of being the first mom when she joined *Conan*'s staff in 2010.

Work on *Warehouse 13* continued. We had a strong season and finished as Syfy's most-watched series. Over hiatus, I teamed up with Tim Carvell (now head writer/Executive Producer of *Last Week Tonight*) to write *Backstabber*, an update of *All About Eve*, set in the fashion industry with a gay male assistant taking over the Eve Harrington role. (The spec script is still available as it appears we misjudged the market for a screenplay starring a woman in her forties and a young gay man.)

Like many Americans in 2010, I started spending lots of time on Facebook. I'd been an early adopter, joining when you still needed a dot edu address. Through the site, I reconnected with Elliot Schrage, a friend from college who was now running Facebook's media and communications. Elliot knew I worked in TV and reached out with some comedy-related questions.

"Should Mark Zuckerberg do a voice on *The Simpsons*?"

Yes!

"What if he doesn't love the pages they sent?"

Ask for new jokes.

"*SNL* wants Mark to do a cameo when Jesse Eisenberg is hosting. Do you have any ideas?"

Yes!

The setup was Mark would stand with Lorne Michaels at the monitors and watch Jesse Eisenberg chat with cast member Andy Samberg. Both had impersonated Mark onscreen. The money shot was all three "Marks" together, so it seemed obvious that the real Mark should want to join the two fakes. The conflict would be that Michaels doesn't think it's a good idea. I pitched this exchange:

> MARK: You leave me no choice.
> *Mark pokes Lorne with a finger.*
> LORNE: What are you doing?
> MARK: Poking you.

LORNE: That's SO annoying.

MARK: I know. I invented it.

Mark shortened the pitch to a much-snappier "I invented poking" and it got a big laugh.

Writing occasional jokes for Mark Zuckerberg was a fun side project. Then in March 2011, Elliot sent an email asking if I'd seen Sheryl Sandberg's TED Talk.

"Seen it?" I wrote back. "I memorized it."

I wrote him that Sheryl had shifted my perspective in a positive way and my P.S. mentioned that I'd sent her a friend request but hadn't heard back. Five minutes later, I smiled as a message flashed on my screen: "Sheryl Sandberg has accepted your friend request."

It was the beginning of a beautiful friendship.

Sheryl was set to deliver the Forrestal lecture at the U.S. Naval Academy in April. She had a partial draft written in bullet points, but as a full-time COO and mother of two small children, she was looking for someone to pull the speech together and make it flow. Although I'd never written a serious speech before, I was eager to do anything to support her. She sent me her draft, which contained this bullet point:

- Get women to lean in—especially during the childbearing years—find a way to get them to get them to lean in to their careerts and give them the flexibility they need to stay in the workforce.
  - Admiral Mullen spoke about the importance of this for the Navy at the While house earlier this year

This was Sheryl's first public mention of the phrase "lean in." Today, the term is so widely used that a friend recently asked me, "What did we say before 'lean in'?"

Speechwriting came easily since it combines two skills I'd already developed. Like a magazine article, a speech needs to present an argument with a strong opening, a logical flow of ideas, and a thoughtful or uplifting conclusion. Like TV dialogue, the speaker needs to sound natural and have a consistent voice. Sheryl has off-the-charts charm and her natural character combines three of my childhood heroes: she has the logic of Mr. Spock, the empathy of Dr. McCoy, and the leadership abilities of Capt. James T. Kirk of the Starship Enterprise.

The Forrestal lecture was followed by the 2011 Barnard Commencement Address. Again, Sheryl asked me to collaborate and we considered what we would have wanted someone to tell us when we graduated from college. Sheryl said she wanted to give young women permission to be ambitious. Too often, our culture discourages that. She also wanted to discuss how women unconsciously hold themselves back out of fear.

I flashed back to my teen years, when I'd listen to Barbra Streisand sing "I'm the Greatest Star" from *Funny Girl* over and over. I also idolized Bette Midler, who radiated confidence. She even dubbed herself "The Divine Miss M." I didn't realize it at the time, but Bette and Barbra were modelling fearlessness and self-esteem. They were teaching me how to "lean in."

The day of the address, Sheryl was battling a cold and her voice was hoarse, but the force of her conviction never wavered. She encouraged the all-female graduating class to aim high and believe in themselves. "Never let your fear overwhelm your desire," she urged at the end. "So please ask yourself: *What would I do if I weren't afraid?* And then go do it."

Watching a livestream of the speech in Santa Monica, I cheered along with the hundreds of new Barnard graduates.

After Barnard, there was buzz about trying to reach a broader audience with a book. At a conference, WME (William Morris Endeavor) book agent extraordinaire Jennifer Rudolph Walsh followed Sheryl into the Women's Room to pitch the project. "Books start conversations," Jennifer insisted.

Sheryl had a packed schedule and couldn't see a way to fit in an additional major project. Then one day, she called, excited.

"Jennifer just called me. She got an offer to write a book and I think I want to do it."

"That's great!"

"I told them I wouldn't do it without you. Are you in?"

A wave of fear hit me.

"You know, Sheryl," I stammered. "I've never written a book."

"Neither have I!" she replied.

Dave Goldberg, Sheryl's brilliant and supportive late husband, saw the importance of the message and together the couple carved out a way forward: Sheryl would write at night after the kids went to bed, pull back on social dinners, and devote vacation and weekend time to the book. I would also work nights and weekends, but my kids were older so it was less of a strain. Researcher Marianne Cooper was recruited from the Clayman Institute for Gender Research to find and vet studies. The three of us all had day jobs and families, but we learned that while work expands to fill the time, time expands to fill a mission.

In December, Knopf editor Jordan Pavlin, Jennifer, Sheryl and I all met in New York. It was supposed to be a let's-get-the-ball-rolling meeting, but Sheryl arrived with a full outline and completed introduction. She'd been writing this book in her head for twenty years.

It was an odd period of my life. As Co-Executive Producer of *Warehouse 13*, I'd spend the day thinking up science fiction scenarios. Then at night, Sheryl would send me chapter drafts and we would iterate through another twenty—or forty—drafts on the barriers that women face. These two worlds collided just once when I was fleshing out a *Lean In* section on "Queen Bees"—a term for women who attain status in a male-dominated industry and keep other women out. I wrote: "Unfortunately, this 'there can be only one' attitude still lingers today."

Sci-fi nerds will recognize this reference to *Highlander*, a 1986 action/fantasy movie starring Christopher Lambert and Sean Connery that I've watched an embarrassing number of times. I figured the line would be edited out of the book, but it managed to survive (much like the Highlander himself). When reading the book in galleys, I realized Sheryl might not know the source of the quote so I sent her an email and included the film clip. She wrote back that she had not gotten the reference, but it was fine to leave in.

Lean In is the book that I wished I'd read at twenty-five, not helped write at fifty-two. It acknowledges that we need better institutional and governmental policies to support and protect all women, especially single moms. We need equal pay, more affordable childcare, better parental-leave policies, more sponsorship, and greater awareness of implicit bias. The book also looked at the internal barriers that can hold women back and urged women to sit at the table, raise their hands, take risks, and seek leadership positions. The hope is that once more women become leaders, they will be in the position to spur faster change for all.

For women to *lean in* at the workplace, men need to *lean in* to their families. Even with parents who both have full-time jobs, moms do about 40 percent more childcare and almost 30 percent more housework than dads. This prompted Sheryl to advise women that "the most important career decision you will ever make is choosing who your partner is."

I nailed that one. Still, it hurt my stomach to work on a section about negotiation. I got it so wrong. My instinct had been to prove my value by listing my personal contributions to a project. That strategy works fine for men who can self-promote with impunity, but women are expected to be nice and communal.

In October 2012, Sheryl hit Send on a final draft to the editor. It had been an intense nine months and we both had our first weekend off in a long time. My plans included seeing a movie with my family and yoga. I didn't expect to hear from Sheryl so I was surprised when my phone rang that Sunday morning.

"I couldn't sleep last night," Sheryl said, sounding more excited than tired. "I want to start a nonprofit to go with the book that would help support women. I've already written the mission statement. Can I send it to you?"

Her mission statement turned into LeanIn.org, which now hosts a community of over 1.5 million and provides materials for creating small support groups called Circles. These Circles truly help members ask for promotions, dump unsupportive partners, and be more ambitious.

Sheryl Sandberg, Marianne Cooper, and me on *Lean In*'s launch day, March 11, 2013

We hoped the launch of the book would change lives. On a personal level, it already had. I'd always been a feminist but relied on my actions to speak louder than my words. Now I was broadcasting my beliefs and it was *awesome*. After a life spent trying to break into boys' clubs where I endlessly had to justify my worth, I was welcomed with open arms into a new club.

Sheryl introduced me to her League of Extraordinary Women. I met Mellody Hobson, the President of Ariel Investments, who inspired us both with her declaration that she wanted to be "unapologetically a woman and unapologetically black." I met Joanna Coles, the funny and formidable editor of *Cosmopolitan*, who is the "universal big sister." And thanks to Sheryl, I met Gloria Steinem. *The* Gloria Steinem.

I'd grown up fascinated by the founder of *Ms.* magazine so it felt surreal to sit in a small room with her and Sheryl as they discussed global issues. Gloria had just returned from India and had horrifying stories to relay.

"There are eight million missing girls in India," she said. "Gone."

Sheryl, who has spent time in India, nodded knowingly.

"What do you mean?" I asked.

"From the age of one to five, girls are almost twice as likely to die as Indian boys," Gloria replied. "Why do you think that is?"

I didn't know. I shook my head.

"When girls get sick, their families don't value them enough to seek medical attention or pay for treatment."

My heart sank. Gloria and Sheryl continued to talk about enslaved women until Sheryl got called away. Alone with Gloria, I felt queasy. Suddenly, I blurted out my existential angst.

"I can't believe I care about getting women hired on late night TV when that's going on in India."

Gloria leaned forward and placed a hand on my arm.

"Oh no. You worry about late night TV. I'll worry about India," she said.

She delivered this advice with a little smile. She knew it sounded flip, but her point was profound. Gender bias is everywhere and we need man-to-man—pardon the expression—defense on each front. We all need to speak up as much as we can with the specific influence we have.

I've seen how women advocating for other women in late night can make a difference. When *Jimmy Kimmel Live!* moved from 12:30 a.m. to 11:30 p.m., ABC Entertainment President Anne Sweeney took an interest in adding more women to the staff. Head writer Molly McNearney, the only female writer on *Kimmel* at the time, reached out to me to get names of women who might want to submit packets. I compiled a list and encouraged Bess Kalb, a sly and hilarious writer at *Wired* magazine, to give it a shot. Dozens of other funny women applied. Standup Nikki Glaser was on my list but passed to focus on her performance career. The night before submissions were due, Nikki emailed me.

☆ Nikki Glaser 🖉   📧 Late Night Submissions   June 1, 2012 at 7:23 AM   NG
A friend's packet...
To: Nell Scovell

🗑 ↩ ↩↩ ↪ 📎1 ⌄

Nell,

I mentioned to a writer friend of mine last week that I was considering getting a packet together for you guy. She said that she was going to try to put something together as well have some manager who is hip-pocketing her submit her. Now that guy is playing dumb and saying he can't get it to the right people.

I know it wasn't my place to spread the word about this - and that wasn't my intention in this case - but she just emailed to ask if I could help in any way. She worked really hard on it and I think she's a very talented writer. So I'm including it in this email and of course you can do what you like with it, but I just wanted to at least do my best as her friend to get it to the right people.

Thank you and I'm truly sorry if this breached any confidentiality!

Nikki

If women who don't help women get a special circle in hell, I think women who *do* help women should get a special cloud in heaven. Thanks to Nikki, Joelle Boucai's packet made it to the show. And thanks to Anne and Molly, both Joelle and Bess were hired and have worked at *Jimmy Kimmel Live!* for more than five years.

In 2013, Laurie Kilmartin suggested I check out the Twitter feed of Jill Twiss, who made quirky observations like, "I'm just going to say it. Bananas are cliquey" and "Pretty worried for gluten-free pigeons." I messaged Jill to learn more about her. During the day, she tutored kids for standardized tests and moonlit as a standup comedian and actress. When *Last Week*

Tonight began staffing up, Tim Carvell asked for names and I mentioned Jill. That show reads submissions "blind," removing any identifying details about the writer. Out of about a hundred submissions, Jill was one of eight people hired. She now has more Emmys than I do. (Although to be fair, anyone with one Emmy has more Emmys than I do.)

Jill Twiss bearing a striking resemblance to "Janice from accounting" on *Last Week Tonight with John Oliver*

Last Week Tonight also hired Juli Weiner who was working at *Vanity Fair*. Juli's blog pieces cracked me up and I emailed her with the same comment that I heard at roughly the same age: "I really think you could write for television."

Unfortunately, my system for tracking down funny female writers isn't methodical. It's mainly based on word-of-mouth, which can cast a limited net. I always wish that I could help more women, and especially women of color.

In an ideal world, awareness would lead to action which would lead to change. But in the real world, awareness more often leads to defensiveness which leads to excuses. Emboldened by the for-

ward motion in late night, I called a showrunner who ran a popular sitcom with a huge staff and only one female writer. We knew
each other socially so I thought he'd be open to a discussion. I
got as far as my observation that his staff had a gender imbalance
before hitting a nerve.

"How dare you accuse me of being sexist," he said. "My
mother was the breadwinner in our family and my wife is one of
the strongest women on the planet."

I tried to salvage the phone call.

"I didn't call you sexist. But just look at the numbers on your
staff—"

"You think I don't notice?" he said, ire rising. "I look around
the room and notice it every . . . single . . . day."

This showrunner bringing up his breadwinner mother
and strong wife is a perfect example of "moral licensing."
Everyone—male and female—is biased. But no one wants to
admit it so our brains search for examples that disprove the ac-
cusation. Moral licensing comes into play when people rely on
past behavior to dismiss current prejudiced behavior. This is
better known as the "Some of my best friends are . . ." defense.
People who believe they are unbiased turn out to be more biased
so it's not enough to be aware that there's a lack of women in a
room; you must also be aware that your knee-jerk defensiveness
is part of the problem.

"When you're used to privilege," the saying goes, "equality
feels like oppression." My showrunner friend felt under attack
and our call ended on a sour note. I was angry with myself for
coming on too strong. On the plus side, it taught me what *not* to
do. It would be so helpful if blurting out, "Obviously, there's a
problem so just fix it!" worked. It doesn't. Ask anyone fighting climate change or gun violence where the stakes are life and death.

Reshaping our culture means reshaping ourselves. We're
raised in a biased culture and that sinks into our psyches in ways

that are hard to escape. A few weeks after the release of *Lean In*, Sheryl's friend Michael Lynton threw a backyard book party for her in LA. It was a fun, festive occasion and at one point, a young woman approached me.

"Would you sign my book?" she asked.

Without thinking, I waved my hand.

"Oh, you don't want my signature," I said. "It's Sheryl's book."

She looked at me strangely. "Please?"

I signed her book, feeling a little freaked out by my reaction. I had just spent eight months cowriting a book encouraging women to "own their success," so why was I backing away from taking any credit? I thought of inscribing the young woman's copy with "Man, this shit is deep." Instead, I wrote, "Don't skim!"

The next day, I emailed Sheryl to tell her about the exchange because it was such a perfect example of how women are socialized to downplay our achievements. Within seconds, Sheryl emailed me back: "You know there's this great book you should read . . ."

CHAPTER 17

Lily Tomlin,
the Kennedy Center . . .
and a Surprise Guest

And no one is more loyal. You get Lily, you have her for life.
Like with her cosmically brilliant collaborator and spouse Jane
Wagner. They've been together for 43 years. (beat) *I don't*
know what that's like but it sounds terrific.

—Jane Fonda celebrating Lily Tomlin at the
2014 Kennedy Center Honors

IT TOOK A COUPLE OF YEARS, BUT SPEAKING OUT ABOUT
the lack of gender diversity in late night went from being
one of the scariest things I'd ever done to one of the best.
It put me on the path to Sheryl and *Lean In,* and my fear that
CBS would never hire me again proved wrong. In the fall of
2014, Tim Carvell gave my name to writer Lewis Friedman,
who emailed me to say that he was looking for someone to help

with the CBS special, *The Kennedy Center Honors*. Now normally I don't work on such classy shows, but it seemed worth a follow-up.

Lewis explained that year's honorees included Sting, Al Green, Patricia McBride, Tom Hanks, and Lily Tomlin. The executive producers were specifically looking for a female writer to help with Lily's tribute. Was I interested?

I said "Yes" so fast I sprained my tongue.

Lily had been part of my life since I was nine. Most of *Rowan & Martin's Laugh-In* went over my head, but I loved Lily's character Edith Ann, a little girl who sat in an oversized rocking chair and had a lot of opinions. She'd end her monologues with "And that's the truth," and then stick out her tongue and make a fat raspberry.

Lily moved from TV to movies, appearing in three of my all-time favorites: *Nashville, All of Me,* and *9 to 5.* Lily also appeared on Broadway playing a dozen different roles in *The Search for Signs of Intelligent Life in the Universe,* written by her now-spouse Jane Wagner. I'm still laughing from lines like: "I worry about things like, if peanut oil comes from peanuts and olive oil comes from olives, then where does baby oil come from?"

The *Kennedy Center Honors* had already booked Jane Fonda, Jane Lynch, and Reba McEntire for Lily's salute. (Dolly Parton was unavailable.) Executive Producers—George Stevens Jr. and his son, Michael Stevens—considered adding one more performer. We batted around ideas over the phone. Sarah Silverman? Sketch gods Keegan-Michael Key and Jordan Peele?

"You know who'd be great?" I said. "Kate McKinnon."

"Who?"

I explained that Kate was a cast member on *Saturday Night Live* and had just received her first Emmy nomination.

"Does she have a connection to Lily Tomlin?" someone asked.

"I don't know, but she plays Justin Bieber and Angela Merkel with equal ease so I'm guessing yes."

They sent me on a fact-finding mission. A few phone calls later and Kate McKinnon was excitedly telling me how much Lily Tomlin meant to her.

"My mom talked about Lily throughout my childhood," Kate said. "She gave me the book [*The Search for Signs of Intelligent Life* . . .] and said, 'You're gonna need this.' Like she was giving me a map. I read the book two hundred times. When I finally saw the video [of the stage show], I was like, 'This is what I want to do.' I thought it was the best thing I'd ever seen . . . It's not a caricature. She's inhabiting those people and makes you really feel for them. That's the standard for sketch characters. She created the field."

The producers worked out the details for Kate's appearance and Lewis and I started shaping Lily's tribute. It would open with Jane Lynch performing one of Lily's most memorable monologues: "I'm Lucille and I'm a rubber freak." Lewis had a fun idea of putting Kate in an Edith Ann rocking chair. She could do some physical comedy, sliding off the chair in her evening gown. Reba would talk about Lily's authenticity. Jane Fonda would talk about their deep friendship that started in the seventies. I assumed that the tribute would conclude with Reba singing a rousing version of Dolly's massive hit *9 to 5*, but when I asked about it, the executive producers said Lily's tribute didn't need to include music. I wrote an impassioned email to try and change their minds.

I can't say enough about how meaningful the movie 9 to 5 *was and still is. It changed the world.* 9 to 5 *helped launch a union—Service Employees International Union—and became an anthem for feminism. Every woman connects with it. It's both emotional and rousing.*

One last thought: How great would it be to have SARAH
SILVERMAN, REBA McENTIRE and KATE
McKINNON walk out on stage from an elevator door
dressed like this to Dolly's thumping vamp? Laughs,
applause, chills.

Still from *9 to 5*

Yeah, that didn't happen. The producers wouldn't budge on
adding the song.

Stephen Colbert was set to host the *Honors* and had his own
writers working on an opening monologue. Documentary filmmaker Sara Lukinson was crafting mini-bios of all the honorees.
Lewis and I were responsible for intros, transitions, and generating additional material for speakers. Since Lewis lives in NYC,
we collaborated through email and over the phone. We'd convene
in DC right before the show. Two days before my flight, Lewis
called.

"Hey, I thought you should know this," he said. "David Letterman just narrated the Hanks film."

"Okay," I said.

A beat.

"That means he'll be appearing on the show and we need to write some jokes for him," Lewis explained.

Adrenaline surged through my body. I didn't expect to ever cross paths with Dave again. My mind started spinning. Would he remember me? Had he read the article? Did he hate me? He probably hated me.

"Since you've written for Dave before, why don't you do a first set of jokes?" Lewis said.

I couldn't respond. I was too busy having a mini-panic attack.

"You'll be great at that," Lewis added.

That's a wonderful boss. Lewis knew my history with *Late Night* and sensed my shaky mood. By giving me a task and encouragement, he refocused me on the work. I started at the beginning, brainstorming an entrance for Dave. The same way a good architect examines the physical landscape before designing a building, a writer examines the cultural landscape. I usually ask myself, "What is the audience thinking when that person walks on stage?"

In Dave's case, there was one major event on everyone's mind. That spring, Dave had announced that he was stepping down after more than thirty years on TV. This announcement triggered roughly 50,000 blog pieces about how CBS should replace him with a person of color or female host. A week later, Stephen Colbert was handed the baton.

After the announcement in April, Colbert stopped by the *Late Show* to chat with Dave, but the hosts hadn't been seen together in over six months. An idea popped into my head. I emailed Lewis with the subject line: "Funny idea?"

On Dec 2, 2014 at 2:13 PM, Nell Scovell wrote:
Have Letterman start the show and then Stephen comes in
and says, "I'll take over."

On Dec 2, 2014 at 2:34 PM, Lewis Friedman wrote:
HAHAHAHAHAHAHAHA

On Dec 2, 2014 at 2:38 PM, Nell Scovell wrote:
One way or another, we should engineer them together on stage. That's the money shot. Alternatively, Stephen could start the Tom Hanks tribute and Dave interrupts and says, "This is my job. Not yours yet."

On Dec 2, 2014 at 3:36 PM, Lewis Friedman wrote:
ANNOUNCER (V.O.)
Ladies and Gentlemen, 2012 Kennedy Center Honors winner, David Letterman.

[LETTERMAN walks to the SR LECTERN.]

[As he's about to speak, STEVEN COLBERT enters, walking right up to him.]

DAVID LETTERMAN
Not yet!
[Colbert sheepishly exits.]

On Dec 2, 2014 at 6:38 PM, Nell Scovell wrote:
Yes! That's all you need to do and it would get such a big laugh.

This was our complete email exchange and it shows the way a notion can quickly refine into a bit.

When I arrived in DC, Lewis told me that Colbert had approved the "Not yet" beat. We just needed to get Dave on board. Lewis sent an email to Tom Keaney, Dave's point person, along with the opening and a couple of pages of jokes. Tom is Chief Strategy Officer at Rubenstein Communications and one of the most brilliant PR reps around. If Tom had been captain of the Titanic, he would have convinced the iceberg to move out of the way.

I was sitting at a desk next to Lewis when Tom wrote back. Lewis read the email out loud. Tom thanked us for the jokes and said Dave was jotting down some of his own. Oh, and they liked the opening.

"Yeah!" I said.

Lewis paused.

"Well, that's interesting," he said in his normal deadpan.

"What?"

"Tom just asked me a question about our meeting with Dave tomorrow—'Now it's just going to be you and the producer in the room, right?'"

Lewis stared at me.

"Do you think he recognized my name?" I said.

Lewis kept staring.

Of course. Tom's job was to protect his client. This news didn't upset me since the thought of sitting across a table from Dave filled me with anxiety. As I was convincing myself that it was all for the best, Lewis typed a response and hit Send.

"I just emailed him back," he said.

"What did you say?"

"That you were working on the show and would be in the meeting."

Again, that's a wonderful boss.

The next morning, I asked a friend who knew Dave well for guidance.

"I think I'm gonna see Dave today on this Kennedy Center Honors thing. Yikes. He scares me," I wrote.

My friend wrote back immediately.

"Just remember, his first thought about everyone is 'They hate me.' If you just smile and say hi and keep going, it will be a relief."

I took my friend's advice . . . and half a beta blocker to keep my heart rate down and minimize sweating.

Lewis, some assistants and I were in a rehearsal hall when Tom Keaney entered, followed by Dave. I jumped out of my chair.

"Hi, Dave," I said, cheerfully. "I'm Nell."

"Nell," he said. "It's good to see you again."

I relaxed (or maybe that was just the beta blocker talking) and we got to work. Dave read some jokes that he'd jotted down.

"I noticed that if you take the T out of Tom and put it up next to Hanks, look what you get," Dave said.

Wordplay. I liked it. Dave asked if we had anything. Since Dave would be sporting his own Kennedy Center medal, I pitched, "What if you listed all the places Tom Hanks went in movies, from

Four Unused Jokes I Wrote for Letterman

- Thank you for including me tonight. I was already in DC to check out the Smithsonian. After my last show, CBS is sending me straight there. They found a nice spot between Marcus Welby's lab coat and the hats from F Troop.

- Tom keeps challenging himself. I think he's covered every story there is: Man versus Man. Man versus Machine. Man versus Volcano.

- And my god, does he deliver. Here are some words that have never been uttered: "Tom Hanks? Eh, I don't care for him."

- Anyone else thinking Tom Hanks 2016?

Note: Last one less funny in retrospect.

a desert island to outer space to Philadelphia. Then you laugh and say, 'I got mine for sitting behind a desk for thirty years.'"

Dave shook his head.

"I don't want to mention that," he said. "Tom Hanks winning after me was just a bookkeeping error."

We discussed the opening moment between him and Colbert. Dave liked the bit but thought we could go beyond "Not yet." Lewis and I offered to come up with some options. Dave left after an hour. His wife and son were in DC and he was eager to get back to them. We'd pick up the discussion tomorrow, which was also show day.

The next morning, Dave arrived at rehearsal with a few new jokes. He didn't like our alternatives for the opener, and suggested that he pull Colbert aside after "Not yet" to say, "You're embarrassing yourself. That's my job." The director tried staging the additional lines, but nixed them for camera purposes. Dave's rehearsal wrapped. He did not seem happy. A few minutes later, Lewis and I were summoned to Dave's dressing room. We raced over, joining Tom Keaney and a *Late Show* writer who'd come to DC to help. Dave was agitated.

"I don't want to do the 'not yet' bit," he said.

I was stunned.

"It got a big laugh in the run-through," I said.

"It's a big laugh," Dave said. "A huge laugh. I understand. But I think if I start on this big laugh, how's the rest of my bit gonna work? I'm just gonna tank."

My brain went into overdrive trying to think of a way to soothe Dave's concerns.

"It's just a light, fun moment," I said. "You know Leno and Conan were never seen having fun together when that show was in transition—"

"Then let Conan do the bit," Dave interjected.

"I just think it makes you look like a good guy to be seen with Stephen," I said.

"But *he* gets the joke," said Dave.

What? No. Dave has the line and Colbert slinks offstage. I didn't know how to react. Flailing, I turned to Lewis.

"You have more experience with the show, Lewis. What do you think?"

"I think people who start on a big laugh gain a lot of good-will," Lewis said.

That didn't appease Dave, either. Just when it seemed like all was lost, the cavalry appeared: George Stevens Jr., who created the *Kennedy Center Honors* in 1978 and was still producing the show in his eighties, heard there was some tension and stopped by to help. George is a consummate diplomat. He listened intently as Dave repeated his concerns, then assured Dave that the exchange was "warm" and "charming."

"There's nothing to worry about," George said.

George soothed and cajoled and eventually, Dave relented. The "Not yet" bit stayed in.

Lewis and I ran back to the stage to watch a rehearsal of the Lily Tomlin tribute. The ending was sweet, as Jane Fonda declared, "We love you, Lily, beyond measure." Then all four actresses added in unison, "And that's the truth!" followed by four loud raspberries. Other parts fell flat, including a bit patterned after a chant Lily had done on *SNL*. Reba McEntire approached me after the rehearsal.

"It's not working," Reba said.

"I know," I said.

"It's just cheesy," her then-husband interjected.

Thanks, dude.

"What do we do?" Reba said, staying focused on finding a solution.

"I don't know," I said. "I just wish they'd let you sing '9 to 5.'"

Her face lit up. "That's a great idea! Why can't I do that?"

I explained that idea had been pitched and rejected. Reba

thought we should try again. We found one of the musical producers and she gave it her all. This would be a much better story
if Reba's passionate plea had worked. Unfortunately, the producer
explained there wasn't time to pull together a musical number
and we just had to make the best of what we had.

I was frustrated that the tributes were so lopsided. The Tom
Hanks salute included Steven Spielberg speaking from the heart,
Martin Short telling jokes, Pentatonix singing "That Thing You
Do," three leading ladies of Broadway—Kelli O'Hara, Laura
Benanti, Jessie Mueller—serenading Hanks with "They Can't
Take That Away From Me," and not one . . . not two . . . but
three marching bands playing "Yankee Doodle Dandy" while
Martin Short and a choir sang freshly tailored lyrics by clever
Amanda Green. While heartfelt, Lily's tribute was decidedly
under-produced. I think most people would agree that when it
comes to cultural relevance, "9 to 5" just barely edges out "That
Thing You Do."

The choreographer made some changes to the blocking
for Lily's chant and improved that moment. Jane, Jane, Reba,
and Kate headed backstage to keep rehearsing. During dinner break, I grabbed my dress bag and headed to the women's
bathroom. I wet a paper towel and washed under my armpits.
I pulled on some control top hose and prayed there wasn't a
run. I slid into a black Max Mara slip dress, and swapped out
my daytime Stuart Weitzman wedges for my sparkly Stuart
Weitzman pumps. I wet my hands and ran them through my
hair to add some curl, slashed at my eyelashes with mascara,
and looked in the mirror.

Cringe. Why hadn't I gotten up early and sprung for a blow
out? Suddenly, I heard Penn Jillette's voice in my head. Penn's
mother, Valda, was a stoic New Englander and whenever her son
had concerns about his appearance, she would respond: "Who's
looking at you?" This thought instantly relaxed me. All I had to

do was stand near the luminous Misty Copeland in the Green Room and nobody would even know I was there.

The black-tie, blue-ribbon audience filtered in. The honorees took their seats. The Obamas entered the Presidential box and the show began. Colbert got huge laughs with his monologue. Usher performed Al Green's "Let's Stay Together," one of my favorite songs. I wanted to soak it all in, but a nagging fear kept me on edge. Tom Hanks's tribute came third in the lineup. As Patricia McBride's segment wrapped up, I leaned over to Lewis.

"I think it's fifty-fifty that Dave will do the 'Not yet' bit."

"It's in the script," Lewis said.

"Yeah, but what if while getting into position, Dave just says to Stephen, 'Let's skip it.'"

"There's nothing we can do about that," Lewis said.

We moved to the wings for a better look as the announcer boomed, "Ladies and Gentlemen, 2012 Kennedy Center Award Honoree David Letterman . . ."

Dave strode across the stage. I held my breath. I'll let the transcribed notes from the performance, which includes the audience's reaction, describe what happened next.

(DAVID LETTERMAN ENTERS)

PROP: MEDALLION   *202214*

(AS HE'S ABOUT TO SPEAK, STEPHEN
COLBERT ENTERS)
                                                202237

DAVID LETTERMAN

Thank you [laughing] thank you so much
[laughing contines . . . more laughter . . .
[Letterman COUGHs] (to Colbert) Not yet [big
Laughter . . . goes on . . . and on . . . clapping . .
. clapping . .]

Dave timed it perfectly. He didn't rush the moment and he didn't milk it. The joke required a cultural knowledge of the backstory and that seemed to connect the crowd. When people laughed and clapped, it was because they were in on the joke. Lewis flashed me a smile.

"Happy?"

I nodded. It feels fantastic when a joke lands—like great sex with no messy cleanup.

Colbert nailed his exit, backing into the wings like a chastised boy. The Hanks tribute was big and flashy. As the three marching bands filled the aisles, the cameras caught Hanks mouthing, "This is over the top." Dave and the Broadway leading ladies came out at the end to wave before the curtains closed for intermission.

Dave wasn't hanging around for the after-party so I texted Tom Keaney to see if I could stop by and say goodbye. Tom texted yes, but warned me that Dave was ready to bolt. I headed straight to his dressing room. Intermission had started maybe five minutes earlier and Dave was already back in his sweats and engaging in a postmortem with his writer and Tom. I complimented Dave on his performance. He had tweaked the ending to a story since rehearsal and made it better. We discussed a couple of jokes and the audience's reaction, then Dave stood up and reached out his hand.

"Nice seeing you," he said. "And congratulations on the book."

"You don't know about my book, Dave," I responded, skeptically.

"Yeah, the one you wrote with that woman," he said.

"That woman." 'Nuff said.

We shook hands and, suddenly, it hit me: this was the moment I never thought would happen. This was my chance to ask Dave about my article. Except I didn't want to bring it up in front of others. I needed a plan. Quickly.

"Dave, could I speak to you for a sec?" I blurted out. "Want to take a walk down the hall with me?"

"Sure," he said.

Before anyone could protest, Dave and I stepped out of the dressing room. I'd done it! I had Dave's ear!

Now what? We started down the hall. Dave is much taller than I am and he stooped a little, curious to hear my private message.

"I have nothing to say to you," I said. "But I thought it would drive Tom crazy that I wanted to speak to you alone. He will always wonder what we discussed. Promise me you will never tell him that it was nothing."

Dave's hand moved instinctively to his chest. "This joke hits me right where I live," he said.

We smiled and made small talk to the end of the hallway, then U-turned back. Now the cool move would've been to just leave it at that. But as always, I wasn't that cool.

"So, I have to ask," I said. "Did you ever read that article I wrote?"

"No. No," Dave said.

"It was about the culture of late night and getting more female writers—"

"I don't worry about that stuff," Dave said, cutting me off.

I bristled at him reducing gender diversity to "that stuff." We neared the dressing room door.

"Let's do another," said Dave.

Like characters in a Sorkin scene, Dave and I walked-and-talked for one more hallway loop. Maybe Dave didn't want the discussion to end on that awkward exchange and we resumed our chit-chat. Back at the dressing room, we shook hands again and Dave slipped inside.

As I returned to the green room, I thought about how quickly Dave had gone into full deflection mode. In a way that helped me. I'd always felt guilty that I hadn't said anything about the show's culture when Dave asked why I was quitting back in 1990. Former *Late Night* head writer Merrill Markoe once assured me that it wouldn't have made any difference. I thought she was trying to make me feel better. Now I believe she was right.

The rest of the Honors passed quickly. Kate McKinnon killed from the moment the spotlight hit her. She struggled to shimmy off Edith Ann's oversized rocking chair in her floor-length gown.

"There's no good way to do that," she said. "It's sort of like getting off the lap of the Lincoln Memorial."

The crowd laughed, but unless you were in the Kennedy Center that night, you didn't get to see this bit. The onstage portion of Lily's tribute was short to begin with and then edited to the bone. The live performance lasted a scant six-and-a-half minutes compared to Hanks's twelve-and-a-half. Now I love Tom Hanks as much as the next human, animal or volleyball. He absolutely deserves twelve-and-a-half minutes of celebration. So did Lily.

Years later, it's still hard for me to let this one go. On my death bed, I'll gesture to Colin to come close and then whisper in his ear, "You and the boys are everything to me. Oh, and they should have sung '9 to 5.'"

At the post-show dinner, I started to crash. The last four hours had been intense. I grabbed a dinner roll and ate it like a Dickensian orphan. They'd seated me off to the side with the lesser donors, but I needed to find someone sitting with the fancy people. I snaked through the crowd, slipping between tuxedos, until I reached the big-ticket tables. I scoured the area. Finally, I spotted her. She was alone and seemed to be searching for her place. I approached.

"Lily?"

She turned and I was looking straight into Lily Tomlin's beautiful and expressive eyes.

"I wanted to introduce myself. I was one of the writers for tonight's show."

Instantly, Lily threw her arms around me and wrapped me in one of the best hugs of my entire life. It wasn't a Hollywood hug;

it was a Mom hug. The kind that makes you feel like everything is all right.

I flew back to LA the next day and put together a package for Tom Keaney. I had promised to send him a copy of *Lean In*. I threw in a spare copy for Dave, selecting the version published in Finland, which I inscribed:

> *Dave—I know you'll never read this book so I'm sending you a copy in Finnish. Nauti!*

About a month later, this came in the mail:

January 8, 2015

Dear Nell,

Thanks for all your help in Washington. Thanks for the book. I think it's even better in Finnish.

All my best,

Dave

DL/mb

LATE SHOW WITH DAVID LETTERMAN
The Ed Sullivan Theater · 1697 Broadway, New York, NY 10019

Hilarious.

The year after he left the air, Dave started advocating for hiring more women in late night. He grabbed headlines when he told Tom Brokaw, "I don't know why they didn't give my show to a woman. That would have been fine." He even grilled two directors during an interview at Ball State on Hollywood's "pervasive sexism." When one of those directors tried to duck the subject, Dave followed up with, "Having been very, very successful, now can't you devote your career to help others who struggle to be successful?"

Since Jay Leno turned over *The Tonight Show* to Jimmy Fallon, he has adopted a similar altruistic tone. "I'm really disappointed there's not more diversity in late night comedy," Jay said in a 2015 interview. Well, I'm disappointed that when Jay went off the air in 2014, he had *zero* female and *zero* African American writers on his very large staff.

It's great to hear these former hosts promoting equality, but why didn't they take any action when they held power? If, in the previous three decades, Dave and Jay had showcased equal numbers of female standups and hired equal numbers of female writers, they would have transformed the comedy world. Maybe Dave truly regrets that he didn't "worry about that stuff" when he had a show, but my sense is that what's irking both him and Jay can be found at the intersection of ageism and sexism. The two former hosts now know something every woman learns early in her career: it sucks to be pushed aside by a less-experienced man.

CHAPTER 18

Our Funny President

People say I'm too cozy with Hollywood. I was just laughing about that with Clooney.

—Joke I contributed to President Obama's
2013 White House Correspondents Dinner, unused

PRESIDENT BARACK OBAMA KNOWS HOW TO TELL A joke, and at the White House Correspondents Dinner, he got to tell a lot of them. The WHCD is a black-tie fundraiser and celebration of the press that used to be known as "Nerd Prom," and has now evolved into the "C-SPAN Oscars." Each year, the dinner books a well-known comedian to play court jester, but first the president is given the chance to dispense with diplomacy and skewer his critics with good humor. For example, in 2011, President Barack Obama said this:

I've even let down my key core constituency: movie stars. Just the other day, Matt Damon—I love Matt Damon, love the guy—Matt Damon said he was disappointed in my performance. Well, Matt, I just saw *The Adjustment Bureau*, so right back atcha, buddy.

Matt Damon missed seeing the joke live, but dozens of his friends emailed him the next day to alert him to the presidential burn. Damon was a good sport.

"I have to say, it was pretty funny," Damon told *GQ* magazine. "Whoever came up with it, it was a terrific joke."

So that was me . . . with some wordsmithing tweaks from the White House speechwriters. The Damon joke almost didn't make it into the final speech. That Saturday morning, Director of Speechwriting Jon Favreau emailed me that the president was wavering. There was concern that the joke was too mean.

"I saw the *Adjustment Bureau* last week," I wrote back. "Truth is a defense!"

I didn't hear anything further from Jon. That afternoon, I boarded a plane to travel home from Toronto where I'd just finished producing an episode of *Warehouse 13*. Minutes before the president rose to speak, I arrived home in Santa Monica, dropped my bags, and fired up C-SPAN. I had no idea if the joke was in or out. Halfway through the speech when I heard President Obama say, "Just the other day, Matt Damon—" I shrieked, "He's doing it!"

The president landed the joke and got a big laugh. Even applause. Then he followed the Matt Damon joke with another line I'd sent in:

Of course, there's someone who I can always count on for support: my wonderful wife, Michelle. We made a terrific team at the Easter Egg Roll this week. I'd give out bags of candy to the kids, and she'd snatch them right back out of their little hands.

The audience roared as the First Lady shook her head and mouthed, "No." Her husband seemed to be enjoying the moment and repeated the phrase "snatched them," stealing a second laugh. The next day, I spoke to Albert Brooks and we both marveled at the president's delivery.

"He has Johnny Carson's timing," Albert said. "The way he repeated 'snatched them' . . . That's what Johnny would have done."

For a girl who grew up in Newton, Massachusetts—arguably the most liberal city in the most liberal state—writing for President Obama was a highlight of my life. And I owe the opportunity to SpongeBob SquarePants.

Ten days before the 2011 dinner, President Obama took a swing through Northern California, which included a visit to the Facebook campus. The communications team asked me to send in some amusing lines that the executives could use in a welcome speech. I thought it would be funny if Mark mentioned that the president had nineteen million Facebook followers—"only half-a-million short of SpongeBob SquarePants."

My Facebook contact gently reminded me that the idea was to *welcome* their guest, not roast him. That line wasn't used, but Sheryl Sandberg shared it with Jon Favreau, who was traveling with the president. Jon instantly recognized that the SpongeBob comment would be funnier coming out of the president's mouth. Sheryl connected Jon and me via email and I was happy to serve my country by contributing a throwaway line. The next evening at a San Francisco fund-raiser, the president used the SpongeBob quip. I know because it was quoted in news outlets. This is one of the differences between writing for a president and writing for a TV character. When the president cracks a joke, it's news.

The timing of Sheryl's introduction turned out to be ideal. The White House Correspondents Dinner was coming up in less than two weeks and Jon invited me to send in jokes. It was the greatest moonlighting job ever. After spending the day on a set in

Toronto, I'd take a pad of paper to the sushi bar and scribble jokes for the leader of the free world.

My jokes fell mainly into two categories: topical humor (based on the news) and character comedy (based on the individual). If the president is willing to be self-deprecating, you have a classic sitcom character: the most powerful man on earth . . . who doesn't always get his way. Here's an example of a character joke I contributed to the Al Smith dinner, which brought together President Obama and GOP nominee Mitt Romney right before the 2012 election.

> Ultimately, though, tonight is not about the disagreements Governor Romney and I may have. It's what we have in common—beginning with our unusual names. Actually, Mitt is his middle name. *(beat)* I wish I could use my middle name.

The president punctuated the joke with tight lips, which made it even funnier. He may have been living in the White House with the nuclear codes, but at that moment, we all felt a little sorry for Barack Hussein Obama.

Since it was my first time contributing to the WHCD, I tried an array of jokes, some character-based and some topical. I also threw in a few absurdist jokes to see if they'd fly. Here's a sampling:

- (At top of speech, POTUS points) Ohmigod, there's Paul Rudd!
- There are now three women on the Supreme Court. You know what that means? For the first time in American history, the Supreme Court can field a double-dutch jump rope team.
- I don't want to scare off any challengers, but anyone running for president should know the White House is

haunted. Late at night, roaming the halls, you bump into former inhabitants, souls who are not at peace. Mary Todd Lincoln . . . Rahm Emanuel . . . One of them mutters the most foul things . . . and it's not the one you'd expect.

- I know some of my advisors are concerned about my current approval rating. But here's the thing—I live with two daughters, a wife and my mother-in-law so having ANY approval rating seems pretty good to me.

None of these jokes made it in and I admit, the Mary Todd one was a stretch. But I'm sharing them because they illustrate why a female perspective can lead to joke areas that male writers might overlook. Again, I don't believe only men can write for men and only women can write for women. Still, the Paul Rudd joke is something that a teenage girl (or I) would scream, which is why it seemed funny to put it in the president's mouth. Double Dutch was popular among the girls in my elementary school so when I was brainstorming about what three women on the Supreme Court could do, that popped into my head. More perspectives lead to more opportunities for finding comedy.

The 2011 WHCD turned out to be notable for two reasons. The next day, the world would learn that President Obama had ordered the Navy SEAL raid on Osama bin Laden's compound in Pakistan before heading to the dinner. His coolness and good humor didn't give away the greater mission. That WHCD also included a joke run that mocked the decision-making ability of reality TV star Donald J. Trump who was sitting in the audience. Judd Apatow and Jon Lovett cooked up the hilarious takedown and the entire room laughed loudly at the ridiculous host of *The Apprentice*. As someone who'd been making fun of Trump since my *SPY* magazine days, I couldn't believe this "Queens-born, failed casino operator" was still in the public eye. Surely after this humiliation, the brass-loving steak peddler would go away for good. Instead, many have pointed to that night as causing the "narcissistic injury," which prompted his decision to seek revenge and run for office.

After the 2011 dinner, Jon Favreau invited me to the White House to meet the other speechwriters. Jon Lovett kindly procured a photo that President Obama inscribed for me. The president thanked me for the jokes and added, "Glad I was able to provide the material."

Sweet, self-deprecating, and funny.

Each year, I looked forward to contributing to that April evening so much that, starting in early March, I'd check my email nervously every morning hoping for a note from the White House. Each year I sweated it out, and each year the email would arrive. In 2013, I attended the dinner as the guest of Josh Marshall, founder and editor of my favorite news site, Talking Points Memo.

The dinner includes a weekend of parties leading up to the main event. Beltway dwellers love the chance to mingle with Hollywood stars. Since I get to do that in my day job, I was more excited to meet politicians. At one party, I watched fans flock to the magnificent Kerry Washington, while I kept my eye on a woman who was chatting with just one other person. When that conversation seemed to be wrapping up, I sidled over.

"I wanted to meet you. I'm Nell Scovell."

"Tammy Baldwin," she said, offering her hand.

"Yes, I know, Senator," I said, shaking the hand of the recently elected, first openly gay member of the Senate. "I'm so glad you won."

Still, the best sighting came right before the dinner. I was milling around outside the ballroom when I saw the crowd start to part. Suddenly, Supreme Court Justice Antonin Scalia swept by me like a Roman Emperor, flanked by bodyguards. He was smiling broadly and seemed almost animated, like a cartoon fireplug come to life with sparks flying all around.

Lovely and talented writers Michael Chabon, Ayelet Waldman, and my host Josh Marshall at the White House Correspondents Dinner, 2013.

My old *Wilton North Report* pal Conan O'Brien delivered the comedy address that night, and I got to congratulate him at the *Vanity Fair* after-party at the French Ambassador's residence. The backyard trees were strewn with blue lights creating a magical setting. It's always a treat to see Graydon Carter and I hugged my editor Mike Hogan. Toward the end, I ran into the delightful Scott Berg by the fireplace. Scott and I had collaborated on a screenplay about a woman's college back in 1988. All my worlds were colliding in the loveliest way.

After President Obama's final WHCD, I figured my presidential joke writing days were over. Then, in October 2016, speechwriter extraordinaire Jeff Nussbaum reached out to me about contributing to Hillary Clinton's upcoming Al Smith dinner address. I'd never written for the former Secretary of State/Senator/First Lady and leapt at the chance. Her opponent Trump would also take part in this white-tie fund-raiser for Catholic charities.

Like President Obama, Secretary Clinton is a good sport and willing to wring comedy from self-deprecation. As with Letterman at the Kennedy Center Honors, I began by brainstorming an opening line. At the time, one of Trump's unfair criticisms was that Secretary Clinton lacked "stamina."

"She'll go home, she'll take a nap for four or five hours then come back," candidate Trump once said at a rally. "No naps for Trump! No naps. I don't take naps."

First, this statement convinces me that Trump takes naps. Second, it struck me as a good jumping-off point. I played around in this area and landed on a line for Clinton: "This is such a special event that I took a break from my rigorous nap schedule to be here."

Amazingly, the way I heard it in my head was *exactly* the way she delivered it a couple of weeks later.

Five Jokes Secretary Clinton Didn't Use at the Al Smith Dinner

1. Donald defines nontraditional marriage as between a man and a brunette.

2. You know we used to be friends. Donald even invited us to his wedding. And believe me I'm sorry now that we didn't spring for the 10-speed blender.

3. On *Dr. Oz*, Donald said that he gets his exercise from moving his arms while he speaks. When I heard that, my eyebrows got a great workout.

4. Mike Pence keeps saying the country needs broad-shouldered leadership. Hey, maybe it's time for some child-bearing-hips leadership.

5. Whoever wins, I think it's fair to say that the quality of basketball in the White House will drop.

Clinton came across as relaxed, funny, and in control. Trump's performance communicated the opposite. During his speech, he delivered one solid joke, which came at the expense of his wife. Then Trump dropped all pretense that he was interested in participating in good-natured fun. He started punching below the belt.

"Here she is tonight, in public, pretending not to hate Catholics," Trump said, viciously. It wasn't a joke. It was a deceitful attack. I will never understand why Cardinal Timothy Dolan didn't stand up and say, "Hey, that's not funny."

Humor can unite people of all faiths and political leanings, but Trump didn't want to be part of that. Or maybe he was incapable. Comedy requires empathy. A joke works because it builds off a shared feeling or perspective. Since Trump can't connect with the thoughts and emotions of anyone not named Donald J. Trump that limits what he can find funny. People have said that Trump has no sense of humor. I disagree. He clearly finds humor in the misfortune of others. He once retweeted a doctored video of him hitting a golf ball and knocking Clinton over. It's schadenfreude with a laugh track.

Despite Trump's nasty comments at the Al Smith dinner, Clinton enjoyed the highest poll numbers of her campaign that week. She was on a roll. Exactly one week later, James Comey released the infamous letter saying some of her emails had surfaced on Anthony Weiner's laptop. None of the emails turned out to contain classified information, but her poll numbers plummeted.

Colin and I were in New York City on Election Day, aka November 8, 2016, aka my fifty-sixth birthday. Ed Solomon, one of Hollywood's funniest writers, invited us to his apartment to watch the returns and eat chili. As polls were closing, I passed the hotel on Sixth Avenue where Trump was holding his post-election party. The white men in their red MAGA hats looked apprehensive, and I briefly allowed myself to think that Clinton was going to win. My spirits soared. Her administration would battle climate change. It would protect those who need protection. A female would finally lead this country. I knew that wouldn't end sexism, but it would signal progress.

The rest of the night was a long slide from jubilation to despair. The most qualified, experienced public servant ever to run for president lost to a racist, draft-dodging, greedy, sexual assaulting, pathological lying, short-fingered vulgarian. I excused myself from Ed's chili party early and walked the four miles from SoHo to the Upper West Side. The very air felt different, polluted by the nation's choice.

The next morning, I called my eighty-eight-year-old father and broke down.

"How could they have voted for him?" I asked, sobbing like a child.

"It'll be okay," Mel said.

I hoped he was right, but it now occurs to me, this may be the only time in my life that my father ever lied to me.

Unused Jokes I Submitted for President Obama's Final WHCD

- Welcome. I know many of you came tonight to see the charismatic leader of North America, but Justin Trudeau couldn't make it.

- I turned fifty while in office which meant I had to have my first colonoscopy and guess what they found? Mitch McConnell. That guy can obstruct anything.

- The Republicans are working hard to change the Constitution. They want to shorten the First Amendment to "Congress shall make no law." *(beat)* That's it.

- If Trump wins, he gets the nuclear code. I'll give him a hint now: it's the same number that's on my Kenyan birth certificate.

- People ask me who I'd like to see as our next president which is touchy—it's a little like asking who I want to see as Michelle's next husband. I mean, c'mon, man, I'm still doing the job.

- After all these years, I'm getting really used to living where I work so post-presidency, Michelle and I are starting to think we may open a bed and breakfast. We're not sure where but we've already got the name: [*show slide*]

CHAPTER 19

Stage Five of a Hollywood Writer's Career

Don't die. It interferes with everything.

—Irving Brecher, 1914–2008

IRV BRECHER AND I MET IN 2005 AND BECAME INSTANT friends. We had no choice. Irv was ninety-two and there really wasn't time to let a relationship "unfold."

We crossed paths at the Aero Theater in Santa Monica where I was sitting in the audience for a showing of a 1939 Marx Brothers film. *At the Circus* is not as well-known as *Duck Soup* or *Horsefeathers*, but it holds its own thanks to the catchy "Lydia, the Tattooed Lady" and Irv Brecher's absurdist script. Remarkably, sixty-five years after Irv thought up the gags, people were still laughing at them. The screening ended and Irv was helped to the stage by an old *SPY* colleague, Hank Rosenfeld. Tall and commanding, Irv opened strong.

"My eyesight's not so good," he said, "but my wife tells me the theater marquee reads, 'Irving Brecher Live.'" He paused. "That'll be a surprise to my doctors."

I fell in love.

Irv's credits are legendary. He received sole writing credit on two Marx Brothers movies. He turned his radio show "Life of Riley" into a sitcom, which launched Jackie Gleason's career and won the very first Emmy for "Best Film Made for and Shown on Television." (Clearly, the industry was still confused about how to label the new medium.) Irv directed Ernie Kovacs's final movie and cowrote the screenplays for *Meet Me in St. Louis*, *Bye Bye Birdie*, and *Shadow of the Thin Man*. He even punched up *The Wizard of Oz*. Groucho Marx and S. J. Perelman once set out to name the three quickest wits in America and landed on George S. Kaufman, Oscar Levant, and Irv Brecher. Since the other two were unavailable, I befriended Irv.

Irving Brecher, aka the Wicked Wit of the West

Irv and his wife, Norma, lived in a high-rise condo on Wilshire Boulevard and I'd visit them on Sunday mornings. Irv would tell me stories about fishing with Groucho and golfing with Jack Benny. His close friends included Harold Arlen and Yip Harburg, songwriters of "Lydia" and "Somewhere Over the Rainbow." We'd talk about subjects we both loved, like old Hollywood, Jewish food, and Broadway shows. One summer, I came back from a trip to New York City.

"I saw a wonderful revival of *South Pacific* at Lincoln Center with Kelli O'Hara," I gushed to Irv.

"I was there for opening night in 1949," he replied. "Al Jolson couldn't use his tickets so he gave them to me. Mary [Martin] was great but I loved Myron McCormick."

It was impossible to one-up Irv.

Often, we discussed politics. Irv was a lifelong Democrat but the world was changing fast and sometimes it was hard to keep up.

"Irv, I've never asked you," I once said. "What's your opinion on gay marriage?"

"I'm fine with it," he said. "I just haven't found the right guy."

Mostly, we talked about show business. Irv's agent had been dead for over twenty-five years, but that didn't stop Irv from complaining about him. Irv even held on to his anger at studio executives for miscasting the female lead in *At the Circus*. "I could have had Kitty Carlisle Hart," he said, shaking his head.

But Irv wasn't living in the past. Six decades after he helped invent the sitcom, his fertile mind was still hatching new premises.

"What if . . ." he would begin. "What if there's a divorced couple and the wife remarries a guy who lives in a luxury apartment so the ex-husband takes a job as the building's concierge in order to be closer to his son."

A solid pitch. And like most writers, Irv had already started casting the series in his mind.

"Louis C.K. would be terrific for the concierge," he said.

"And for the wife, I'd cast that young, blond girl. You know, whatshername . . ."

"Amy Poehler?"

"Bette Midler!"

Bette was sixty-five but to Irv, she was still an ingenue.

Irv asked me if I'd be interested in writing the pilot with him.

"I'd be honored," I said.

"Good," he said. He paused and then added, "I just want one more shot."

Those six words pierced my heart. Irv's fervent desire was either the most inspiring or the most depressing comment I'd ever heard. At ninety-three, Irv still felt the pull of Hollywood.

We are all seduced by the softly whispered come-ons of success, even when we know the odds of creating a hit movie or TV show are ridiculously low. Success in Hollywood requires the right concept, the right execution, the right casting, the right production team, the right outlet, the right marketing, and it all needs to come together at the right cultural moment. There are so many variables and writers don't fully control any of them.

In his seminal 1983 book, *Adventures in the Screen Trade*, William Goldman leveled Hollywood in three words: "Nobody knows anything." Specifically, Goldman meant that nobody knows anything about how a movie will perform at the box office. His book offers examples, including Universal turning down George Lucas's proposed space opera called—what was it?—oh yeah, *Star Wars*.

Rejection and failure are the bread and butter of this gluten-free, nondairy town. Over a decade ago, I bumped into a talented comedy writer who had recently turned forty. Work was not coming as easily, and his agent was no longer responding quickly to his calls. My friend was shifting into the "Get me a younger, cheaper" phase of his career. I was struggling too. We commiserated.

"I need a new paradigm for success," he sighed.

I knew exactly what he meant. In the previous decade, I had spun through a dozen "paradigms" desperate to duplicate the success of *Sabrina*. I tried high-concept shows. I tried low-concept shows. I teamed up with talent. I ran with the studio's idea. I ran with the network's idea. I ran with my passion project. I developed TV shows based on books . . . movies . . . and even a sales video. (One year, CBS digitally inserted Leslie Moonves into old TV shows for the annual advertising upfronts, and the video was so well received that the network hired me to write a pilot about a modern-day sheriff who gets advice from a rotoscoped Andy Griffith.)

I was trying—and failing—to crack the Hollywood code. Then in 2008, I gained some clarity. At the height of *Desperate Housewives*, I got a call to meet with Teri Hatcher who had a development deal at ABC. The actress had sold a concept to the network about a woman who discovers that her daily horoscope is remarkably accurate. I thought it was a clever device and a terrific way to create internal conflict. For example, what if one morning the woman's horoscope tells her, "Avoid major decisions today" and then at dinner, her boyfriend proposes?

Teri gave me the thumbs-up to develop her premise. I made the lead a lawyer who loves rules and resists the notion that the stars affect her life. The network approved our pitch and I went off to write. Two months and many drafts later, all signs were positive as the script landed on the desk of the network president. He read it that night and passed the next morning.

According to my agent, the network president liked the characters. He liked the setup. He just didn't care for the horoscope concept.

"You're kidding me?" I said.

The rejection didn't stun me, but the reason given did. It meant the *exact* thing that sold the project in the first place led to its downfall in the end. If you're confused, imagine how I felt after two solid months of work.

I called my friend Rob Bragin to vent. Rob is wise and judicious—his nickname at *Murphy Brown* was "the Professor"—and I trusted him to make sense of what had happened. He pondered my story for a moment.

"Well," he said. "There's nothing to be learned from that."

I gasped audibly.

Instantly, I knew Rob was right, not just about this situation, but about most situations in Hollywood. Like Los Angeles itself, the entertainment business is built on shifting ground. Each experience is unique, shaped by personalities, emotions, timing and, for all we know, the stars. There's no code to crack. There's no paradigm to follow. Instead, the system operates on gambler's reinforcement where intermittent success becomes a motivator.

Studies show that if a rat presses a lever and randomly receives a food pellet tied to that action, the rat will keep pressing that lever all day long. *This time. No, this time. Maybe, this time. Please, this time. What about this time? Yes! Whoo! Now again.* Pressing the lever may lead to insanity, but how else are you gonna get a pellet? So the rat spends his day in a nice cage with some water to sip. It's really not that much different from a writers' room. And lever-pressing isn't the worst job in the world—sure beats maze running. I can even picture two old rats sitting around, telling stories: "Remember the time three food pellets came out *in a row*? Man, that was something."

This mentality explains why Irv still longed for "one more shot." The flip side of the depressing "Nobody knows anything" is the far more optimistic and Jewish-y, "You never know . . ."

That's why I continue to churn out scripts. I expect nothing, hope for something, and am delighted when my efforts are rewarded.

There's opportunity in confusion and Hollywood has *a lot* of opportunity. Even after three decades, I truly don't understand how the system works. But I do know that the only paradigm for success is to keep looking for a paradigm for success.

In 2014, after some furious lever-pressing, a nice fat pellet popped out and I went back on a sitcom staff for the first time in almost two decades. *Big Bang Theory* cocreator Bill Prady came up with a brilliant way to reboot *The Muppet Show*, making Miss Piggy a talk show host and shooting the series documentary-style. Like everyone with a soul, I grew up loving Jim Henson's creations and swooned at the chance to add to the Muppets canon. I joined the series as a Co-Executive Producer.

My first week on the show, I approached Bill Barretta, the Muppets' wildly gifted producer/director/performer who voices Pepe the King Prawn, Rowlf the dog, and the Swedish Chef (among many others). I had an idea, but it required one small, curly piece of information.

"Bill," I said. "Does Miss Piggy have a tail?"

"Huh," he said unsure. "I guess." Then he grew more confident. "Yes. She's a pig. She must."

"But we've never seen it?" I asked.

"Not that I know of," he said.

"*Could* we see it?" I asked.

"I don't see why not," he said, flashing a mischievous smile.

I set off to develop a story I was dying to write. It began with Miss Piggy on the red carpet, posing for photographers. Suddenly, she experiences the pig equivalent of Janet Jackson's "nip slip" and her tail pops out. The newspapers plaster the embarrassing photo on the front page.

Prop from "A Tail of Two Piggies"

Normally confident, Piggy is embarrassed by the mishap. She's not some tail-flashing, barnyard animal. She explains her discomfort to her costumer Uncle Deadly.

```
                    MISS PIGGY
          My whole life, I've tried to cover
          the fact that I'm a . . .
               (drops voice)
          pig.
                  UNCLE DEADLY
               (a beat; then)
          You are aware that your name is Miss Piggy?
```

The issue, Piggy explains, is that her fans see her "as a lady, not a pig."

Piggy plans to publicly apologize for the incident until a "family values" group starts body shaming her and picketing the show. The protest backfires when Piggy wakes up to our culture's double standards.

> **MISS PIGGY**
> What's so offensive about my tail?
> Look around.

PIGGY STARTS POINTING OUT MUPPETS AND THEIR TAILS.

> **MISS PIGGY (CONT'D)**
> Fozzie's tail is out. Bobo's, too.
> And Yolanda's. Or is that okay because
> hers is long and thin?

> **YOLANDA**
> Thanks for noticing.

> **KERMIT**
> Piggy, I see your point but it'll blow
> over a lot faster if you just apologize.

> **MISS PIGGY**
> I refuse. I've been hiding for too long.
> (takes off sunglasses)
> The fact is, I grunt and snort and have a
> tail. That is who I am. I'm a lady *and* a pig!
> And it's time the world caught up with me!

"A Tail of Two Piggies," which I cowrote with Steve Rudnick, was a joy to produce. Watching Eric Jacobson perform Miss Piggy was a master class in both puppeteering and acting. There's an obvious irony that a human man plays a female pig, but Eric takes the responsibility seriously. At one point, he came over to me on set, uncertain how to play the line, "I'm a lady *and* a pig."

I explained that I saw this as a moment of self-actualization rooted in my own experience.

"All my life, I hated it when people called me a 'female writer,'" I said. "I wanted to be perceived as just a writer. The world saw me as my gender and I saw myself as my accomplishments. But as I've aged, I've embraced my identity more. Now I'm happy stating, 'I'm a woman *and* a writer.' That's who I am.

And I want Piggy to stop denying who she is, too. I want her to realize that her pigginess is part of what makes her special."

Eric understood and delivered the line beautifully. He also added a great gag to button the scene. As Piggy becomes radicalized, she declares, "I'm off to change the world!" She starts to exit in one direction then, a beat later, does a 180.

"The world is *that* way," she says, scurrying off.

The Muppets was cancelled after a partial season. It's a long story so let's just say there were too many Swedish Chefs in the kitchen. I took a break from TV to edit *Option B,* written by Sheryl Sandberg and Adam Grant. The project was a sobering look at how to face adversity and build resilience. Sheryl shared the overwhelming grief that she and her family felt after her extraordinary husband Dave Goldberg died suddenly at 47. She also shared her determination to recapture meaning and joy. The book could not have been a bigger tonal departure from writing for the Muppets. Like Piggy, I pulled a total 180: "The world is *that* way."

★   ★   ★

I have no idea what the future holds for me, which is both exciting and frightening. Irv once told me that his biggest regret was that he stopped writing at around age fifty. He urged me to keep being creative with one caveat.

"Promise me, honey," he said to me in the hospital, "that you won't take any project that your heart isn't in."

I promised him that I wouldn't.

Irv died the next day. I think he would want me to recount his last joke. That same visit, the hospital phone rang and I answered. The kitchen needed Irv's lunch order. I passed along their questions:

"Any allergies?"

He shook his head.

"Any dislikes?"

"George Bush," he replied loudly and without hesitation. I held the phone up so he could hear the hospital worker laughing on the other end.

I hated leaving his side that day, but Irv was tired. The next day, I called to see if I could come back. Irv said he didn't feel up for a visit.

"I love you," I said.

"I love you, too," he replied.

I miss Irv and wish I'd met him twenty years earlier. I think often of his advice to work only on projects that my heart is in. Sheryl said something similar in her commencement address at Barnard. She urged each graduate to "try and find a job that matters to you and matters to others. It's a luxury to combine passion and contribution. It's also a clear path to happiness."

Sheryl definitely wrote those sentences herself, because I didn't know this principle was true until after we worked together on *Lean In*. Combining passion and mission *is* a clear path to happiness. Nothing is more satisfying than having a positive impact on people's lives.

This realization also helps explain why I love writing jokes. On a much smaller scale, laughter is a sign of impact. That impact may be fleeting. A laugh may be over in the wink of a president's eye. But for me, that moment is bliss.

Thirty years after I broke into Hollywood, I'm still pressing that lever hoping for a pellet. In an ideal world, I'd get to direct another movie. Or maybe I'll create and run another show. I just want one more shot.

And then one more shot after that.

And then . . .

THE END

*Job Timeline**

1987	*It's Garry Shandling's Show*, freelance episode, unshot
Nov 1987–Jan 1988	*The Wilton North Report*, FOX
March–May 1988	*The Smothers Brothers Comedy Hour*, CBS
	Funny Girls, pilot for Disney New Writers program, unshot
	Reunions, feature, cowritten with A. Scott Berg, FOX, unshot
June 1989–Mar 90	*Newhart*, story editor
	It Was One of Us, spec movie cowritten with Claire Scovell LaZebnik
	Jody Hartman and the News, Act 3 (Norman Lear), unshot
June 1990	*The Simpsons*, freelance episode ("*One Fish Two Fish, Blowfish, Blue Fish*")
July 1990–Nov 1990	*Late Night with David Letterman*
1990	*Three Girls and a Genii*, pilot, unshot
Jan 1991	*Princesses*, consultant on pilot, CBS
Feb 1991–1993	*Coach*, Co-Producer, Producer, ABC
	Sibs, freelance episode, shot but unaired
1992	*Mighty Ducks* punch up
1993–1994	*Murphy Brown*, Supervising Producer
	Fred and Frieda, spec movie, unsold
1993	*The Critic*, freelance episode, "A little Deb Will Do Ya"

1994	Brillstein two script deal
	The Good Stuff, pilot, ABC, unshot
	Nebraska, pilot for Christine Taylor, unshot
	The Bags, spec movie with Joel Hodgson, unsold
1995	*Space Ghost: Coast to Coast* with Joel Hodgson, freelance episode, TBS
	Pandora's Box, movie treatment, Turner Animation
1995–1996	20th Century Fox overall deal/TV pilots
	Microserfs sitcom pitch with Douglas Coupland
	The Love Lab, unshot
	Prudy and Judy, WB
	Honey, We Shrunk Ourselves, with Joel Hodgson, Karey Kirkpatrick, Disney
	The TV Wheel, writer, HBO
	George of the Jungle, rewrite with Joel Hodgson, Disney
Jan 1996	Rudy Summers born
April 1996–1997	*Sabrina the Teenage Witch*, creator, Executive Producer, ABC
1997	Paul Sorvino project, rewrite, showrunner, ABC
	Teen Angel, consultant, ABC
	Times Like These, (live-action *Jetsons*) WB, unshot
May 1998	Dexter Summers born
1998–1999	*Nellie Bly*, The Wonderful World of Disney, unshot
	Providence, Consulting Producer, CBS
	Trust Me, spec pilot developed for Hugh Laurie, unshot
1999	*Hayley Wagner Star*, writer, director, producer, Showtime
2000	*The War Next Door*, three freelance episodes, USA
	Hidden Celebrity Webcam (web series), creator
2001	*Princess and the Pauper*, cable movie, unshot
2001–2002	*Charmed*, Co-Executive Producer, WB
2002	*Honor*, pilot, Spelling Television, CBS, unshot
	Split Second, pilot rewrite, Lifetime, unshot
2002–2003	*Presidio Med*, Consulting Producer, CBS
2003	*Without A Clue*, pilot, CBS

McCloud, updated for Brett Butler, USA, unshot
Jealous Type, spec movie sold to Dimension, unshot
Behind Bars, pilot, FOX, unshot

2004 *Monk*, two freelance episodes, USA
The Rich Girl, pilot, CBS, unshot

2005 *Same As It Never Was* (became *Hello Sister, Goodbye Life*), ABC Family
Girl in the Curl, rewrite movie, cowritten with Andrew Hill Newman, Paramount, unshot

2006 *Split Decision*, spec movie, unshot
Untitled Marley Shelton Pilot with Bruce Helford, unshot

2006–2007 *NCIS*, Consulting Producer, CBS

2007 *It Was One of Us*, Director, Lifetime

2008 *Monk*, freelance episode, USA
Mercury Rising, hourlong pilot, ABC, unshot
Sheriff, half-hour pilot, CBS, unshot

2009 *Dance Lessons*, cable movie rewrite, Lifetime, unshot
81st Annual Academy Awards Red Carpet preshow, ABC

2010 *Man Up*, half-hour pilot, ABC, unshot

2010–2012 *Warehouse 13*, Co-Executive Producer, Syfy

2011 *Backstabber*, spec movie cowritten with Tim Carvell, unsold
F8 with Mark Zuckerberg and Andy Samberg, opening sketch

2012 *Lean In* (book), Sheryl Sandberg

2013 *Lean in* (movie), Sony, unshot
Mac and Celerie, spec half-hour pilot, unsold
Last Gasp, spec drama pilot, unsold
Meet the Morales, spec animation pilot, unsold

2014 *Awkward*, director, episode
Win/Win web series, director
The Kennedy Center Honors, writer

2015–2016 *The Muppets*, Co-Executive Producer, ABC

2015 Bette Midler, "It's the Girls!" tour, writer

2016   *Option B*, edited book written by Sheryl Sandberg
and Adam Grant

Mystery Science Theater 3000, "Carnival Magic,"
writer

The Wand Percent, pilot, Disney Channel, unshot

2017   *Just the Funny Parts*, book

Trophy Sister, pilot, CBS

*Doesn't include journalism, speeches or half-written scripts

Acknowledgments

Sheryl Sandberg gave me a seat on her rocket ship and changed my life forever. I could not be more grateful for her friendship and all the opportunities that our working together has provided. You'd think that after collaborating with someone closely for seven years, you'd get accustomed to how they think and act, but Sheryl's kindness, generosity, and brilliance still amaze me.

Editor Jessica Sindler was lovely and patient throughout this long process. Her guidance was invaluable. I am indebted to Julia Cheiffetz for being the first to believe in this project. And a boatload of thanks to the steady stewardship of Lynn Grady, as well as Ben Steinberg, Kendra Newton, Kell Wilson, Kelly Rudolph, Jeanne Reina, Beth Silfin, Andrea Molitor, Suet Chong, Alivia Lopez, and the rest of the team at Dey Street.

Lacy Lynch was a delight to work with and so much more than an agent. She was a partner, and I depended on her advice, sense of humor, and judgment in all matters, both creative and practical. She encouraged me and challenged me in the best possible ways. Miller/Dupree super agent Jan Miller was this book's fairy godmother. She should write her own book. I bet she'd get a good deal.

Jill Twiss was my first reader and has seen sentences no human should have to read. Her thoughtful and funny feedback made every chapter better. I met Lewis Friedman in 2014 and he instantly became one of my most trusted friends. Since he hadn't heard all my stories, he proved to be an important and insightful reader. Rachel Dry is funny and wise and was there at the beginning. Laura Zigman is wise and funny and was there at the end.

Years ago, I told Barry Kemp that I was thinking of writing a memoir. He tapped his fingers against his lips and said, "You should call it 'Just the Funny Parts.'" I know a good pitch when I hear it.

Alex Isley designed the cover. He is an artistic genius, as well as one of the kindest and funniest people I know. I cherish our long friendship. Robert Trachtenberg deeply understands comedy and is as good a writer as he is a photographer. I'm lucky that he shot the cover and author photo. Kurt Anderson and Anne Kreamer deserve a special thank-you for being there from the proposal to the cover selection. They were my heroes before they were my friends.

Most of my friends are writers and I leaned heavily on them. Many are mentioned in the book so I won't double up. Some deserved to be mentioned but there wasn't space. Lots of love and thanks to: Scott Alexander, Beth Armogida, Neena Beber, Aimee Bell, David Dreyer, Quentin Hardy, Jenny Jaffe, David Kamp, Larry Karaszewksi, Leah Krinsky, Nell Minow, Kay Oyegun, Tony Rogers, Erin Gloria Ryan, Krista Vernoff, Jessica Yellin, and James Andrew Miller, who is as brilliant as he is supportive. And heaps of gratitude to nonwriter pals Hannah Zackson, Carol Krol, Anthea Liontos, David Shaw, Ashley Zandy, Aileen Boyle, Reade Fahs, Gina Wangrycht, and Rachel Klayman for invaluable input.

Thanks to all the members of the Jungle. I'm glad I crashed there. To my fellow IJC members, I offer a hearty "Juice!" Everyone on TMTS is a goddamn delight. And hugs to all the WHEN-ers, including Kate Mullaney, Jessica Bennett, and especially Amanda McCall, who made me happy when skies were gray.

I am grateful to lawyers Heather King and Jonathan Sherman of Boies Schiller & Flexner LLP for offering expert advice and overall kindness. They gave me the gift of peace of mind. Marty Schwimmer of Leason Ellis helped me understand the complexities of copyright law while making me laugh. Lawyer Ghen Laraya Long did incredible work, giving her full attention to every legal detail. Her dedication and enthusiasm for the project meant the world to me. Leigh Brecheen is a world-class entertainment lawyer *and* a world-class friend.

Many thanks to all my agents over the years and to the last ones standing: WME's Simon Faber and Nancy Josephson. I am lucky to have them in my corner. I'm grateful that Barry Greenfield and David Altman have kept Finishing the Hat Productions running smoothly over three decades. Lauren Johnson was indispensable.

Mellody Hobson and George Lucas generously provided inspiration and a gorgeous place to write at Skywalker Ranch. I loved my time at "Yaddo for Nerds." Many thanks to Connie Wethington who took great care of me while there.

My siblings—Julie, Alice, Ted, and Claire—have kept me laughing my entire life. It's been an honor and a privilege to be their middle sister.

Finally, my love for Colin Summers cannot be summed up in a single sentence. Or even two.

Photo Credits

Courtesy of the author: pp. 4, 6, 12, 22, 66, 70, 88, 117, 122, 132, 139, 145, 155, 164, 167, 168, 169 (second photo), 184, 185, 199, 208, 244, 247, 260, and 287; **Jill Miller/Vanity Fair** © 2015 Conde Nast: p. 5; © 2011 Getty Images. **Reprinted with permission**: p. 6; © **Tim Sheaffer**: p. 15; **Courtesy of Sussex Publishers LLC**: pp. 30, 32; **Karen Kuehn. Provided courtesy of Sussex Publishers LLC**: p. 31; **Courtesy of New London Barn Playhouse**: p. 37; **Courtesy of the *Wilton North Report***: p. 46; © 1987 *San Francisco Chronicle*: p. 46; **Artwork by Conan O'Brien. Reprinted with permission**: p. 47; **Courtesy Comedic Productions**: pp. 54, 59, and 60; *Newhart* © 1989 Twentieth Century Fox Television. All rights reserved: pp. 74 and 77; **Courtesy of the author. *Newhart*** © 1989 Twentieth Century Fox Television. All rights reserved: p. 80; ***The Simpsons*™ and © 1990 written by Nell Scovell. Twentieth Century Fox Film Corporation. All rights reserved**: pp. 94 and 100; **Courtesy of Colin Summers**: pp. 112, 219, and 294; *Late Night with David Letterman* courtesy of Universal Television LLC: p. 117; **Artwork by Joel Hodgson. Used with permission**: pp. 126 and 130; **Courtesy of Joel Hodgson and the author**: pp. 128 and 129; **Courtesy of Mike Saltzman**:

Permissions

Dialogue from *Sabrina the Teenage Witch* on pages 151 and 154–155 courtesy of CBS Television Studios.

Quote from *Washington Post* review of *Sabrina the Teenage Witch* on page 160 courtesy of Tom Shales, *Washington Post*.

Quote from *Rolling Stone* review of *Sabrina the Teenage Witch* on page 160 courtesy of David Wild, *Rolling Stone*.

Quote from *Los Angeles Times* review of *Sabrina the Teenage Witch* on page 160 courtesy of Howard Rosenberg, *Los Angeles Times*.

Kurt Vonnegut quote on page 203 courtesy Kurt Vonnegut LLC. Quoted from the *New York Times*, April 22, 1990 "Notes From My Bed of Gloom or Why the Joking Had to Stop."

Jane Fonda's quoted speech celebrating Lily Tomlin, Kennedy Center Honors on page 263 courtesy of Kennedy Center Honors.

President Barack Obama's WHCD speech on pages 281–82 © 2011. "The President's Speech" at the White House Correspondents' Dinner" by Kori Schulman available at https://obama whitehouse.archives.gov/blog/2011/05/01/president-s-speech-